D1379911

EVEREST: THE UNFINISHED ADVENTURE

E. E. Shipton   *F. S. Smythe*

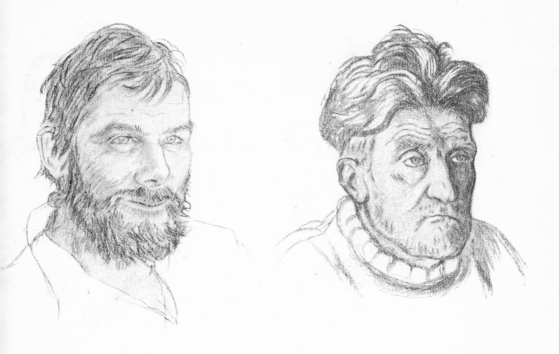

P. Wyn Harris   *G. Noel Humphreys*

J. M. L. Gavin   *E. H. L. Wigram*

C. B. M. Warren   W. R. Smijth-Windham

C. J. Morris   *E. G. H. Kempson*

P. R. Oliver   Tibetan Type

Hugh Ruttledge

EVEREST: THE UNFINISHED ADVENTURE

BY HUGH RUTTLEDGE

HODDER & STOUGHTON

FIRST PUBLISHED . . . . NOVEMBER 1937

Made and Printed in Great Britain for
Hodder and Stoughton Limited by
Hazell, Watson & Viney, Ltd., London and Aylesbury.

AUTHOR'S
ACKNOWLEDGMENT

I AM deeply indebted to my comrades who have contributed the scientific chapters in this book; to my wife, who encouraged me in the difficult task of writing, for the second time, the story of an expedition to Mount Everest, and who has read through the proofs with me; to Mr. A. R. Hinks and the staff of the Royal Geographical Society, who have taken much trouble over maps and references; to our Publishers, whose patience and courtesy are inexhaustible; and to Mrs. Wade, who has for the second time type-written my manuscript with scrupulous accuracy.

I wish to pay a tribute to the memory of the late Sir Percy Cox, who as Chairman of the Mount Everest Committee was a tower of strength to the Expedition of 1936, and to whom I never went for counsel or support in vain.

HUGH RUTTLEDGE.

YACHT 'EQUINOXE,'
  BRIXHAM,
      June 30, 1937.

CONTENTS

CHRONOLOGY

1936

February	1.	First party of expedition left England.
March	19.	Expedition left Gangtok for march to Mount Everest.
April	2.	Expedition crossed over into Tibet.
„	26.	Base Camp established.
„	27.	Camp I established.
May	6.	Camp II occupied.
„	7.	Camp III occupied.
„	13.	Route to North Col completed.
„	15.	Camp IV on North Col occupied by Smythe and Shipton.
„	18.	Camp IV evacuated.
„	19.	Expedition returned to Camp I. First news of monsoon.
„	23.	Monsoon reached the Everest region.
„	24.	Camp III reoccupied.
„	28.	Expedition returned to Camp I.
„	30–June 3.	Party weather-bound at Camp II.
June	3.	Camp III reoccupied.
„	5.	Attempt to re-establish Camp IV.
„	6.	Shipton and Wyn Harris involved in avalanche.
„	7.	Camp III finally evacuated.

1936

June	8.	Expedition started up Main Rongbuk glacier, halting at " Lake Camp."
„	9.	" North Face Camp " established.
„	10.	First reconnaissance of west side of North Col.
„	12.	Smythe and Wyn Harris to high camp near final slope of North Col.
„	14.	Party returned to Camp I. Shipton's party gave up attempt on North Peak and descended to Camp I.
„	17.	March home begun.
July	6.	Expedition returned to Gangtok.

NARRATIVE

Chapter I

WHEN, sixteen years ago, the possibility of attempting Mount Everest was translated with startling abruptness
from abstract speculation to concrete fact, the event stimulated
mountaineers, geographers and surveyors, but excited little
beyond a mild interest in the general public. As a nation we
are not concerned with mountains, the secrets of which are
supposed to be investigated by esoteric and amiably eccentric
bodies of men who, for reasons best known to themselves,
would rather risk their necks unaccountably on a mountain
than respectably in the hunting field and who prefer frost-bite
to sun-bathing.

Signs are evident, however, that this attitude of mind is
not static : people in all walks of life, who might have been
indifferent to an immediate success, are beginning to observe
that a section of their fellow-countrymen has embarked upon
an enterprise of great difficulty, and is now engaged in the
peculiarly British pastime of enduring a number of reverses
preparatory to achievement. The very strangeness of the
ambition affords an added interest in a mechanical age which
has long accepted the inefficiency of muscle as a means of
getting anywhere. Curiosity therefore prompts the eternal
question, " Why do you do it ? " From this transition may
be easy to self-identification with the whole project if a

3

rational answer can be given to the question. I propose, therefore, to begin this book with an attempt to appreciate some widely separated points of view and to explain the ideals or motives which inspire the effort. The analysis will, I fear, be anything but exhaustive, for I can in any case speak only of such evidence as has come to my notice ; but it may serve to give perspective to the account of the 1935–1936 expedition, and may afford an *apologia* sufficient to enlist the sympathy, if not the active co-operation, of the sceptical.

The approach of Science to the subject is direct, and may be considered first. Geographers have, from the beginning, collaborated with mountaineers, for the line of march to Mount Everest ran through a region of Tibet partly unsur-veyed before 1921, and for the mapping of the environs of the mountain itself considerable mountaineering ability was required. In fact, the enterprise was launched by a joint committee of the Royal Geographical Society and the Alpine Club. One could wish that more strictly geographical work could have been done by the six parties which have visited Mount Everest, but there have been two handicaps : the strongly-expressed wish of the Tibetan authorities that there should be no straying from the direct route to the mountain, and the gradual realisation that Mount Everest is so difficult to climb that the whole energies of an expedition have to be concentrated on this single purpose. The Reconnaissance of 1921, being fully equipped for survey, covered more ground than any subsequent expedition, with the result that Majors Morshead and Wheeler between them revised a previous tentative $\frac{1}{4}$-inch survey of 4,000 square miles, and made a new $\frac{1}{4}$-inch map of 12,000 square miles, and a detail photo-survey of 600 square miles of the environs of the mountain, supple-mented by a $\frac{1}{2}$-inch preliminary sketch-map of the same area for the use of climbers.

In 1922 Major Morshead was put out of action by frost-bite while climbing, and could do no more survey work. The

4

Kharta valley was again visited, and one party penetrated some distance down the Arun gorge. In 1924 the Rongshar valley was examined but not surveyed. In 1933 and 1936 attention was focused entirely on the mountain itself, but in the Reconnaissance of 1935 Michael Spender, with assistance from Shipton and his climbing party, was able to begin a survey of the Nyönno Ri range, and to make an improved map of the environs in general, and of the North Face in particular, of Mount Everest. Much geographical work remains to be done, if only the Tibetan authorities will lift their ban. This applies with greater force to the South Face of the mountain, to which access is not permitted by Nepal. Such knowledge as we have of this side is due mainly to the successful Houston Mount Everest flight of 1933.

Other branches of science have not been neglected : geological surveys have been remarkably comprehensive, considering the difficulties under which they were made. Botany and entomology received a fair share of attention; and physiology knows more about the capacity of the human system to adapt itself to exotic conditions. Again, the possibilities of wireless transmission and reception among high mountains have been explored. It may be claimed, therefore, that these expeditions to Mount Everest have made some contribution to the sum of human knowledge; not perhaps equal to that of Arctic and Antarctic explorers, who have more time in which to pursue their researches, but sufficient to rebut a charge of extravagant inconsequence from people for whom scientific values are paramount.

The sportsman, in a general sense, is prepared to apply a less exacting test, even though he specialises in one form of sport and has a good-humoured contempt for those outside his orbit. The player of ball games is perhaps a little puzzled, at first contact, by a form of activity which implies little or no competition, which follows no prescribed rules, and is unfettered by boundary lines or by well-defined time limits.

5

Moreover, the application of a team spirit is not clearly obvious. On the other hand, the hunting or shooting man is not without some affinity of ideas. His philosophy is by no means summed up, as many people think, in the desire to kill something. Indeed, his chief pleasures are to be found in adventure, the pitting of his skill and resources against danger and the unforeseen, and his close communion with Nature. It is here that he is on common ground with the mountaineers; indeed, the man who makes the ibex, the markhor and the thar his quarry soon finds that without an apprenticeship in climbing he is practically helpless. Again, the capacity of Mount Everest to " hit back " appeals to all that is best in men of this stamp. Risk and chance are the very essence of good sport, transcending success itself. So here we are preaching to the already converted.

By way of contrast, let us consider people as far removed from sport as it seems possible to be: the old and the infirm. During my five years' intimate association with Everest affairs, nothing has affected me more than the many letters received from lonely men and women cut off for ever from the fierce joy of action, but interested in even vicarious adventure. They understand, through the willing spirit to which expression is denied, the full measure of our privilege.

Then there are those happily incurable romanticists even to-day, the very young. They have been born into a world in which machinery seems to dominate man, and speed is the criterion of value. Yet some instinct prompts them to find room in their Valhalla of aviators and racing drivers for the men who calculate their resources in terms, not of mechanical horse-power, but of human strength, and mountaineering skill, and resolution; whose advance is reckoned in feet per day rather than in miles per hour. All honour to those who can control the Frankenstein monster of modern machinery, but youth can still respect the perfect co-ordination of muscle and mind and the indifference to hardship needed to reach those far-off

6

summits of the Himalaya. The school-boys and girls from whom so many letters of hope and encouragement have been received know all about the splendid achievement of the flight over Everest in 1933; their great charity embraces the climbers also, as they fight their way unaided up the pitiless slabs of the North Face, beaten back time and again, but always ready for the next attempt. I have yet to meet a critic in this company—not one has ever asked me that question, "Why do you do it?" They have the faith that moves mountains, and regard for the qualities demanded of our ancestors when the world itself was young.

I turn now to some very different observers. The Press, for instance; that clearing-house of fact, fiction and opinion. I have met a great variety of reporters—good fellows, nearly all of them, and broadminded. Unfortunately, they cannot approach the subject of Mount Everest in a subjective way; their personal reactions must be subordinated to professional needs. Their interest in facts appears to be at perpetual war with their dramatic sense, which may explain the circumstance that, too often, they refrain from learning up the subject beforehand and make a fearful " marmalade," as the French realistically call it, of their interviews, even when their informant has been at pains to give them accurate details. They are obliged, of course, to provide a story, and in our case this is a sorry business of making bricks without straw unless we can oblige them with a fine full-blooded accident, or by taking a lady on the expedition, with romantic sequel. They must long to galvanise us into some show of personality in the newspaper sense, when we exasperate them by prosaic understatement and an obvious desire to escape. The result is, I think, that the general public is given a wrong impression of what an attempt on Mount Everest implies; for values are distorted and false sentiment obscures the true nature of the quest. Exuberant headlines, personalities and mock heroics are a sad inversion of the message we want to give.

Surely the public interest in this kind of adventure is in no need of artificial stimulation.

We are fair game for the inventors and those mechanically-minded persons whose mission in life it is to impose gadgets upon their friends. The most enterprising I have met was the man who, in 1932, proffered a man-raising kite, on the broad wings of which " buy New Zealand butter " was inscribed in large letters. Last year an Indian student in Calcutta was desperately anxious that each climber should attach himself to a balloon with a lifting capacity exactly equal to his weight. This might certainly neutralise the effects of a fall off a precipice, but I had awful visions of Smythe, for example, suspended in space for all eternity, and scrabbling in a very undignified way at the rocks to regain his footing. Besides, a strong wind would have the last say in the matter of direction, and the climber might find himself half-way up Makalu, ever so many points off his course.

I have been informed of a very fine thing in windlasses (method of installation not specified); of a system of pipes through which oxygen could be pumped to an indefinite height; of rocket-grapnels, and of a splendid little engine which would supply electrical heat to those suffering from low temperatures.

Gratitude is due to our would-be benefactors, whose attitude of mind may be logical enough. But why not fly over the mountain again and be done with it? We prefer to try to climb in as normal a manner as possible; accepting with good grace the argument that ice-axes, ropes, pitons and crampons are also gadgets.

Generalisations are notoriously unsafe, but I seem to detect signs that the public is beginning to answer its own question, to which I have already referred. The enormous development of transport facilities since the War has made possible the discovery of the country by our urban population, and the re-discovery of the joys of rambling. That the process

8

is still in its infancy may be deduced from the output of humour directed at " hiking " and cognate activities ; but the child grows rapidly towards manhood—one has only to keep one's eyes open at holiday time to realise that our young men and women now want to get out into the open, away from towns, away even from the playing-fields. First the roads, then the moors, the hills, the mountains. Henceforward it is just a question of degree, and of opportunity. Nor does the spell bind only the very active—wild Nature calls to every age, and can give to each according to his capacity. The consequence of all this is a growing interest in adventures which are but a logical evolution ; and the eccentric mountaineers of yester-day are seen to be reasonably normal people who carry a pleasurable pastime to the limit. In short, they climb the Himalaya because they like doing it, and that is an acceptable explanation. There will always be found, of course, the superior person who prides himself on his sanity and wants to know, " Why do you idiots risk your necks and permanently damage your hearts and get frost-bitten climbing up a very high mountain in Tibet, with no advantage to anybody ? You would be better employed sprawling on the sands under an August sun or fishing with evergreen optimism from the end of a pier." And the cynic says, " Quite simple, my dear fellow : they just want the notoriety—everyone wants notoriety to-day." Fortunately the public is not made up of cynics and superior persons, so my generalisation may serve.

For the perspectives which I have tried to describe the material has been drawn from conversation with the hundreds of people, in all walks of life, who have voluntarily discussed this subject with me. They include, in addition to the types already mentioned, administrators, scholars, artists, members of the fighting services, teachers, policemen, fisher-men, shepherds, bookmakers and pugilists ; and that list is by no means exhaustive. I have been astonished by the direct and unprejudiced method of approach which these people have adopted, and again and again have received encouragement from their comments. Quite often they knew a great deal more about Mount Everest than I expected, but the main thing was that they were interested and anything but intolerant. Another generalisation may be ventured here— women show a very keen and appreciative sympathy with our aims. Many, of course, are not only energetic travellers, but extremely capable and bold mountaineers, whose co-operation is assured. Others, who may never have set foot on a mountain in their lives, are prepared to give us their full confidence, being persuaded that any honourable quest of adventure is worthy of support. None, so far as my experience goes, cavil at or decry such ambitions. It has ever been so—the more quixotic the venture, the more have men received the priceless loyalty and inspiration of women. It is a privilege which I hope they will never lose.

One more point of view should perhaps be considered before the second part of this analysis. I am thinking of those fellow-mountaineers who are not themselves directly connected with Everest expeditions; and I crave their indulgence. It goes without saying that they have closely followed the fortunes of each party that has gone to the mountain and returned unsuccessful; many must be contemplating, not only the method and organisation of these attempts, but the implications. Mountaineering has always been the sport of lovers of Nature, of men who preferred the quiet hills to the clamorous arena. Is there not danger that the inevitable growth of specialisation, competition, publicity, will destroy the ideals which informed the founders of this essentially unostentatious sport? And are not these very things magnified by the cumulative effort to reach the highest summit in the world? What is the effect upon our very best young climbers, who alone can make this effort? These are some of the questions that suggest themselves.

Again, the spirit of nationalism has already invaded most

sports ; on the Continent in particular it is responsible for a very disquieting attitude towards mountaineering. Some may think that the composition of Everest parties is due to it, but that is not really the case : in the first place, the Tibetan authorities have so far invariably made it a condition that all European members should be British ; secondly, experience has shown that international expeditions, lacking as they do the homogeneity vital to high-altitude work, are not really efficient. That is a digression : the point is, that a national-istic spirit, though absent at headquarters, may very well distort the public mind.

It has another effect, already patent in many sports— professionalism, sometimes open, sometimes thinly veiled. Modern efficiency demands an intense concentration that already is almost beyond the resources of the amateur. Is that sacrifice to be demanded of us by Mount Everest ? Already we know that the climber who has several Himalayan seasons to his credit is the best man to take, for the simple reason that he is acclimatised. But how many young men, in an unleisured world, can compass this ? It is too terrible to contemplate that wonderful mountain as the objective of striving nationalist organisations, employing each a professional team of experts. One more thing : with an attitude of mind turned to success at any cost, we are committed to the ruthlessness of modern war ; those ideals of honour and conduct for which the Alpine Club has always stood will take second place. Change our principles in respect of Everest, and—*facilis descensus Averno*.

I think that, with all the wish in the world to bless, many mountaineers are distressed by some such considerations as I have suggested. For myself, I believe that, in spite of all difficulties, we *can* maintain the good old ways without im-pairing efficiency. I will go farther and say that Mount Everest is far more likely to admit us to her topmost pinnacle if we approach her as votaries of a cult untinged by materialism.

What of the men who climb ? An attempt has been made, in the first part of this chapter, to interpret other people's points of view : will any single formula suffice to demonstrate the motives and ideals which send a man to try himself against the mountain ? I think not. *Quot homines, tot sententiæ* applies no less to the very few who can be chosen than to mankind in general. We speak of a homogeneous party, and strive for the closest possible approximation to that ideal, but that can at its best only imply unselfish team work—the willing self-subordination of each member to the common interest ; we cannot deny to each his individuality, and it will be found that in most men of this type that individuality is strongly marked, for they are not exactly gregarious by nature. The sport of mountaineering fosters independence of character.

Reference was made above to the facile and, for its purpose, adequate explanation that men go to Everest because they like doing so. Of course they do—the climbing of this mountain may be fairly regarded by mountaineers as the arrival at Mecca is regarded by adherents of Islam. Selection for the party implies recognition that a man has qualified himself by the hardest preparation and is possessed of exceptional skill and endurance. He will wish, not only to demonstrate that the confidence in him has not been misplaced, but to put to the test, on the biggest of them all, everything that he has learnt of mountains. What could give greater satisfaction to a keen man ? I do not mean to convey that, in a technical mountaineering sense, Everest is the most difficult of all mountains ; but the fact that five first-rate expeditions have failed is sufficient indication of her quality. This is a challenge to the very best, to be taken up for its own sake.

So much for a motive shared by every man and requiring no embellishment. Even in its best form it cannot be altogether dissociated from personal ambition, which is harmless and even praiseworthy if kept within bounds. I have had the good fortune to find in Everest parties a remarkable absence of

12

this quality carried to the length of egotism. Members would not be human if they did not hope themselves to reach the summit; but I had the impression that, provided they could do well enough to secure or retain the respect of fellow-climbers, they were content—for publicity they cared very little. The proposal has more than once been made—and not in British mountaineering circles only—that the names of those who reached a summit should not be published, on the ground that every man had done his duty and made success possible; so that equal credit was due to all.

When a spirit like this animates men, you have not far to go to find ideals; expressed in conduct rather than in speech. I suppose we have changed very much in this respect; in the seventeenth century men were prone to analyse and proclaim their ideals; they still do so in the East; in the twentieth century it is more usual to find reticence. Matters of the spirit are jealously guarded within, and to the world is presented an appearance of lighthearted flippancy. But there is no disguising conduct, especially when all veneers have been stripped away by the chisel of hardship.

It may be taken as axiomatic that each man has joined an expedition resolved, not only to prove his own capacity, but to think of his companions and of the expedition before himself. The execution of that resolve must depend on ideals which are not formed in a day, but are the outcome of long self-discipline and meditation. From a subjective standpoint he may, if very advanced, be like Kipling's hero, and accept triumph or disaster as equal impostors, regarding his duty as an end in itself. A more positive attitude may be adopted by the man who regards the effort he is about to make as the highest expression of himself, and as a test rather than a demonstration. Another will be sensitive to the age-old belief of the East, that mountains are holy ground, with all that that implies of sacrifice. Yet another will be psychic, seeing visions and dreaming dreams, but ever pressing on, like Tennyson's

13

Ulysses, through the arch of experience towards the ever-fading margin of the untrodden world.

The mere healthy materialist has no place in such company, and I think that Everest will have none of him. When the real strain comes, his appetites will hold him back while the men of ideals go forward, supported at the last by that power of the spirit which surpasses the physical. Bayard in the Middle Ages, Mallory in our time : study them, understand them, and you have the key to Everest.

Chapter II

RECONNAISSANCE, 1935

I WELL remember a day in the early spring of 1935, when news was received from our very good friend at the India Office, Mr. J. C. Walton, that the Tibetan Government was prepared to allow another attempt to be made on Mount Everest. Shipton and I happened to lunch together ; we realised that there was not time to organise a full expedition in that year, but it occurred to us that if a small party could go out in May a great deal of useful work could be done by way of preparation.

At a meeting of the Mount Everest Committee that afternoon I propounded this scheme, suggesting that Shipton should lead the party. The upshot was that the Secretary of State for India was approached with the proposal that the Tibetan Government should be asked to extend its permission over a period of one year, from June 1935 to June 1936, covering a reconnaissance followed by a complete expedition. This would ensure a more thorough examination of the environs of the mountain than had hitherto been possible, with a view to possible alternate lines of attack ; and a test of new men, whose ability to acclimatise at high altitudes would thus be observed in the only practical way—on the spot.

Thanks to the cordial relations existing between Tibet and the Government of India, the proposal was sanctioned.

15

The Committee then drew up the following statement of the objects of the Reconnaissance :

1. To collect data about snow conditions at high altitudes and investigate the possibility of a monsoon or post-monsoon attempt. This would necessitate the party remaining in the vicinity of the mountain during the whole period of the monsoon.

2. To examine the possibility of alternative routes from the west. Two had been suggested : the north-west ridge which rises from the head of the Central Rongbuk glacier ; and the practically unknown western Cwm, which is really a tributary of the valley that contains the Khumbu glacier.

3. To report on the present ice formations on the North Col. This would be of use in deciding what apparatus would be necessary for the main expedition in the following year.

4. To try out new men as possible candidates for the main expedition and to secure for them preliminary acclimatisation.

5. To try out new designs of tents and other equipment ; and also new ideas for provisioning high-altitude expeditions. In respect of the latter, Shipton received much help from Dr. S. S. Zilva, of the Lister Institute.

6. To carry out a stereo-photogrammetric examination of the northern aspect and valleys of Mount Everest, and to continue the work of the Reconnaissance of 1921. The contours of the North Face, and the exact height of its prominent features, had still to be accurately determined.

No better man could have been found for the conduct of this Reconnaissance than Shipton, whose temperament and abilities it exactly suited. His love of exploration is only equalled by his horror of large expeditions ; the former was clearly going to have full scope, and considerations of finance and diplomacy set the latter at rest. Moreover, he is a past master in the art of living off the country and of exploring a mountain region at a minimum of expense but with the utmost rapidity.

16

Of the party selected by him and approved by the Mount Everest Committee, two besides himself had previous experience of the Himalaya : H. W. Tilman, his companion in 1934, when that wonderful exploration of the Nanda Devi basin was made which made possible the climbing of the peak in 1936 ; and Dr. Charles Warren, who was a member of Marco Pallis' expedition to the Tehri-Garhwal Himalaya in 1933. The other climbers were E. G. H. Kempson, with twelve years' summer and winter experience in the Alps and a consequently wide knowledge of snow ; L. V. Bryant, perhaps the finest mountaineer that New Zealand has produced, and E. H. L. Wigram, a former President of the Cambridge University Mountaineering Club.

The seventh—and very important—member of the party was Michael Spender : not a trained mountaineer, but an exceedingly able surveyor, who was soon to prove that work in Greenland had prepared him, not only for rough travel and exposure, but for the particular difficulties of making survey stations in all sorts of mountain country. Thanks to the generosity of the Danish authorities at Copenhagen, he was able to postpone certain work on which he was engaged there, and to bring with him a light Zeiss photo-theodolite lent by the Danish Geodetic Institute. He also took the Wild photo-theodolite used by Professor Kenneth Mason in the Karakoram in 1926.

This expedition must have been able to recapture some of the splendid romance of the Reconnaissance of 1921. Untrammelled by the duty to expend its strength, to the exclusion of everything else, on the terrible higher face of Everest, where altitude and cold and exhaustion must inevitably take their toll, the party could devote itself to genuine exploration and to mountaineering in its most delightful form, sure of bringing back some tangible result to justify the effort. It was free, in a sense which no climber of Everest can possibly feel.

Shipton budgeted for an inclusive expenditure of £200

C

per man. This implied, of course, the cheaper but not necessarily less amusing forms of travel, and a definitely Spartan
regimen while in the field ; with resultant lack of transport
worry, and great mobility. Shipton maintains that this
simpler way of conducting a campaign evokes an understanding sympathy from thinking Tibetans, who consider that large
expeditions unsettle the people and bring about a dislocation
of their social system.

A party of even these modest dimensions takes quite a long
time to organise. The start was eventually made from Darjeeling on May 24 ; not without anxiety, because the Tibetan
passport had not yet been received. No time could be lost, so
a provisional permit to cross the frontier was obtained from
Rai Norbu Bahadur, the Personal Assistant to the Political
Officer in Sikkim. The Rai Bahadur holds high rank at
Lhasa, and doubtless felt that it was safe to anticipate the passport, knowing as he did the prevailing sentiment in Tibet.

Shipton realised the potential superiority of the route via
the Kongra La and Sebu La as compared with the Phari plain.
We had considered this in 1933, and were to follow it in 1936,
with complete success. The passport having not yet arrived
a certain latitude in guessing its probable contents was thought
justifiable ; anyhow, wish being father to the thought, the
well-beaten track through Kampa Dzong and Tengkye Dzong
was avoided, and the party turned off westwards from the
farther side of the frontier, with a view to exploring the
Nyönno Ri range, temporary headquarters being established
at the village of Sar on June 8. Here the most friendly relations were cultivated with the headman, who was hospitality
itself and apparently did not consider himself accountable to
Lhasa for the party's movements. His hospitality often took
a very fluid form. Until June 20, when a very definite expression of disapproval arrived from the Tibetan Government,
coupled with the remark that as Rongbuk was the ostensible
object it had better be reached by the most direct route, three

18

separate parties were able to begin the exploration of this Nyönno Ri range. Spender photographed it from the east, occupying five stations in ten days; Tilman, Kempson and Warren, taking the Zeiss theodolite, attempted Nyönno Ri itself; finding it too difficult, they surveyed part of the southern range. Shipton and Bryant crossed a high pass to the north; explored a wonderful basin which is surrounded by snow peaks but provides pasturage for the people of the Kharta valley, and returned by another pass on the south. From several points they saw Everest and Makalu free from cloud, at a time when by normal standards the monsoon should have been in full blast. If only we could have made an attempt on the mountain at the usual time in 1935, we might have had a very different story to tell. Shipton considers that the monsoon did not break till June 26, the day on which he left Sar.

Rongbuk was reached on July 4, and on the 6th, in perfect weather, the climbers went straight through to Camp I, leaving Spender with experienced porters and apparatus at the old Base Camp. Altitude was beginning to tell upon Bryant, who had to be left at Camp I while the rest, in two days, went on to Camp III. The rapidity of their advance clearly shows that the early work in the Nyönno Ri had given them a considerable measure of acclimatisation. For the moment the mountain, fickle as ever, was as clear of snow as it should be in May; there was no wind, and the nights were clear and cold. The possibilities of a high climb were most encouraging. But that mood changed the very day after Camp III was established.

Forty Tibetans had been employed to take five weeks' provisions as far as Camp II. Above that, the Sherpa porters who were not needed for Spender's camp, and the climbers themselves, were able to carry equipment and food for three weeks; and a move was made to a spot some 500 feet higher than Camp III, near which a food dump was left in 1933. On the way there they suddenly came upon the body of Maurice

19

Wilson, who was known to have perished in this neighbour-hood during his solitary attempt on Everest in 1934. It has always been very difficult to extract any detailed and connected statement from the two or three porters who accompanied him thus far but declined, very wisely, to try the North Col with a man who was obviously not a mountaineer. So Shipton and his companions were obliged to seek evidence on the spot. Wilson's diary appeared to have been kept up to within a short time of his death, and indicated that he had made more than one attempt to reach the North Col, alone. The wonder is that he did not kill himself while so doing ; but it was clear that he had died from exhaustion in his tent. The porters had shown him our old food dump, so hunger was not the cause. Subsequently the wind blew the tent to rags.

The party had now to examine the slopes of the North Col. As might be expected, these had altered considerably since 1933, so that the route adopted in that year had to be revised. The comparatively easy snowslope a little less than half-way up, and the ice-wall above it which gave Smythe and Shipton such a tussle in 1933, were now, as Shipton puts it, " a mass of tottering séracs," and obviously must be left well alone. But a tongue of ice was found some distance to the right, by way of which the point was reached where in 1933 we established Camp IV on an ice-ledge which was really the lower lip of a crevasse, some 240 feet from the crest of the Col. The downward movement of the ice here (it is in fact a steep falling glacier) had obliterated the ledge, the slopes and bulging ice-cliffs above were far too difficult for direct ascent, and there was nothing for it but to traverse in a southerly direction across the face to a point almost immediately below the old Camp IVa on the Col itself, and then climb straight up.

The party worked for three days on these slopes. On July 12, only six days after leaving Rongbuk, Shipton, Kempson and Warren occupied the North Col with nine Sherpas and supplies for fifteen days. It was a fine performance,

20

accomplished not without difficulties other than those of the ground ; for some of the Sherpas, perhaps upset by the discovery of Wilson's body, refused work on one day ; and Shipton was forced to read the riot act.

It will be observed that these North Col slopes were climbed during the monsoon—three highly experienced men, well aware of the dangers of avalanche at this time of year and of the disaster in June 1922, when seven porters were killed, used all their skill and knowledge to test the snow section by section ; to all appearances it was in good condition, and safe. By Alpine—and most Himalayan—standards, the climb was justified. The plan now was to take a light camp up to 26,000 feet and from there to examine the condition of the snow on the upper slabs and generally reconnoitre the ground. If circumstances permitted, it might even be possible to attempt the summit.

Unfortunately the weather now turned against them, and four very windy nights caused great discomfort. After going a short distance up the North Ridge, Shipton decided that it was not worth while trying to go farther while this weather lasted. He knew well the effects of staying too long at this altitude. Some of the tents and stores could be left on the North Col, and the party could climb elsewhere, intending to return at the first good opportunity.

Now came the counterstroke for which the North Col had been biding its time—one of the many it had made and was still to make. It was observed that during the last four tempestuous days only a few inches of new snow had fallen. There was no particular reason to anticipate danger, yet the descent on the morning of July 16 was commenced with the greatest caution ; Shipton and Kempson leading with five Sherpas, and Warren following with the other four. A short distance down, the leading men suddenly found themselves on the brink of a cut-off which stretched for several hundred yards in either direction. Plainly an enormous

21

avalanche had broken away, probably the night before and in complete silence. It had swept the line of the ascending tracks, carrying with it the snow surface to a depth of at least six feet. Nobody in the camp above had heard a sound, and this is a mystery to which no solution has been discovered. All that can be said is that Himalayan snow in general and the North Col in particular have yet a good many lessons to teach us ; and that this party was extremely fortunate not to have been caught during their previous ascent, or at the moment of descent.

Shipton displayed fine judgment in descending along the track of the avalanche without delay, assuming that another immediate fall was improbable ; and brought his party back safe to Camp III. He resolved then and there to abandon everything left on the North Col and to leave the place alone for the remainder of the Reconnaissance. He was quite right.

A move was now made across to a little glacier under Khartaphu, 23,600 feet : and this peak was climbed on the following day. Difficult ice delayed arrival at the summit so much that clouds had come up before any useful work could be done with the light Zeiss theodolite. However, some exceptionally good telephotographs were obtained of Everest and Makalu. Those of the former, taken from this eastern viewpoint, give a very different impression of the mountain from those taken from the north ; and a grim impression it is. The north-east arête, which looks comparatively easy from the Base Camp, is seen in a truer perspective.

On return to Camp II it was found that Tilman and Wigram had meanwhile climbed two peaks of over 22,000 feet ; and Spender had done a splendid bit of work : from several stations on both sides of the Main Rongbuk glacier he had surveyed the North Face in detail, making possible a large-scale map and the accurate determination of the height of prominent features. This was a great contribution to the data required for planning an assault. Bryant, unhappily,

22

was still far from well, and therefore unable at present to join in the operations.

For the next phase of work the party was divided into two. Kempson, Warren and Spender set off to explore the country between the East Rongbuk glacier and the Doya La. The remainder based themselves on Camp II, and began by climbing the mountain generally known as " Kellas " Rock Peak, 23,180 feet. As Shipton says, photographs of this peak have so often appeared in the newspapers over the name of Mount Everest that he experienced quite a thrill on reaching the summit. During the climb, as on Khartaphu, it was found that a sudden and dangerous change occurred in the condition of the snow above 23,000 feet. This was in July ; later on the snow was bad far below that altitude. No attempt is here made to generalise in respect of the Himalayan range ; the point is that in the Everest region the snow at any considerable height is not safe after the monsoon has developed.

Next came the ascent of the 22,580-foot peak west of Camp II—a particularly good ice climb ; followed by two 21,000 footers to the east, from which photographs were required to supplement Spender's survey.

Returning to Rongbuk on July 31, they found that things had not gone so well with the other party. Bad weather and a partial failure of the commissariat had prevented a completion of the work, while two porters were down with dysentery and Spender had symptoms of it. In spite of these setbacks, Spender surveyed a considerable area in the neighbourhood of the Kharta Changri pass, and Kempson and Warren took the light theodolite to the summit of two peaks over 22,000 feet high and then climbed Kharta Changri itself, 23,070 feet.

It might be supposed that even these men had by now earned a rest. They were so far human as to allow themselves two days at Rongbuk, during which time they performed some almost equally remarkable feats in the way of absorbing

23

Tibetan fresh food which Karma Paul, who ought to have been a sutler in Massena's army in Spain, contrived to amass. Shipton's tally is : twenty-one dozen eggs, two sheep, and a little rancid butter. His justification is that the party maintained its weight and strength.

The third phase was to be an expedition up the Main Rongbuk glacier, followed by an attempt to cross the watershed over into some of the western valleys of Everest. Kempson had now to return home ; the rest divided up into three parties. Shipton and Bryant (now much better) went up the West Rongbuk glacier ; Tilman and Wigram were to attempt to cross the Lho La (at the head of the Main Rongbuk glacier) and also to examine the north-west ridge of Everest, which Hazard recommended to our attention in 1933 ; a few days later, when Spender had recovered, he and Warren went off for some more survey in this region.

Shipton and Bryant led off with characteristic energy, climbing three peaks in the Lingtren group, including the triangulated summit of 21,730 feet. On one of these—Lingtren Nup—they were able to use their theodolite. On the last, trouble nearly overtook them during the descent in bad weather. Shipton says : " While we were making our way along a narrow ice-ridge I heard a roar like a heavy gun going off, felt a jerk of the rope round my waist which nearly cut me in two, and found myself standing alone on the ridge. Bryant had broken away a bit of the cornice, had gone down with it, and was now almost hanging on the other end of the rope some way below the crest of the ridge ; but he had retained possession of his axe and was thus able to cut his way back to me. Later in the descent we got involved in a small snow avalanche which, fortunately, we were expecting."

From a pass next day they were able to look over into the Sola Khombu district of Nepal, from which most of the porters come ; and to see the Western Cwm of Everest. Shipton thinks this side of the mountain does not look impossible, though very steep ; but access from the watershed is extremely difficult, and in any case we are not yet allowed to enter Nepalese territory.

Meanwhile Tilman and Wigram, finding no possible route southward from the Lho La, climbed a peak close by in order to get a good view of the north-west ridge, which they pronounced to be utterly impracticable in its lower section. They then crossed the difficult pass immediately north of the North Peak, descending to Camp II on the East Rongbuk glacier ; and finished their work in this region by climbing two more 22,000-foot peaks (it all sounds so easy) before the general rendezvous at Rongbuk on August 14.

Again two days' rest was considered sufficient, after which the whole party except Spender reascended the East Rongbuk glacier to try their luck on the North Peak, which is also called Changtse, 24,730 feet. The chief objects of this attempt were to take telephotographs of Everest, and to obtain further data regarding the behaviour of monsoon snow at these extreme altitudes. About the latter they were soon informed : three camps were made on the North Peak, and to reach the highest, at about 23,200 feet, they were obliged to flog their way up to their waists in soft snow. This became so much worse next day, even at dawn, that little further progress could be made, and the ascent was abandoned. The men could look down on the North Col and see that the tents left there in July were hidden under fresh snow.

The reunited party now entered on the last phase—exploration of the mountain region between the East Rongbuk glacier and the Doya La, already partly seen by Kempson, Warren and Spender. An improvement in the weather enabled them to combine enjoyment of wonderful scenery with really good survey work. Crossing the Kharta Changri pass, all heavily laden, they reached what Spender named the Ice Cap station, from the resemblance of the great sheet of névé west of Kharta Changri to the ice formations in Greenland. Bryant and

25

Warren branched off to climb the triangulated peak, 22,470 feet; and when they rejoined the whole party proceeded north-east to cross the glacier at the head of the Kharta Chu. Here a peak of 20,750 feet was climbed, affording magnificent views of all the higher mountains in the neighbourhood.

They now found themselves in a district which was practically unknown and therefore very sketchily mapped. It contained, however, one triangulated peak, 22,150 feet, to which the name " Dent Blanche " was applied at the time, owing to its resemblance to the peak above Zermatt. The plan for an immediate assault by the whole strength of the climbing party was frustrated by a strike of the Sherpa porters, who were convinced that they were faced with inevitable starvation in this wilderness—a situation largely brought about by their having jettisoned tsampa in favour of extra clothing and various treasure trove, such as two of the 1922 oxygen cylinders. Shipton was obliged to send Tilman, Bryant and Wigram over into the Kharta valley, while he and Warren remained to tackle the peak and see Spender off towards the Lang Chu.

The " Dent Blanche " was a very hard nut to crack, and at the outset there was nearly an accident. At one place a very steep snow gully had to be descended; Shipton and Warren decided to glissade down it, but instructed the Sherpa porters, who knew nothing about glissading and were also heavily laden, to climb down the easy rocks at the side. All did so in complete safety except Pasang who, convinced that he could do anything of which his leaders were capable, disobeyed orders and tried his luck glissading. In a sense, his luck was good, and better than he deserved. Very soon he lost control and terminated a series of somersaults by crashing into the rocks at the bottom. Miraculously he escaped with a badly bruised leg, and was with difficulty sent off to the Kharta to recover. His load, which included a much-prized pressure cooker, was completely shattered.

Shipton and Warren camped at 20,000 feet on a promising

ridge of the mountain, but encountered bad weather and serious difficulty higher up, and were beaten. They are sure that after adequate reconnaissance the climb will go. They now got into very tangled country, all arêtes and glaciers, among which a way was far from easy and direction-finding gave many anxious moments. In the end, however, they descended to lakes and flowers and pastures, and found that they were, as they had hoped, in the Lang Chu.

Any hopes of continuing the survey of the Nyönno Ri range were put an end to by the refusal of the Tibetan authorities. The party travelled eastward at top speed, reckless of the suffering entailed by the Tibetan wooden saddles, and crossed the Choten Nyima La, to finish up with some climbing in the little-known Dodang Nyima range of North Sikkim, where the snow was appalling. Spender's proposed survey of the country north of Kangchenjau was made impossible by severe monsoon weather.

Shipton's last comment on this astounding reconnaissance is characteristic : " As is generally the case, the results of the expedition fell short of our hopes, but our inability to wander far afield enabled us to do more mountaineering than we had intended. Twenty-six peaks, all over 20,000 feet high, had been climbed, the summits of only two of these had been previously reached." I think there is more to be said than that, for the party achieved a success for which it is difficult to find a parallel in the history of Himalayan exploration, and that on the slenderest resources. Taking the objects of the Reconnaissance as originally stated :

1. The difficulties and dangers of monsoon snow conditions at high altitudes in the Everest region were brought to light ; and additional evidence was found to prove that the only season for attempting Mount Everest is between spring and summer.

2. The practicability of the north-west ridge was assessed ; and the Western Cwm was examined so far as conditions per-

27

mitted. Here I venture to make my one and only criticism—
I could have wished that the western slopes of the North Col
had been more closely examined.

3. The ice-formations on the North Col were studied;
this saved time in 1936.

4. The capacities of new men to acclimatise were thoroughly tested.

5. Equipment was further tried; and Shipton at least was
convinced on the subject of provisions.

6. An excellent stereo-photogrammetric survey was made
by Spender of the North Face; the environs of the mountain
were better mapped; and a beginning was made with survey
in the Nyönno Ri range. Spender has paid warm tribute to
the help he received from the climbers, all of whom contributed
to this success.

Of the purely mountaineering aspects of the expedition it
is difficult to write without hyperbole. The number of peaks
climbed evokes an admiration intensified by the skill displayed
—some of these mountains were exceedingly difficult; and
by the endurance, the energy, and the judgment which carried
through these climbs without a single serious accident. Once
again Shipton has given proofs of exceptional enterprise,
organising ability and powers of leadership.

Chapter III

ENGLISH winter weather was quite up to standard on the morning of February 1, 1936, when the advance party of the fifth Mount Everest Expedition left Waterloo Station to join the P. & O. mail ship *Ranchi* at Southampton. Rain had been falling for many hours during the night, and visibility was what the shipping forecasts call " poor." A few dejected porters accepted without enthusiasm the small amount of luggage which had not been sent forward ; and for our part we and our relations and friends, having arrived with time in hand, kept nervously away from any group of our fellow-citizens who might betoken that enterprising body the Press. Sir William Goodenough and Sir Percy Cox, past and present Chairmen of the Mount Everest Committee, and other members of that body very kindly came to say a few parting words of encouragement. Half an hour passed pleasantly away in their company, and as the time for departure grew near we had some hopes of being able to get into our carriages without any fuss. Disillusion followed : I was presently recognised by my friend the representative of the *Daily Telegraph*, and then the fat was fairly in the fire. Doctor Humphreys and I, our respective wives, and Gavin each became the centre of a ring of striving Pressmen ; cameras clicked, flashlights exploded under our very noses, and we were en-

29

treated to " say a few words." Inspiration failing us, we were ingeniously driven into some show of spirit by the most excruciatingly inaccurate suggestions, some reporters being firmly persuaded that we were the relics of the Houston Mount Everest Expedition and intended to fly over the mountain again. One bright little incident lingers in my memory : a strong, determined-looking man with a red face drew me out of my ring by main force and delivered himself of the following remarkable sentiment in a husky voice : " See here, guv'nor, I'm a bookie, and I've come a long way to do you a good turn ; Belted 'Ero's your horse for the Grand National, because you *are* a blinking 'ero." I have never been so flattered in my life. I am not in the habit of betting, but both my wife and I backed Belted Hero both ways for the Grand National, and I regret to add that the horse did not start. Nevertheless, I have nothing but friendly feelings for that bookie ; he meant well.

After this the Press gradually dwindled away, in despair at our extreme dullness, and we were able to say good-bye to the many friends who had come to wish us luck. But we were by no means out of the wood yet : at Southampton an exceedingly amiable official of the Harbour Trust looked after us with the utmost kindness, but prefaced his good deeds with the whispered warning that we had to face a movietone camera. We were bundled up on to the boat deck of the ship and introduced to the Captain, whose feelings must have been even more painful than mine, if that were possible. Despite the heroic efforts of two members of the Committee, Mr. Hinks and Professor Mason, who had come all this way to bid us a final farewell, we were taken in hand by an aggressive person who besought us to consider the Great British Public. The Captain and I were compelled to shake hands warmly, and to mumble phrases which it would never have occurred to either of us to utter ; we cursed freely under our breath, but there was no escape and we got the business over as quickly as possible. Happily I have never met anyone who saw the result. The publicity surrounding these big expeditions is undoubtedly one of their most painful aspects.

Shipton and Smijth-Windham were to follow by the next ship and Smythe, Warren, Kempson and Wigram a week later. I believe that they too suffered in their turn ; but I treasure the remark addressed to one of them : " So you are going to Everest ! That must be *quite* in the wilds ! "

The idea of bringing the party out to India in echelon as it were was that both time and money would be saved if the preliminary work of organisation at Darjeeling could be done by a few, after which the whole party would assemble at Kalimpong for the march. Morris had already gone ahead and was hard at work selecting porters ; Wyn Harris would meet us in Calcutta from Kenya ; Oliver would come direct from Jandola, where he was serving with the South Waziristan Scouts. Most of our heavy stuff was sent forward by cargo steamer, but Warren had to bring with him the oxygen apparatus, which was tested up to the last possible moment by him and Shipton. I gather that some of their practical tests on Boxhill caused a good deal of alarm as their masked figures appeared unexpectedly over the brow of some steep rise.

At Bombay, on February 20, I was very glad to place our party in the competent hands of Mr. C. E. Boreham, Manager of the Army & Navy Stores, Ltd., who rendered us such efficient service in 1933. The Government of India again most kindly agreed to the admission of all equipment free of customs duty, and with a minimum of fuss we were off to Calcutta, where we arrived via Agra on February 23. Here it seemed that the whole resources of the Eastern Section of the Himalayan Club had been mobilised in our favour by their most efficient honorary secretary, Mrs. Townend, to whom the expedition owes a debt of gratitude for the endless trouble she took to help us on our way. I had the pleasure of staying with Colonel and Mrs. E. O. Wheeler ; and of hearing at first hand of the great adventure of the Reconnaissance of 1921 when Colonel Wheeler made the first map of the Everest region. I had also the honour of lunching with H.E. the Governor of Bengal, Sir John Anderson, who takes a strong and practical interest in the enterprise and has shown great kindness to two expeditions.

There were long discussions with Mr. T. S. Bowman of *The Statesman,* to whom our expedition news was to be sent, and to be forwarded by him to the *Daily Telegraph.* Then arrangements had to be made with Messrs. Kodak, Ltd., who were to process the expedition photographs.

Wyn Harris joined us in Calcutta, very cheerful yet lamenting an increase of weight during the last three years. Long-distance running in Kenya had entirely failed to keep it down, but he had great hopes of the Tibetan plateau. We spent a most enjoyable evening as guests of Dr. A. M. Heron, the geologist of the 1921 Reconnaissance. Next morning it was time to do a little serious work : Wyn Harris and I interviewed Dr. S. N. Sen, the meteorologist who was so helpful to us in 1933. I had already met Dr. C. W. B. Normand, Director-General of Observatories, at Bombay. As in 1933, he made special arrangements for weather observation, and I now wanted to consult Dr. Sen on points of detail. The latter has always told me that the early prediction of weather conditions on Mount Everest in a given year is an almost impossible feat ; but on this occasion he very willingly gave us the result of observations up to date. They amounted to this : " There are no indications at present that there will be an abnormally early monsoon in the neighbourhood of Everest. Western disturbances from the Persian side may give very bad weather at intervals ; but these periods are likely to be short. The monsoon should take between a fortnight and three weeks to reach Mount Everest from Ceylon. The equatorial current in the Bay of Bengal is rather strong this year, and is likely to increase the rain-bearing capacity of western disturbances. It splits up in the neighbourhood of Orissa, one part going towards the United Provinces and one towards Assam. Up to now the frequency of western currents has been low. On the whole, we may reasonably expect better weather than in 1933. It is impossible to say whether there will be an interval of comparative quiet between the first arrival of the monsoon and its full establishment, but that is expected."

Unfortunately Dr. Sen himself would not be able to help us throughout the expedition, being under orders of transfer, but the work would be carried on by his successor, Dr. Roy. Messages would be sent to us at the Base Camp every evening, followed by special telegrams at the observer's discretion in the mornings.

For our part we undertook to assist the department by reporting weekly during the march across Tibet and twice daily from the Base Camp ; dealing specially with temperature, precipitation, wind movements and strength, cloud formations and general descriptions of weather. Though naturally tentative, the information so far gained was distinctly reassuring, and we were able to tackle with cheerfulness our next task, transport to Darjeeling. This was made easy by the cordial co-operation of the Bengal and Darjeeling-Himalayan railway authorities, and especially by the most generous and practical assistance given by Mr. G. B. Gourlay, who volunteered to receive, clear through the customs and despatch to Kalimpong the whole of our equipment and stores. As may well be imagined, this was a tremendous task, undertaken and carried through in a manner beyond praise. Gourlay, who is himself a good mountaineer, has twice been on the verge of inclusion in Everest parties. In 1936 the choice of a transport officer lay between him and Morris. The latter served on the 1922 Expedition, and is a first-rate Nepali scholar. Gourlay in the most generous spirit recognised these qualifications in his friendly rival, and

D

accepted his own disappointment in a way that has earned him our highest respect and regard.

With friends such as these, there could be no delay and no strain. By February 26 we were in Darjeeling, knowing full well that there was no need to look back and see if our arrangements were maturing.

At Siliguri, where the Darjeeling-Himalayan railway begins, we were met by our hard-headed interpreter, Karma Paul, who has served with every expedition except the first. He was just in time to prevent me, on the station platform, from precipitating myself into the arms of a total stranger, whom I mistook for a porter friend of 1933, and whose incipient alarm was most amusing to witness. Karma Paul took Dr. and Mrs. Humphreys up in his car (when not engaged in trying to put us on the summit of Mount Everest, he is a flourishing car and lorry proprietor at Darjeeling). Wyn Harris and I preferred to go up by that quaint little railway which climbs terrifying gradients until the angle becomes so severe that you seem to be on the point of rushing cata-strophically backwards to the plains ; it then takes to a rack and pinion arrangement and clatters noisily upwards, crossing the road at frequent intervals to the embarrassment of bullock cart drivers and negotiating hairpin bends where, from your carriage, you can very nearly shake hands with the engine driver in his cab. At critical points, where the question of forward or backward movement seems to be in the balance, a man stands on the front plate of the engine and scatters sand in large quantities on the rails to prevent wheel-slip. It is all very primitive and very delightful, as we climb up from the hot plains of Bengal, through the densely wooded foothills, to the 7,000-foot ridge on which Darjeeling stands.

Morris was awaiting us at the little hill terminus with several of the 1933 porters, all of whom he already knew by name, and who were clearly on the best of terms with him. It is inexpressibly delightful after a period of years again to

34

meet the men with whom you have climbed. There is no preliminary awkwardness : you just take up the threads where you dropped them and begin a new pattern. I particularly enjoyed watching Ang Tarkey, Rinzing and Tsering Tarkey, three " tigers " of 1933, whom Wyn Harris had led up the North Face. With me they were friends, with him they were brothers. Then there was that big strong country bumpkin, Jingmi, who carried Birnie on his back down from Camp II. Many others also, all of them most merry and bright, and decked with flowers. It was quite a triumphal little procession up to the Planters' Club at Darjeeling, where we were again most kindly made honorary members and were welcomed by Mr. and Mrs. Wrangham-Hardy.

At Darjeeling the two most important things to be done were the recruitment of porters and the organisation of transport. The former was taken first ; news that a fresh expedition is to go to Mount Everest travels with an efficiency which must be the despair of wireless engineers ; and I think it highly probable that the Sherpa community, far away in Sola Khombu near the southern slopes of the mountain, were aware of the Tibetan Government's decision long before we received it in England. Anyhow, porters had been coming in for a long time past, and Morris had completed sifting the grain from the chaff before my arrival. Service in a Gurkha regiment, and a masterly knowledge of Nepali, had given him a remarkable understanding of eastern Himalayan people. We wanted about sixty men to accompany us throughout the march ; Morris carefully made his first selections up to this number, keeping a second line ready in case I should, for any particular reason, reject any of the first lot or lose them as a result of an unfavourable medical report. Among the first selections were, naturally, the majority of the best men we had in 1933. The character rolls which I wrote out at the end of that expedition, supplemented by Mrs. Townend's

careful notes on each man's subsequent history, gave Morris
data upon which to work, and his own judgment after personal
interviews was a valuable addition. Most of the " tigers " of
1933 were accepted without hesitation; fortunately none of
them had departed from the straight and narrow way, and
they were both fit and keen. I must except poor Kipa Lama,
that eccentric though gallant sportsman who, having carried
his load to Camp VI, threw it down with a grunt and demanded
on the spot a written certificate of conduct; and afterwards,
during a descent from the North Col, embarrassed his convoy
by the firm assertion that he was dead. On this occasion I
was obliged to tell him that, much as I liked him and appreciated his past services, it would not be a kindness to take him
again. He was too old for this kind of work. Though
grievously disappointed, he accepted my ruling, but asked
for another certificate of conduct, to supplement the very
florid one I had written for him in 1933. I did this, and
added a long letter to Mr. W. J. Kydd, who looks after our
porters' interests during their absence. I hoped that thereby
local employment would be found for Kipa, but the letter
was never delivered. I think poor Kipa, his slightly un-
balanced mind working in a channel of its own, must have
put both certificate and letter into the charm box slung round
his neck and have gone off into the blue, trusting rather to
their abstract than to their concrete effect.

Darjeeling was almost *en fête* for this occasion, and I very
much doubt if any work was done in the bazaar on this day.
Certainly all traffic along the road below the Planters' Club
was held up. Everybody had brought his wife and children,
most of the less useful men had partaken freely of the raw
bazaar *chang*, and along one side of the road all the inveterate
gamblers pursued their avocations with complete indifference
to their surroundings.

With a great deal of trouble Morris's first and second
selections were carved out of the crowd and stood in two long

lines, both ends of which wobbled nervously as unacceptable candidates forced themselves in among the ranks from time to time. We passed along, and considered each man individually; the accepted ones were formed into a fresh line and securely guarded from unofficial interruption. Morris's choice had been so good that within an hour his first line was enrolled, and it only remained to take a few from the second line to replace possible casualties. I regretted my inability to leave some of the really good men for Monsieur de Segogne and the French Himalayan expedition, on whose behalf Mademoiselle Odette Bruhl, of the G.H.M., was present in Darjeeling. I gave her the best list I could, but Everest had to come first.

We do not take porters to Mount Everest without previous medical examination, though very few, in spite of the very strenuous life they lead from early childhood, are afflicted by heart trouble, or indeed any other serious complaint. You cannot be sure. Further, they are extremely partial to a diet of pork, lightly singed in the fire for the sake of appearances; and in consequence are liable to infection by various organisms which must be eliminated if their host is to be efficient. Accordingly our candidates were at once marched off to the Darjeeling hospital, where the Civil Surgeon, Major T. S. Thomas, I.M.S., and Dr. Yen Sing most kindly collaborated with Humphreys in examining them. The men who had been through this ordeal before lost no opportunity of telling their new colleagues what a frightful time they were going to have; and several amusing incidents occurred. Humphreys called upon one young man to cough. The young man did so with extreme violence, straight into Humphreys' face, and then laughed immoderately at the result. Another young man, taken aside into a private ward for an inquisition of a more intimate nature, thought this altogether too much of a good thing and came bouncing out of the door among his agitated comrades, protesting against the indignity. How he was

37

appeased I know not, but in the end all the men were given doses of an extremely searching medicine and spent the next two days in a state of high curiosity.

There was a pathetic side to the situation : Pasang, who did extremely well in 1933, was found to have a murmur in his heart, and was at first rejected. I could see him edging his way back into the line, wearing an expression of such profound anxiety that I could not resist asking the doctors to overhaul him once more. Happily he was given the benefit of the doubt, and he never failed us on the mountain. Others, again, one had to harden one's heart and refuse. Some were too old, some bore scars of severe frost-bite on Kangchenjunga or Nanga Parbat, and too many with good previous reputations had allowed the temptations of the bazaar and of so-called civilisation to ruin their constitutions.

More men would be needed on the mountain, and it would obviously be of great advantage if they could be recruited direct from Sola Khombu and join us at Rongbuk. During the winter Morris sent out Ang Tarkey and Ang Tsering to select about a hundred of the best on the spot ; and Ang Tsering remained with orders to bring the whole lot over the Nangpa La to meet us in April. Of them more anon. Meanwhile arrangements were very kindly made by Mr. Laden La, who always helps us on these occasions, for the Lamas of the Ghoom monastery to bless the expedition—a ceremony by which the porters set considerable store.

This was the time of the Holi festival, celebrated by Hindus of certain classes with a good deal of horseplay and conviviality. The Sherpas are not, of course, Hindus, but in the East you need not refrain from joining in your neighbour's merrymaking because you hold a different creed ; and in general Hinduism is widely tolerant. But our porters were going to Everest and had no intention of " missing the bus " for the sake of ephemeral pleasure. They looked on with an air of virtuous aloofness, cocking an eye to see if this exemplary conduct was observed. So there were no returns of "drunk and incapable" to worry about. Instead, they crowded in full force into the Planters' Club, where it had occurred to Wyn Harris to show them his 1933 cinema film. The men brought their wives and families—even little babies, each in a wicker-work basket. A few chairs were provided for us, but most of the audience sat on the floor or stood. It must have been the atmosphere which broke three window-panes, because the behaviour of the crowd was beyond reproach. True, they knocked over the projector-tripod three times before the performance began, but we were packed like sardines in the semi-darkness and any movement anywhere was transmitted with hydraulic effect. Jemadar Lachiman Singh and Karma Paul undertook between them the task of commentators on the film. It was not really essential, because the audience were extremely quick to recognise both action and scenery. I was squeezed in between Ang Tarkey and Ondi, with sundry children prancing on my feet and holding on to my collar ; and could hear most of the delighted chatter as the film unrolled. " Why, that's Pasang " ; " Look at me climbing up to Camp IV " ; " See, that's just what the place looked like—steep enough, isn't it ? " ; " There go Ishsmythe Sahib and Shipton Sahib, and there's Ramro Sahib " (Longland) ; " Oh, and the great Lama of Rongbuk " ; " You wait till you get on to snow like that " (this to a novice) ; " Don't be a damned fool—*we* fixed that rope." So it went on, for two mortal hours of semi-suffocation but unalloyed delight. Wyn Harris will never have a more appreciative audience.

I think it will always be difficult to find good cooks for expeditions, yet they are an important factor which is apt to be neglected till the last moment. In 1933 we had a very fair artist in Tencheddar, who had some gift of organisation and a courageous persistence in times of difficulty. He was one of the first men I asked for on arrival at Darjeeling, only to find that he was dead. His understudy Chun-Chun, whose

39

pink pyjamas for daywear we remembered better than his cooking, was taken on at once, for at least he had held the fort at Camp II for many days and given us something better than the monotonous food of the higher camps. Two other men—Lhakpa and Pasang—had to be engaged on very slender credentials. Such available trained cooks as were prepared to join demanded impossible wages, and one knew that men who have been accustomed to work in civilised houses may function well enough for the first few days; after that they develop anxiety about their families, followed rapidly by hypochondria. Chun-Chun evinced readiness to learn the art of bread-making after we had bought him a wonderful camp oven; and some of his early menus contained strange items such as " Beef classic " and " Apricot Mall." It all seemed very promising.

Practically all the porters made family allotments before leaving. Under this system, by which they set much store, Mr. Kydd pays out a weekly sum to their dependants and nearest of kin, to be deducted from wages when the expedition returns to Darjeeling. It would never do to pay the men in full during the campaign, as they cannot resist the temptation for a carouse in every village they pass through.

Morris and I now set about the second part of our work, namely transport. To arrange for this we had to go first to Kalimpong, where Mr. and Mrs. Odling gave us the very warmest of welcomes and as before took upon their shoulders the task of securing the safe arrival from railhead and the storing of all our expedition boxes. Here also I made a tentative arrangement with the firm of Pangda Tsang, the Tibetan Government trader, for transport across Tibet. Next day we proceeded to Gangtok, the capital of Sikkim, where there was a good deal of business to be transacted and discussed with Mr. B. J. Gould, the Political Officer in Sikkim. Mr. Gould had had a good deal of trouble over our passport. It seemed that one or two unauthorised travellers had entered

Tibet, and that the Tibetan authorities were much annoyed. However, Mr. Gould was able to persuade them that we were after all officially accredited, and he guaranteed that we would faithfully abide by the terms of our permission. The Tibetan Government thereupon honourably implemented its promise, and the passport arrived punctually.

This time I devoted much thought to the possibility of taking a full Everest expedition, for the first time, straight up through North Sikkim and over the two 17,000-foot passes on the frontier to Kampa Dzong. This would save the party the long trudge up the Chumbi Valley and the extremely severe conditions prevalent on the Tibetan plateau in the Phari district early in the year. Those conditions, I knew, took a great deal out of both Europeans and porters. The project was somewhat frowned upon by General Bruce, who feared that we might find the mountain paths and bridges out of order in the spring, and that we might get held up by a heavy fall of snow on the passes. Certainly the route should not be embarked upon without a great deal of previous enquiry. Here we were to find a most generous friend in His Highness Sir Tashi Namgyal, K.C.I.E., the Maharaja of Sikkim. He not only welcomed us to his country, but undertook that the roads and bridges should be repaired, and that his people should provide ample transport.

Matters being thus satisfactorily in train, Morris and I hurried back to Darjeeling to complete our work there. Shipton had meanwhile arrived from England, and set to work getting our expedition boxes ready for transport from Kalimpong. Smijth-Windham, who had a very hard time in England preparing single-handed his wireless equipment, was looking more than a little tired; but he lost no time in organising the wireless station at Darjeeling which was to be manned by Serjeant W. J. Frawley, Indian Army Ordnance Corps, and Lance-Corporal Maudsley, Royal Corps of Signals, whose services had been very kindly lent to the expedition by the

Officers Commanding Rawalpindi Arsenal and "A" Corps Signals, respectively.

Though without any previous experience of wireless work, Gavin undertook to help Smijth-Windham, and most efficiently did he do it throughout the expedition. We were also fortunate in receiving valuable help of all kinds from the Posts and Telegraphs Department of Bengal, thanks to whom there was never any leakage of news.

The blessing of the expedition by the Ghoom Lamas was now carried out with full ceremony and to the complete satisfaction of the porters; and was followed by a general parade at which the German Red Cross was conferred upon Pasang "Picture" in recognition of gallantry displayed by him during the ill-fated German Nanga Parbat expedition of 1934. The presentation was made by Herr Hartlmaier, the leader of an enterprising little German party which was touring India by car.

After this, matters of finance remained to be discussed with Mr. A. Y. Russell of the Imperial Bank of India, from whom I began by drawing Rs 24,000 for expenses in Tibet. Wyn Harris again made himself responsible for the expedition accounts, and the treasury chest was placed in the safe hands of Jemadar Lachiman Singh Sahi of the 1/3rd Q.A.O. Gurkha Rifles, assisted by Lance-Naik Lilambar Rana and Lance-Naik Gopal Gurung of the 2nd Battalion of the same regiment, whose services had been kindly placed at our disposal by the Commander-in-Chief in India. These Gurkha soldiers, besides doing a lot of sound though unspectacular work, always provide much fun by reason of their quaint comments on men and things. For instance, on the first occasion that I met Lance-Naik Gopal Gurung he was presented with a photograph of himself recently taken by Morris. He stared at this for some time with an utterly inscrutable countenance: then, suddenly brightening up, he said, "I don't know anything about my face, but it's an uncommonly good photograph of my shirt."

The expedition may be said to have started when we left
Darjeeling for Kalimpong on the morning of March 9. We
did not get away altogether unscathed : Morris was stopped on
the Mall by an old lady who censured him for being " one of
those nasty horrid men who try to climb Mount Everest and
thereby cause the earthquakes in India and Nepal." But it
was cheering to have a last few words with a planter friend who
thought that although we might have some disturbed weather
when crossing the high passes into Tibet, conditions looked
favourable for a fine season after that. So far, there had been
nothing abnormal in the Darjeeling weather. Days were
sunny and warm, nights cold. Away to the north, clouds
not infrequently concealed that marvellous mountain panorama which, once seen, can never be forgotten ; but this
was quite usual, and when the mists cleared away one could
see Kangchenjunga from base to summit, the latter flying a
long streamer to the south-east—proof that the expected
north-west wind was blowing hard. One had reason to suppose that this wind was rapidly clearing the winter snow from
the slabs of Everest. We were able to go direct to Kalimpong
by means of some admirable light Ford cars, which negotiated
the terrific gradients of the Tista Valley with the utmost un-
concern ; but the heavy treasury chest with its guardian
Gurkhas had to go a long way round by the main road in a
lorry, everything being transhipped by hand over the bridge
near Riyang, which was reported to be in an exceedingly
delicate state of health. All turned up safely at Kalimpong
that night. Mrs. Odling had, as in 1933, arranged " Cawnpore House " for our reception ; but she would not hear of
our dining anywhere but in her own lovely home. Here we
found Oliver awaiting us, and I am ashamed to say that in
my general preoccupation and absent-mindedness I entirely
failed to recognise him at first—a *bêtise* which he condoned
with the utmost good humour.

A cyclone of activity now raged at Panda Tsang's godown

in Kalimpong, where Morris and Shipton spent their days in sorting out the great masses of equipment and despatching it by the fine mule transport which was now available. We were joined on March 11 by Smythe, Kempson, Warren and Wigram, all looking very fit. They brought with them no less than 60 maunds (a maund is 80 lb.) of baggage, much of it oxygen apparatus. Mr. Gould came over from Gangtok for further discussion about our passport, and to help at a conference with the Pipen of Lachen, an individual with a remarkable eye for business who organised the baggage train. On March 12 we made an issue of kit to the porters, and had a great fright when it was found that large numbers of the marching boots supplied for them from Cawnpore were too small. How this had happened I do not know, for Morris had taken the trouble at Darjeeling to measure the feet of several typical Sherpas and Bhutias, and to send measurements and outlines to Messrs. Cooper Allen at Cawnpore. I was obliged to send off a long telegram to Messrs. Cooper Allen ordering 110 fresh pairs, with little hope that they would catch us up until we had proceeded a considerable distance on our way. But I had reckoned without the firm's goodwill and resources: on the next day they telegraphed a reply, undertaking to keep their factory working all night and to send off the required boots by passenger train within twenty-four hours. What is more, they kept their undertaking, supplied us with a splendid lot of new boots, and even agreed to take back those which had been found too small.

Morris and I had a difficult morning interview with the firm of Pangda Tsang. We were using their godown, and they were confidently expecting that we would employ their transport round via Phari to Kampa Dzong. This arrangement had been only tentative, and I had been careful to explain this before, but the firm had been obliged to make certain arrangements in advance in Tibet, and were naturally very disappointed when we made the decision to go up through

44

Sikkim, where only Sikkimese transport could be used. However, after a great deal of diplomacy they professed themselves satisfied with the compensation which I was able to offer.

Meanwhile the Sikkim people made themselves entirely responsible for the safe conveyance of our goods as far as Tangu, where we should join them later. But Smijth-Windham, conscientious as ever, was not going to commit his delicate machinery to the tender mercies of mule drivers, and he persisted in accompanying it for the first part of the journey, to meet us at Gangtok.

There was a great day when the whole expedition, the Odlings, Dr. Graham and other friends had the pleasure of lunching with Raja Topgye Dorje and his wife. Our host and hostess had evidently taken immense trouble over this affair ; we were privileged to enjoy their national food, perfectly cooked and served in lovely china bowls. As was only right and proper, we were expected to use ivory chop-sticks ; after a little practice this was found to be no deterrent, and Oliver is credibly asserted to have consumed seven bowls in rapid succession. Altogether it was a most enjoyable party ; and to stifle any premature thoughts of training at this early stage, Mrs. Odling gave next day a wonderful dinner at which some eighteen people were present. It is impossible to exaggerate the kindness which met us at every turn in Kalimpong.

Pangda Tsang's godown was now rapidly emptying, and half the party were able to push off to Gangtok, to be followed on the 16th by the remainder. The day before that final departure Morris, Shipton, Wyn Harris and I attended divine service at the Kalimpong Homes, where Dr. Graham asked Wyn Harris and me to read the lessons and organised a delightful farewell gathering at his house.

On arrival at Gangtok we found Mr. Gould hospitably occupied in putting up the whole expedition in relays. We owe him a debt of gratitude, for he took an infinity of trouble to make us comfortable, and then was most careful to see that there was no obstacle on the political side of the expedition's affairs. I remember how, when handing over the passport, he impressed upon me the necessity for keeping strictly to its terms. Many people do not realise the vital importance of deferring to the wishes of the Tibetan authorities, if future visitors are to be welcome. Tibet is still, for general purposes, a closed country, and we are bound to respect the wish of its rulers to maintain their isolation. Lastly, Mr. Gould went out of his way to help us in the matter of Sikkim transport, negotiating both in person and through his able Personal Assistant, Rai Norbu Bahadur.

We lost no time in paying a formal call upon the Maharaja, who most kindly invited us all to dinner to meet everyone in Gangtok. I cannot forget the warmth of his welcome, nor the quiet, practical way in which he placed the resources of his staff and country at our disposal. Under his direction the State Engineer, Rai Fakir Chand Sahib, put the roads and bridges of North Sikkim into a state of complete repair, no mean undertaking in a region where the heavy monsoon rains, followed by winter gales and snowfall, cause havoc on a cataclysmic scale. After this there could be no anxiety about our communications. The dinner at the palace was altogether delightful, in a room hung with priceless Tibetan " banners "; but speeches had to be made, and in my nervousness I referred to His Highness as the Maharaja of Tibet !

At Gangtok I decided to form a small staff of the most experienced mountaineers—Smythe, Shipton, Wyn Harris and Kempson, and to work out, at least in outline, our strategic plan. We had a long conversation on the 17th in the room which Mr. Gould had thoughtfully set aside for such purposes, and I was delighted with the splendid spirit which prevailed on this occasion. Everybody was most reasonable and helpful, so discussion never degenerated into argument, and practically complete agreement was reached. The main conclusions were :

1. Base Camp should be reached about April 24 and left on April 27. Our real base this time would be made at the old Camp I. Operation headquarters would be at Camp III, which must be completely stocked by May 15. A new Camp II would be placed in the medial trough of the East Rongbuk glacier, at a place observed by the reconnaissance party of 1935. Camp III would be moved nearer to the base of the North Col slopes.

2. Smythe, Wyn Harris, Shipton and Kempson would, on arrival at Camp III, advise on the best route up the North Col, but would do no step-cutting themselves. This work would be taken on by the other climbers and by selected porters, thus conserving the energy of the probable first two assault parties.

3. The first assault party would endeavour to occupy Camp IV on the North Col on May 22, and to commence their assault on May 25.

4. The second assault party would go up to Camp IV on May 24, and start their climb on the 27th.

5. Oxygen would be taken up to the high camps by porters and used at their discretion by the first two parties. If they failed, the third party would definitely use oxygen.

6. There would be three camps above the North Col, so as to shorten the carries above Camp V. Camp VI would be placed at the foot of the yellow band on the North Face, at about 27,000 feet. Camp VII would be below the first step at a height of about 27,800 feet. I should say here that this decision was something of a compromise. Some of us, notably Wyn Harris, adhered to Norton's opinion that there should never be more than two camps above the North Col ; whereas Smythe, after discussion at home with Somervell, thought it might be possible to place a final camp in or near the great couloir east of the final pyramid, or even on the top of the great buttress beyond the couloir.

47

7. The capacity and morale of our best porters having now improved so markedly, it was thought justifiable to permit them to descend unattended from the highest camps except in the worst conditions.

8. During the final assault any climber who found his powers failing must turn whilst still strong enough to get down to camp by himself. His companion must use his own discretion about proceeding.

These decisions were, of course, subject to modification in accordance with circumstances and, anyhow, they would be worked out in more complete detail later on. So far as they went, they represented a reconciliation of some divergent opinions, and it was clear that each member of the staff was thinking more of the objective than of a dialectical triumph. The great point was that we could now set out on the march without the dismal prospect of continuous, unprofitable and exhausting argument.

March 18 was devoted firstly to sundry experiments with the wireless, secondly in allocation of work throughout the party : Smythe and Wigram undertook the messing ; Morris and Oliver the transport ; Shipton was made O.C. porters, and was to work out in detail a tactical plan and the loads required for the assaults ; Wyn Harris would be fully occupied with the accounts ; Humphreys and Warren, in addition to their medical duties, would interest themselves respectively in botany, and in physiology and the oxygen apparatus ; Smijth-Windham and Gavin would, of course, be responsible for the wireless. Lastly, Kempson undertook two important duties, the management of our postal arrangements and the control of kerosene supplies. He and I visited the postmaster at Gangtok and left with him a deposit of Rs 500 to be used for stamping our homeward mail. I regret to say that, as will subsequently appear, this arrangement was a total failure. Meanwhile, a service of postal runners, or rather riders, was organised ; they were to work under the general direction

48

of a Tibetan who had been well recommended to us, Sandup by name. Kempson, with the utmost thoroughness, worked out a scheme under which mails might and should succeed each other, both outwards and homewards, at intervals of about a week. As for kerosene fuel, he was obliged to put into operation a fairly severe system of rationing; this time we had about 200 gallons of kerosene with us, to save the expense and inefficiency of the usual Tibetan fuel, and we knew that the Sherpa porter, and particularly the Sherpa cook, had but little idea of economy in this respect.

A more complete organisation of the porters had to be made; and this year it was decided to make an experiment which it was hoped, with justice, would have admirable results in discipline and efficiency. Men who did well in 1933 were to have N.C.O.'s rank and to be put in charge of particular sections of the men; and among their duties would be included responsibility for the safe transport and arrival at the end of each march of specified equipment and store boxes. These under-sardars, as they were called, were to receive special pay and special equipment, and to be distinguished by the stripes of their rank. For sardar—serjeant-major, as it were— we selected Nursang, who did very well in 1933 and had previously served with a hospital unit of the Indian Army. Nursang is a man of great energy, courage and resource, with some little failings which compelled me to qualify the favourable remarks I entered in his character roll in 1933. Before leaving Darjeeling this time I read him a severe lecture and impressed upon him his great responsibilities as sardar; and undertook to erase the unfavourable part of his record if he served us well. He certainly did take himself in hand after this, and he never spared himself—or his men—throughout the operations. His character is as hard as his face, which is saying a good deal; but he has humour, which generally gets him out of tight places. Broadly speaking, the men thought of him as the Eton boy thought of his headmaster : " a beast, but a just

E

beast," and that is a pretty good testimonial for a man who has to control those high-spirited people, the Everest porters.

The new scheme took on at once, and was greatly appreciated by the men. The only snag was that Nursang, to the horror of two of the party, adopted a very military demeanour, clicking his heels and saluting both in and out of season, and parading the men on the slightest provocation—I don't think he ever quite succeeded in making them form fours. However, one must judge by results, and these were wholly admirable. On the evening of the 18th we collected the porters in the garden of the Residency to hear a message from General Bruce and an announcement of the special rewards which would be given to those men who distinguished themselves on the mountain. Left to their own devices on this occasion, they would probably have loafed up in twos and threes, and have strolled through the tidy flower-beds and spat on the lawn ; leaving several comrades behind in the bazaar. Anyhow, Nursang was running no risks. He turned them out in good order, and we were complimented on our discipline.

Chapter IV

OUTWARD BOUND

ON the 19th the real march to Tibet began ; not without ceremony, for the Maharaja with his whole staff and escort came to the Residency to wish us good luck, himself presenting us with silk scarves : an honour which was very greatly appreciated.   Mr. Gould proposed our health and success, and the assembled residents of the place heaped good wishes upon us. Then, after a perfect orgy of photography, the expedition was off along the road to Dikchu.   Morris and I started last, having a few final details to attend to, and were able to meet at lunch Major-General W. L. O. Twiss, who was such a good friend to us at Army Headquarters in 1933.   Morris had a very bad time with a sore foot descending the seemingly interminable 9 miles of steep hill down to Dikchu.   Smythe thoughtfully sent out porters with a lantern to help us through the thick woods at the bottom of the valley.

Now for the first time the expedition found itself alone, and I well remember on that first evening at Dikchu the self-consciousness which seemed to assail us all as we took stock of each other.   In such a party, however, that state of things could not last long.   It would, I think, be difficult to find a more urbane collection of men, and in a very short time there was established a harmony which was never lost throughout the expedition.   The majority were by no means strangers to each other. Five served on Everest in 1933 ; four were on the Reconnaissance in 1935. The newcomers, except Humphreys, climbed with Smythe in Switzerland in 1935. The very diversity of our professions ensured a cosmopolitan and therefore interesting—and interested—outlook. Smythe, before settling down (at intervals) to an author's life, was an electrical engineer and afterwards an R.A.F. officer ; Shipton, when not exploring the world, plants coffee in Kenya ; Morris, Smijth-Windham, Oliver and Gavin are soldiers (Morris, having now retired from the Army, devotes himself to anthropology and ethnology) ; Kempson is a master at Marlborough College, and a fine mathematician ; Wyn Harris and I belong to the Kenya and Indian Civil Services respectively ; Humphreys, Warren and Wigram are of the medical persuasion. Humphreys must forgive me if I single him out for more particular exposure : he holds one of the first hundred British airpilots' tickets, which date back to before the War, and recalls with positive but uncanny delight that his first forty landings were all crashes, in those days of empirical design. Shot down in France in 1915, he survived undismayed the years of imprisonment in Germany before the Armistice ; he did air survey in Africa, and then studied medicine and botany with a view to exploration work—anywhere and everywhere, with a special hope of Everest. Lastly, he commanded the British Ellesmere Land Expedition, which returned just in time for him to join us. From a life of many hardships he has extracted a humour entirely *sui generis*. One of my permanent impressions of 1936 is Humphreys in a mess-tent reducing his hearers to the agony of immoderate laughter by some impromptu tale of his experiences—told without one single smile but with perfect artistry. Not that he ever tried to " catch the Speaker's eye "—far from it. Everybody had something to contribute : Wyn Harris' stories of Kenya administration, for instance, though unlikely to find their way into the pages of Blue Books, lacked nothing of realism ; and Oliver, whose life in the South

Waziristan Scouts has not been without incident, was also discovered to be a portrait artist of very considerable promise. As the Mess was installed in three tents, and as we made up, informally, a different marching order every day, there was ample variety of contacts.

Those early days up the Sikkim valleys were extraordinarily pleasant. Later on, we knew, the narrow paths above the river would be streaming with rain-water and alive with leeches, but now we marched up through lovely scenery with nothing to worry us but the fact that we badly needed exercise. That scenery is interesting as well as beautiful. From Dikchu, at about 2,000 feet above sea-level, to Tangu, at about 13,500 feet, is a distance of 40-odd miles; the path climbs up for the most part through narrow, steepsided gorges, which are thickly wooded in the lower reaches. Down by the river, which is never far away, flourishes the heavy sub-tropical growth induced by a warm climate and abundant rainfall. This gradually thins out towards the crests of the ridges, where the great Himalayan pines emerge as individuals from the crowd. Behind them the blue of the sky always looks deeper, yet more luminous where it reflects the sheen of distant ice. We are passing through the main chain of the Himalaya. The narrow, steep nature of the gorge is explained by the fact that these mountains are, in a geological sense, of modern origin and do not form the true watershed. The Tista river, like so many others in this part of the world, is of greater antiquity and its source is farther to the north. As the great southern thrust developed, fashioning the Himalaya, this and other rivers fought their way through along their original channels downward to the Indian plains, carving in the process the tremendous clefts which often are so difficult to pass. One has only to see the rush of water during the monsoon, and to hear the thunder of its passage and the savage rumble of boulders turning over and over below the surface, to realise the forces at work. In their lower sections

53

the hillsides are frequently true precipices, where the road-engineer is obliged to blast a track across the face—sometimes even to shore his path up on logs for which holes are drilled in the living rock. It is impossible to keep permanently to one side of the river, and every kind of suspension bridge is brought into play, from the primitive, giddily swinging affair of rope and bamboo, which for centuries has sufficed a people who do not suffer from vertigo, to the ambitious bastions and steel cables of the bridge above Dikchu.

There is an unforgettable view westwards up the Talung valley towards the mighty Kangchenjunga, Simvu and perhaps the loveliest of all peaks—Siniolchu, which inspired Sella's photographic masterpiece. This little valley is the home of a fast-disappearing race, the Lepchas : a gentle, shy people who seem to have a marvellous aptitude for botany. It is a tragic pity that they have been unable to hold their own against hardier races, for the singular beauty of form and feature which can be seen in individuals of both sexes is a sure indication of something which the striving modern world can ill afford to lose. I am only glad that Morris has undertaken to make an ethnological and cultural study of so charming a people, before it is too late.

At Singhik I read out the strategic plan, which was most favourably received ; and appointed Smythe second in command. Much encouraged by my reception, I even ventured on a little homily which included, I remember, the hope that we could hold together as well as the Bavarians had done on Kangchenjunga, and placed a taboo upon the word " deterioration." Even these sentiments were accepted in the best part, and we reached Lachen in high spirits. Here the Pipen had good news of his transport, which was working well and smoothly ; but we very nearly lost Morris, who began to run a temperature up to alarming altitudes and was pronounced to be suffering from a very severe attack of malaria. At one point there seemed to be nothing for it but to send him back to Darjeeling and out of the hunt; but Humphreys and Warren persevered, and ultimately he was able to carry on, at what cost to himself only he can tell. We should sorely have missed so pleasant a companion and so competent a transport officer.

Above Lachen those who had been this way before knew of a certain bed of watercress, in a little stream flanking the path above the river. Smijth-Windham, who was doing the day's march with Humphreys, approached this place in a state of pleasurable anticipation, for watercress is not only said to be full of the right vitamins but is much appreciated by thirsty travellers. Arrived on the spot, he observed the formality of consulting our M.O. as to any possible risk from enteric or other infection. Humphreys, quite reasonably in such wild surroundings, declared the watercress fit for human consumption; and a large bagful was collected. A hundred yards farther upstream a dead and very decadent pony was found lying in the water. The cress was hastily abandoned.

It was decided to make a stay of several days at Tangu, at a height of about 13,500 feet. At this place stands the last of the rest-houses in Northern Sikkim, built on a small terrace high above the river. During the approach one is conscious of a sense of freedom, as the valley opens out considerably for a few miles. Ever since leaving Lachen and crossing, just above that, the deep gorge of the Zemu (the way to Kangchenjunga), the hillsides have begun to slope back at gentler angles. Even beyond Tangu, at the place where the road finds an unexpected way between the shoulders of Chomiomo and Kangchenjau, they will not converge so nearly again. At the end of March we find snow here and there. Trees are rapidly diminishing, though such as can brave this altitude are sturdy enough. Away on the seemingly bare hillsides are clusters of little black dots—these are the yaks which will take our heavy baggage over the passes to Kampa Dzong. The music of their bells comes pleasantly to the ear

55

as one struggles up the last few hundred yards to the rest-house, knowing that tea and a good fire are waiting. This is the last house we shall stay in for many a long day, and must be made the most of, however primitive the furniture or draughty the rooms. First impressions are startling, for some traveller—possibly a cynic—has pasted round the match-boarding of the principal room a whole series of photographs from the illustrated papers of 1901. Here are the reigning beauties of those days; lovely faces, some of them, free from the look of strain so common nowadays. But the dresses! Can I possibly have spent a happy childhood seeing these horrors every day? Yet who knows? Perchance even now the pendulum is swinging back to leg-of-mutton sleeves. "*Plus ça change, plus c'est la même chose.*" From here Karma Paul and Nursang could go on over the passes with the transport and begin negotiations with the Dzongpen at Kampa Dzong, while we stretched our legs on the surrounding mountains and began the not always simple process of acclimatisation. Fearing excessive enthusiasm and subsequent staleness, I imposed a self-denying ordinance in the shape of a height limit of 18,000 feet. Kempson and Oliver took a light camp up one of the side valleys towards the Lungnak La, in the course of which little trek it was soon found that we had in Oliver an already fit mountaineer. The others spent most of their time on the mountain north of the rest-house, where a good deal of work was done on the high-altitude wireless sets and with the oxygen. I could not take much share in all this owing to a severe cold which had hit me hard in the throat as I crossed the bridge at Tsuntang, below Lachen. But I could unobtrusively watch the style in which each man walked uphill—this can convey a lot to one who knows the value of rhythm and balance at high altitudes. To observe Smythe and Shipton, for instance, starting off for a morning's exercise, was a lesson in effortless climbing; and I have seen Shipton descend 3,000 feet in less than twenty-five

56

minutes, down the long bare slopes, never putting a foot wrong.

The light wireless sets promised very well. Smijth-Windham would take a couple of porters and ascend about 1,500 feet with one set, leaving us to work another outside the rest-house. Presently we would see the little mast go up, and within a few minutes conversation would begin. All that was necessary was that there should be no intervening obstacle to interfere with the wireless waves, and that we should turn the right knob to the right place. Presently porters would be put on at both ends and told to say something. They had some vague ideas about telephones with interconnecting wires—that might pass muster ; but Kusang Pagla's face when some ribaldry from Sentenzing drifted down through empty space and smote his ear was a study in bewilderment. His first instinct was to snatch off his earphones ; his next to replace them and think up some suitable repartee, continuing the game till he was removed.

In the afternoons Smythe, Shipton, Wyn Harris and I worked away at the problem of porter transport to the high camps on Everest. We reckoned that the first assault party would require thirty-eight men, who should carry 25 lb. from the North Col; except those selected for Camp VII, who would carry 20 lb. throughout. In 1933 they carried only 15, and sometimes 12. Ang Tarkey and other tigers stoutly maintained that they could manage 30. This gives some idea of their spirit, to say nothing of their strength.

The spell of cloudy, snowy weather prophesied by my planter friend at Darjeeling came exactly to time, and it was just as well that we were under shelter while Morris was on the mend. As soon as he appeared sufficiently recovered to ride some long marches we set off, on April 1, for the Kongra La and Sebu La, the two 17,000-foot passes which separated us from Tibet proper. Snow was lying everywhere, but not at a sufficient depth to give any trouble, and we already knew that

57

the heavy transport had got over safely. I do not think that, whatever the conditions, we should have been stopped, because the valleys here are not steepsided and there is no danger from avalanches. If the snow had been particularly thick, a herd of yaks could soon have stamped a trail. We had not to face anything like the blizzards of the exposed Phari plain. True, it was fairly cold at Gayokang, our first camp in the open before the passes were crossed, but each man had to himself a most excellent pattern of Meade tent which gave splendid shelter though only weighing 16 lb.; and on April 2, with a following wind but a bright sun, we crossed both passes and completed the fifteen miles to Giru; not one man suffering from altitude. I believe that things were very different in 1935 when the Reconnaissance party, without previous acclimatisation, suffered a good deal.

Tibet was bright with all the lovely colouring that one remembered so well, blues and reds and browns predominating; a complete change from the more obvious or more familiar attractions of the southern side of the Himalaya. Looking down northwards from the Sebu La, one seems to be entering a new world. Atmosphere, which makes scenery as most people know it, is entirely absent until the warm monsoon currents reach the Tibetan plateau. The effect of distance is therefore annihilated, and snowy summits which the map tells us are sixty miles away appear as close as Kampa Dzong which we must reach after a few hours' marching. Kampa indeed, its steep rock-face standing out clear-cut against a dark background as the sun strikes down, looks as if one could cast a stone upon it, and I have to adjust my sense of scale to realise that it is fourteen miles away. Yet there is beauty apart from the riot of colour, a beauty perhaps of things imagined as well as seen, of distance and immensity rather than of form. Wave upon wave seems to come rolling up from far-away Siberia, to break silently upon these Himalayan shores. There is no crash of breakers, but the wind is whistling across the pass,

58

and the illusion serves. We are, if not in a new world, at least seeing our old one as she was in the dim past. Those steppes were ridden over by the Mongol horde; they might well be a primæval ocean.

But it is cold up here, and Kempson, who has good-naturedly moderated his usual tremendous walking pace to accompany me over the passes, must be wondering why I linger. The porters straggle past, each adding a stone to the little cairn on the summit—some walking round the bright prayer-flags which flutter in the wind and may keep them safe in time of peril. We follow down the six-mile easy slope towards Giru; able, now that trees and gorges are left behind, to see the whole expedition strung out over leagues of country.

It was far warmer at Giru than we expected, and I find in my diary that on this day there was a great deal of cloud and confused weather on Chomiomo and Kangchenjunga and pre-sumably right along the main chain. For some time past Smythe had been worried by stomachic trouble, and it did seem a shame that he should, on the night of our stay at Giru, become the victim of circumstances. His porter servant, usually steady enough, dined not wisely but much too well in the village, and then returned to camp with the laudable intention of resuming duty and preparing Smythe's tent for the night. Among other things he had to do was the blowing up of the Li-Lo air mattress. With powerful but liquor-charged exhalations from his lungs he blew this up until it was as hard as a drum, and Smythe kept on falling off it during the night. At last, in despair, he got up and pulled out the little stopper in order to let out some of the air; and was very nearly asphyxiated by the appalling fumes which at once filled the tent.

The next day's march of eight miles to Kampa Dzong was wholly delightful, though bad weather persisted over the Himalaya. Karma Paul, who had been negotiating for trans-port, rode out to meet us with the welcome information that

59

it had been procured at the old rates, and that Nursang had been working hard and had got all our boxes ready in order for inspection and despatch. A check made by the transport officers showed that nothing was missing. The Dzongpen was away at Lhasa, but the old Nyapala who served us well in 1933, though not now present in an official capacity, turned out to help us to the best of his power and introduced us to the two subordinate officers who were carrying on. They certainly did their best, but this was the season of a spring festival in Tibet, and we had to remain four days at Kampa for further transport to Tengkye Dzong. We were thereby enabled to witness some exceptionally good dancing, and a kind of tournament which took one right back to the Middle Ages. The riders turned out in mediæval uniform and rode at something like " Turk's heads " fixed on posts in the ground. They fired at these with muzzle-loading guns as they passed, or struck at them with their whips, or threw stones at them. The stone appeared to be the most efficient weapon. The chief object of the horsemen appeared, however, to be a demonstration of their ability to ride at a gallop with both hands off the reins. They would sway from side to side with their arms held rigidly at right angles to their bodies, and would sometimes endeavour to pick things off the ground. To all appearance they were wretchedly mounted, yet one knew the tremendous distances which these hardy little Tibetan ponies can cover without distress.

It was thought necessary to contribute something to this entertainment in spite of our drab costume, so Smijth-Windham, Oliver and Gavin, having armed themselves with sharpened bamboos and persuaded the puzzled Tibetans to stick pieces of paper in the ground as marks, borrowed their hosts' ponies and gave an exhibition of tent-pegging, which was very well received by the crowd. Various members of the party, distrusting the effects of the Capuan luxury at Kampa Dzong, began at this period to take light camps for the night up the surrounding hills, from which, despite the cold, they obtained some very fine dawn photographs of the peaks to the south. Smythe, who was testing out the new Kodak colour film, took a particularly good telephotograph of Mount Everest, eighty miles away. I shall never tire of seeing that picture : the grey monotones before dawn, the dim mass of Everest rising head and shoulders above her Court of giants, cold as Space itself. Suddenly that far-off summit glows red ; minutes seem to pass before the sky turns paler and the light begins to steal, ever so slowly, down the white shoulders. Then, one by one, the lesser summits burst into flame ; the ridges are caught and held, and at last the eastern sunlight comes striding over the plain, calling us to work.

On most evenings Smijth-Windham held a Morse class, in case of the failure of our light high-altitude wireless sets to transmit speech on the mountain. Humphreys had begun teaching Gavin and me on the way out, and it was found that Oliver already had some experience. Eventually Gavin made such rapid progress that he was left to himself to master the code and run the wireless at Camp III.

April 4 was a day of difficulties : it began with the discovery by Smijth-Windham that his expedition box key was missing from his ring. Someone suggested that I should fine all the porters on the principle of including the guilty one somehow. This method undoubtedly does command considerable support in the East, but it does not appeal to me. Generally speaking, our porters were a splendid lot, and I was not going to subject them to indiscriminate suspicion. Again, we did not doubt Smijth-Windham's servant Pasang " Picture," who had never got into trouble of any kind, but I felt obliged to order his temporary suspension on the ground that he must be held generally responsible for his master's things. Meanwhile every effort was made to do a little C.I.D. work through the sardars ; Nursang, with an air of profound wisdom, hung a little bag upon a post in the middle of the camp and assured me that the missing property would be found in the bag next morning. Nothing of the sort occurred.

Then Morris, Wyn Harris and I got down to accounts with the old Pipen of Lachen, whose transport animals had brought us so far. I regret to say that the old gentleman made a barefaced attempt to overcharge us in spite of the definite agreement made at Gangtok. I was obliged therefore to announce that I would pay him now according to our own figures and notes of the agreement; if he did not accept this and sign a receipt for full payment, I would send a copy of our accounts to the Maharaja of Sikkim asking him to appoint his Chief Justice as arbiter. This worked well, and the Pipen gave way.

After so much haggling it seemed about time for a rest, but Karma Paul, feeling possibly that he must contribute something to the day's alarms, now announced that he had seen a number of Tibetan lamas wandering about adorned with expedition snow-goggles. We had warned our men that there would be periodical kit inspections and this was obviously the occasion for one. I first called up the sardars and told them that they were trusted to keep their own affairs in order. This pleased them mightily, and they set to work to ensure the most rigorous turn out of everybody else's things. The upshot was that practically no kit was missing; probably the lamas had got hold of a few pairs of goggles during the return march of the 1933 Expedition.

Other little troubles there were, serving no doubt to keep us up to the mark. Pangda Tsang's men turned up with only 64 of the 100 maunds of *tsampa* which had been ordered for the porters, and no proper bags to put them in; of course, a lot more chat was needed before this was settled. Then Smythe's slumbers were disturbed by the barking of " Tendrup " (the bear), a young Tibetan mastiff which had been bought by Oliver at Tangu. Tendrup possessed a strong character and a sense of humour all his own. He readily accepted Oliver's instructions to refrain from barking at night, though all his instincts and training pointed to this as part of his duty. But woe betide any Tibetan who was found prowling round our dump. When short of real malefactors, Tendrup kept himself fit, and his teeth in good condition, by mimic warfare with us.

Tengkye Dzong was reached on April 8, after a terribly dusty march across the Lingga plain. Distances on this plain are deceptive, and vary from time to time in accordance with the state of the surface, which can be treacherous and boggy after rain. Remembering the frightful morning in 1933 when Raymond Green, Wood-Johnson and I spent several hours falling into mud-holes, I sought local advice and was directed along a route uncommonly like that selected by the Israelites who, as Kinglake dryly remarks in *Eöthen*, spent forty years in traversing a distance which anyone can accomplish in a few days. The actual distance between Lingga and Tengkye is perhaps eight miles. We made it about fourteen, being forced to cross an endless series of small hill spurs, all covered with wind-blown sand, instead of passing over the plain. Our custom was to " ride and tie," finances not allowing of a pony each. I except tough guys like Humphreys, who always walked. On the way Kempson with an air of happy remembrance pointed out to me, far away to the south, a little white heap which he asserted must be the débris of the 140 eggs which three members of the Reconnaissance are alleged to have devoured in one day.

The resident Dzongpen of Tengkye being away, everything was done for us by his Nyapala, who had been rather suspicious of us in 1933 but has now become the best of friends. I did very much miss that charming old boulevardier, the Dzongpen, who was so pathetically pleased to welcome even English strangers in his exile. Tengkye Dzong expected a good deal of us, after the Olympic games which made such a sensation there before. This time we had no Longland to

63

demonstrate pole jumping, and no Boustead to teach the art of self-defence. Football, however, and even a very primitive kind of cricket were something to go on with, and then we bethought ourselves of the lake, on which to our astonishment were several black-headed gulls, presumably visitors from the Bay of Bengal. Now Wyn-Harris, Smijth-Windham, Gavin and I happened to be interested in sailing, our discussions on which had often reduced poor Morris to silent despair. Could we now manage a regatta ? Of boats, of course, there were none ; I forget to whom occurred the brilliant idea of Li-Lo mattresses reinforced with struts from the Arctic tents, with the refinement of a cockpit in the shape of a canvas bath. Blankets provided some kind of sail. Smijth-Windham's yacht suffered a puncture before she could be launched and he was out of it ; but Wyn Harris and Gavin put up a very sporting show which was intensely appreciated by the locals and the porters, and gave the former something more to remember us by.

We were not *always* frivolous during this march across Tibet. Above Tengkye Dzong there are a number of fairly steep rocky hills, on which Warren was able to observe the reaction of various men to the use of the oxygen apparatus. Most of us were tested, and I think we were agreed that the oxygen enabled one to climb without distress, once proper adjustments had been made. Apart from oxygen, some of the rock masses provided some really difficult climbing, of the kind that is distinctly needed if men are to reach Mount Everest with their muscles in good condition. As is well known, ordinary walking, although it may and does conduce to general fitness, does not train the climbing muscles. It is not improbable that on the buttress which forms the western wall of the great couloir on Mount Everest, and on the slopes of the final pyramid, the angle of the slabs will be found sufficiently severe to demand from the climber considerable use of his arms. Anyhow, where men have not done any rock work for a fairly long time, as is the case in Everest parties, both their muscles and their balance are improved by a little exercise of the kind enjoyed at Tengkye Dzong.

In all, a stay of four and a half days became necessary at this place. The harsh climate and the poor grazing at this time of year, as well as the sparsely populated character of the country, make the collection of transport for a large expedition by no means easy, though the Tibetan authorities have a well-organised system which provides for the calling up of transport animals in rotation for Government needs ; fortunately no movements of troops were taking place, so there was no clash between Government requisitions and our own. I made a considerable number of enquiries whether this system, when applied for our benefit, bore hardly on the people. I gathered that at this particular season it did not, because it was a little too early for agricultural operations. Owners of animals showed no resentment at being called up, and the responsible officials assured me repeatedly that, inasmuch as we paid for all transport promptly, the consequent remissions of Government revenue much more than counterbalanced any inconvenience caused by our passage. But we could not secure anything like the splendid mule transport of Sikkim ; anything available had to be accepted thankfully—yaks, zos, donkeys and occasional mules. Unfortunately the R.S.P.C.A. has no footing in Tibet ; animals, whatever their species and condition, are expected to carry the standard load of 160 lb. This is all very well for the massive yak, but bears hardly on the little donkeys, despite their remarkable strength and spirit. It is only too clear that their life is one of hardship and misery. The Tibetan driver is completely indifferent to sore backs and exhaustion, and many a time we had to interfere and do our poor best to mitigate suffering.

The stay at Tengkye Dzong was made memorable by an unusual event : about 4 p.m. on April 11 our postal riders came into camp from distant Gangtok, evidently carrying

F

something which they had been charged to deliver speedily and with care. It was a telegram which had left Delhi on April 4, and which ran as follows : " I am commanded by His Majesty to convey to you and all members of expedition both British and Indian His Majesty's best wishes for success of your forthcoming attempt. May I also wish you every possible good fortune in your great adventure. Very much wish I had seen you before you started. Viceroy."

In 1933 his late Majesty, King George V, had shown a strong personal interest in our effort, and it was pleasant to know that we were honoured in the same way by his successor ; and Lord Willingdon was, as always, a very good friend to us. Obviously the message must be read out to the whole expedition, even if this entailed a little more militarism. The porters were drawn up with their sardars in front and the British members facing them. I read the message in English first, Jemadar Lachiman Singh then translated it into Nepali and Karma Paul followed with a Tibetan version for the benefit of those who speak only their mother tongue. Our porters are not British subjects, but I could see that they were tremendously impressed by this message from the Sovereign ; I therefore took a chance and called for three cheers for His Majesty. The response was terrific and caused considerable disturbance in peaceful Tengkye Dzong, where heads popped up on all the roofs, while the sea-gulls went wheeling and crying over the lake. Afterwards many of the porters assured me that they considered this a most auspicious event and they were convinced that all would now be well. The effect on their general morale was evidently good.

Social events were limited to a formal payment and return of calls, at which presents were exchanged ; and to a memorable tea-party at the Dzong, attended by Shipton, Humphreys, Gavin and myself. The Nyapala and his wife are splendid hosts, and would not let us go until long after dark. We had to establish a precarious equilibrium between taking as little *chang* as possible and the avoidance of offence. Karma Paul and two under-sardars must have drawn a wonderful picture of our talents and virtues, as formality of the stiffer kind disappeared in the first five minutes, and it was a most jovial evening. By request we had brought the expedition gramophone; the playing of which was shortly entrusted to the Nyapala's son, aged about fifteen. Only with the greatest difficulty could he be persuaded to stop playing it for a moment, and he pleaded most pitifully to be allowed to accompany the expedition as far as the Base Camp in the capacity of musical director.

Social relationships are not, it seems, allowed to over-ride business realities in Tibet. I am not sure what the Nyapala's own views were, but in the matter of transport rates he was evidently guided by a highly intelligent lama who was not going to allow sentiment to interfere with profit. The day before our departure, the lama tried to raise our transport rates to Shekar Dzong by one rupee per animal, in spite of an agreement reached two days before. Here was an opportunity for Karma Paul to show his metal; he immediately rose to the occasion with a florid Tibetan idiom to the effect that he could already see the blush of shame mantling in the cheeks of hospitality. This magnificent effort produced an immediate, good-humoured capitulation. I followed up the advantage with a cup of Navy rum all round and some illustrated papers, and the incident closed.

On the 13th we were off towards Shekar Dzong, having first to cross the Bahman Dopte Pass. I enjoyed the first march more than any hitherto, because I at last threw off a cough that had worried me all the way from Lachen; and began to hope, for the first time, that I should be able to hold my own with my very fit companions. They were all going like stags, so it was pretty evident that the stay at Tangu, and the occasional climbing, had been very beneficial. At Khenga, Morris and Nursang were just in time to frustrate a

barefaced attempt at theft—the only one that occurred throughout the journey to the Base Camp. They observed a muleteer
quietly driving his animal into a byre in the village, from which
he was ejected with a rapidity that must have been observed by
his fellows, for we had no more trouble. From Dochen Mega,
and again from Jikyop, it was observed that violent weather
was harassing the Everest region. With us conditions remained on the whole mild and pleasant, though Kiyshong,
twelve miles short of Shekar, was as liberal as ever with its dust,
and met us with something rather remarkable in the way of
squalls, while in the morning we observed a watery sun with
a big ring round it and two " sun dogs " on its rim. Here
Shipton, remembering that awful camp in 1933, selected a
much better position.

At Shekar we met, for the first time, a genuine Dzongpen ;
the same who had done his best to unravel our difficulties in
1933, when serious thefts of expedition equipment had
occurred. This time he met us with undisguised pleasure and
gave permission to occupy his treasured willow grove, provided that none of the wood was used for the fires. Nothing
would satisfy him but to have the entire British personnel to
tea at the earliest opportunity. Here our Kalimpong experience stood us in good stead, for we used our chop-sticks with
more discretion than our host possibly expected—indeed, he
commented favourably. His singers and dancers were in
great form, especially a gigantic swivel-eyed person to whom
speed was obviously necessary to enable him to retain his
equilibrium towards the end of the evening. The festivities
were interrupted by the dramatic entry of Nursang with the
news that the lamas of the place, who appeared to be both in-
quisitive and riotous, had fallen foul of our porters and were
throwing stones into the camp. Nursang revels in a situation
of this kind : he announced that he was a bachelor—I have
frequently met his wife at Darjeeling—and that his life was of
no moment to him ; if the lamas wanted a fight, he and his
68

porters were perfectly willing to accommodate them. The little Dzongpen, doubtless experienced in this kind of thing, never turned a hair. He simply dictated a polite but pressing request to the head lama of the place to keep his monks in order and Nursang went out with the honours of war.

Feeling that we might be expected to take an active part in the entertainment, we had brought along the gramophone, which I do not think our host really enjoyed, though much too polite to say so; and of course he could not complain when Smythe played his accordion at him. I must do justice to Smythe in this matter: he makes no claim to mastery of his instrument, which indeed he only acquired shortly before sailing. It afforded him an innocent distraction after hours of delving into food boxes, preparation of menus, and the kind of disappointment which Chun-Chun inflicts. Every evening Smythe would be observed to seat himself upon an upturned box, pass rapidly into a trance as his fingers touched the keys, and burst into shattering dissonance. I found this routine very instructive, once my material ear had been pounded into insensibility. Smythe, who can work as hard as anybody when occasion demands, understands the value of detachment. What possible connection could there be between these fearful discords and even the harmony of our relations in the Mess? The social life imposes a certain strain, however well adjusted. Forget it and other mundane matters; ascend for the time to another plane, keeping your comrades away by these defensive measures; you will find peace. Sooner or later the accidental achievement of a true chord, and the acclamation which greets it, will be the ladder by which you can return to earth and resume your normal personality. Smythe was quite right to bring along that accordion. I believe he still has it.

Not to be outdone, we invited the Dzongpen to lunch. Our chief cook, Chun-Chun, had not been very successful of late; indeed, Morris roundly asserted that his name merely meant "tin opener." We felt that a real effort was now necessary,

69

and Smythe and Wigram spent an exceedingly busy morning
thinking out a menu and driving it into Chun-Chun's head.
The expedition tables were set up in line in the willow grove,
the orange-coloured bandalasta ware made a brave show in the
sun; the knives, forks and spoons were less inadequately
polished, and Tendrup, whose nerves were affected to such an
extent that he had already savagely bitten two porter mess-
men, was banished in disgrace. Our guests arrived and were
installed with great ceremony. They were, of course, dressed
in the most beautiful Chinese silks, beside which our mufti
displayed us to the poorest advantage. Karma Paul, however,
whom I had privately instructed to bring along from Darjeeling his national costume, more than held his own. The
Dzongpen was delighted; he struggled manfully with alien
food and with knives, forks and spoons, watching me out of the
corner of his eye and conforming with great skill. He praised
everything, especially the " cleanly service." Happily he
could not see Chun-Chun and his associates in the background,
where doubtless they were washing up in dirty water and,
ignoring the tea-cloths provided, drying the dishes in their
homely way on the tail of their shirts.

After this there was no difficulty over transport. The
Dzongpen arranged for the best we had ever had, at the old
rates, began the preparation of *tsampa* for feeding porters on
the mountains, and announced that we could go anywhere we
liked within his jurisdiction (which includes the Everest
region) provided only that we sent him beforehand a programme of our intended movements. Most happily there
was no need to invoke his aid for the recovery of missing
things. We made a very thorough check at Shekar, finding
our boxes intact, and none of them rifled and then filled up
with stones.

News now came in from Sola Khombu, on the other side
of the range. The hundred or so recruits for whom provision had been made during the winter were most anxious

not to be late, and were coming over the Nangpa La while we were still five marches from Everest. They would not even wait for us at Rongbuk, but charged into our camp at Shekar, full of enthusiasm and good cheer. This zeal was distinctly embarrassing, but the men were so keen that they were perfectly willing to forgo any pay until they actually began work on the mountain, and it was possible to obtain food for them locally. First of all they had to be sorted out, formally engaged and medically examined. Roughly equal numbers had been selected by Ang Tarkey and Ang Tsering, who stood up their protégés opposite each other for inspection. Then there were several free-lances who had turned up on their own and had to be disappointed. I soon found that there was considerable rivalry between Ang Tarkey and Ang Tsering and that one had to be on one's guard against nepotism. The proceedings took a whole day, during which the wind and dust were extremely trying. I may add here that Everest, which could be seen, fifty miles distant, from the hill above, was now the focus of a severe disturbance. Morris and I were having a busy time, but he can find humour everywhere. I well remember his cry of delight when he called to me to come and examine a living specimen of Neanderthal man. Certainly the man in question was of the most primitive type, with squat features and hair hanging low over his anything but lofty brow. He seemed to lack intelligence and his vocabulary was very limited ; but his fellow-men regarded him as a kind of mascot, and they assured us that his carrying powers were exceptional, a statement that was well borne out later on. The medical examinations were soon over—nearly all the men had a splendid physique—and by the end of the day we had a hundred superb porters to supplement those we had brought from Darjeeling.

The evening of our last day at Shekar was spent in a long conversation with Morris, Smythe, Shipton, Wyn Harris and Karma Paul, at which we worked out all details necessary to the establishment of Camp I as our real base this year. Transport had been promised for next morning and everything seemed to be well in hand. But you never can be sure : we had already lost one day because the Dzongpen said that the drivers had a superstitious fear of travelling at the time of the new moon ; this had an unfortunate sequel which might have had very serious results for us. So far our porters had refrained from the orgies with which some of them celebrated, in 1933, their last glimpse of town life ; but on the night of April 22 at least two got very drunk and bombarded the second Dzongpen with stones in his own house. One of these men, I regret to say, was my own servant Namgya, who had never before given any trouble. His family live in Shekar Dzong and in the evening he had obtained a small advance of pay on the pretext of helping them. The whole sum must have gone in the local public house, and Namgya became very obstreperous. He was supported by Rinzing, " the wild Irishman," who never seems to quarrel on his own account but cannot resist the pleasure of a fight in which one of his friends is involved. So next morning, in place of the expected transport, there appeared raging through the camp a justly incensed officer with a bloody nose, demanding justice and retribution ; his face bore a distinctly jazz pattern where he had industriously rubbed the blood from a slight cut all over it, and he was literally gibbering with rage. A pity, for he was a really handsome young man. I hauled Karma Paul out of his tent and immediately set to work with him and Morris to deal with the affair. It was necessary to be prompt, for we were threatened with reports to Lhasa and an indefinite stoppage of the expedition. A note was hastily despatched to the senior Dzongpen, invoking his good offices. A full parade of the porters was called, and a formal trial instituted. Namgya, a man evidently of swift decisions, realised that this was no place for him and absconded during the first confusion, which made things no easier and also meant that poor Rinzing, who was not the prime delinquent, had to bear the full brunt. On the arrival of the senior Dzongpen, looking very serious, Karma Paul led off briskly. With his usual intelligence, he realised he had to get the expedition out of a bad scrape and could only do so by an appearance of extreme horror of the dastardly conduct of its black sheep. To all seeming he was the public prosecutor acting on behalf of the Tibetan authorities. Such witnesses as could be found were all for the prosecution, and their cross-examination was perfunctory. Things began to look very black for us, as Karma Paul intended they should. With apparent recklessness, and certain disregard of the ordinary rules of procedure, he heaped opprobrium upon the unlucky Rinzing, who offered no defence. The effect was that the Tibetan officials considered we were looking at the matter from their point of view, and they relented visibly. At last the senior Dzongpen said that as we were clearly prepared to do all in our power to make reparation he would, out of pure friendship, consent to overlook the affair provided we would punish Namgya whom he realised to be the chief offender. I replied at once that, present or absent, Namgya was dismissed from the expedition with ignominy. Karma Paul then presented the injured second Dzongpen with Rs 5 and a silk scarf as a ceremonial appeasement. I fined Rinzing Rs 30, and this sum, together with another silk scarf, was also handed over to the sufferer. This action was pronounced to be definitely noble and things brightened up at once. Transport appeared as if by magic; the report to Lhasa was cancelled, and we were invited to pay a farewell visit to the Dzong. After ceremoniously conducting the officials to the confines of the camp, with many mutual expressions of goodwill, Morris and I took the errant Rinzing aside, and Morris gave him a severe talking to in fluent Nepali. It was as good as a play to watch Rinzing's face; he professed the utmost penitence, but there was a merry twinkle in his eye which made it impossible for either of us to remain serious for long. Then Shipton,

73

Warren and I went off to the Dzong, leaving Morris to wrestle with the transport. As a special mark of favour, we were shown into the senior Dzongpen's inner sanctum and given tea, *chang* and an excellent omelette. The second Dzongpen was called in after a short interval, still looking much shaken. Warren, who had brought along the necessary things, made a great impression by tidying up the damaged nose and offering a considerable variety of medicines which might be found useful in the future. Harmony was now completely re-established. The senior Dzongpen affirmed that it was a positive pleasure to associate with people like us, gave me a cordial invitation to visit him some day in his home at Lhasa and, accompanying us to the front door, ceremoniously offered the use of his own mounting block, an act which Karma Paul assured me was a particular sign of friendship. So ended a very anxious morning's work.

We had now only one more pass to cross before entering the Everest region ; this was the Pang La, over 18,000 feet, which would afford a sort of final test of the party's condition. We crossed it on April 23, hoping to get a good view of the mountain. In this we were disappointed as another disturbance was evidently at work and there were heavy clouds obscuring most of the higher summits. But there was compensation in observing the complete absence of distress with which everybody arrived on the pass. Wigram, Oliver and Gavin, who took the opportunity of a little climbing along the ridge to the south-west, eventually obtained a view of Everest through a break in the clouds.

Tashidzöm, with its willow groves, was as peaceful as ever, though there was a little flooding of the meadows during the night and Morris nearly floated away on his Li-Lo mattress. We were entertained by some admirable strolling minstrels during tea. As a counterbalance, we turned on the gramophone and played the " Emperor Concerto " to the assembled villagers, whose expressions were most edifying to watch.   Neanderthal was here joined by Piltdown, Heidelberg, Peking and other primitive types.

I was particularly pleased on the march between Tashidzöm and Chödzong to obtain at last a view of Mount Everest which Brigadier Norton has many times pressed upon my attention.   It appeared suddenly up a side valley on the left, and was worth a prolonged halt for study with telescope and binoculars.   The mountain was evidently in splendid condition in spite of the recent disturbed weather, for a strong north-west wind had blown the slopes clear.   The great couloir was more empty of snow than I have ever seen it ; I could not help wondering if this would make things more difficult for an assault party.   In 1933 good hard wind-impacted snow was found in this couloir, affording excellent foothold.   Norton, on the other hand, in 1924 was much bothered by powdery, incoherent snow, into which he had to plunge blindly, trusting that his boot-nails would find anchorage on the underlying slabs.   The rock in the bed of the couloir may well have been polished smooth by countless avalanches.   The final pyramid, seen from this angle, looked forbidding enough, and it was impossible from a distance of over twenty miles to form any satisfactory conclusion about the best way of tackling it.   But there was one encouraging feature : the eastern sun shone full upon the buttress by which access must be found from the couloir to the pyramid, at about 28,100 feet.   Probably this is the most difficult part of the climb ; seen in these conditions, it looked feasible.   If only this weather would hold, there could be nothing to stop us from getting to grips with it.

As usual, there was considerable impatience to be off from Chödzong to Rongbuk on the morning of April 25, and the transport was on the move at 5.30 a.m.   It was a lovely march, completely different from anything we had experienced before. As we passed the mouth of the little valley down which the Sherpas come on their way from Sola Khombu, and in which there is a village of the familiar name of Zambuk, those great peaks Cho-oyu and Gyachung Kang seemed to fill the western horizon and to bar all further progress. But the rough track continued up through a narrow gorge, and at last we reached the corner from which it turns due south to Rongbuk; and there, long before we expected to see her, was Everest towering into the sky. Immediately the sense of scale altered. We had seemed to be moving round the feet of giants, but here was something transcending them all. Never, from any place, have I seen Everest look so gigantic. Later we should be too much underneath her to see in true perspective. Wyn Harris, Kempson and Oliver must have had an even finer view, for they forced a way over to Rongbuk by the hills on the east, by way of a final training effort; and a very strenuous day they had of it.

Everything was so different this time: no snow lying in the valley; no bitter wind blowing in our faces off the great North Face; a brilliant, even hot, sun, and the glorious sight of Everest clear and shining black from base to summit as we turned the last bend to Rongbuk monastery. I wonder if ever again a party will be able, on April 25, to lunch out in the open, at this 16,000-foot camp, and enjoy undisturbed that splendid vision. Certainly this is not what one can expect so early in the year; in 1933, only a few days earlier, the cold and the wind together had made life anything but pleasant. We were brought back to realities about 5 p.m. when the sun sank behind the western hills and the drop in temperature was immediate and severe. There was plenty of wind higher up; Smijth-Windham and Gavin attempted to calculate its speed from the great plume of ice and snow and condensed vapour which was rolling away from the summit to the south-east; basing their estimate on the time that a given portion of the plume took to reach and pass the eastern shoulder, the distance of which from the summit is of course known. They concluded that the speed of the wind was about 40–50 m.p.h.,

76

which would have meant very severe conditions for any party at work on the mountain.

Rongbuk, of course, never changes. The life of that great monastery carries on from year to year, absorbed in religious exercises and completely indifferent to the outside world, even to Everest expeditions. Perhaps I should modify that last statement : the old Head Lama, though he prefers solitude, seems to have come to the belief that we seek something other than material gain. He knows now that Everest is the highest mountain in the world, and that expedition after expedition has come and struggled and suffered to reach the summit, and will continue to do so until success is attained. We have tried to explain to him our motives, many of which are such that he can appreciate and sympathise with. In the course of two expeditions, I seemed to notice a change in his attitude. In 1933 his welcome was modified by a certain reluctance : he completely disapproved of our object, though he would not hinder us. Possibly in the interval since then he has thought over certain things that we said to him during interviews ; certainly he received us in a different spirit this time. Now, at the age of seventy-one, he very rarely leaves the little upper room from which he has ruled his monastery for something like fifty years, and in which his meditations become ever more prolonged. But this time he was resolved to show us that he understood : we were to be received as friends, not as passing travellers on sufferance. The great courtyard of the monastery was swept and garnished. Tea-tables were set out facing the Lama's throne. The 300-odd lamas, who in this monastery are under a stricter discipline than I have seen elsewhere, were to be assembled round the sides of the balconies above ; and I was informed that the whole expedition would receive the old man's blessing with full ceremonial on the morning of April 26. For this occasion the porters were paraded with more than usual care and were marched into the courtyard in an order which they of their own free will were most scrupulous to observe. Each man had been given a small money offering, and had done his poor best to dress well. The old Lama was assisted up on to his throne by his attendants and surveyed us benevolently. Karma Paul, in purple and fine linen, advanced with the silk scarves of ceremony, and with a present of two Petromax lamps and a supply of oil. Our host was delighted, for he had often commented upon the poor illumination of his monastery. At his request we advanced one by one, murmured the formula " *Om mane padme hum* " and were touched on the head with the silver thunderbolt and blessed. Then we returned to our seats at the tea-tables and it was the turn of the porters. Incense from juniper bushes filled the air as they prostrated themselves one after the other and were blessed. One could not have seen anywhere a more sincerely devout congregation. There followed a really effective address, in which the old gentleman, obviously moved, exhorted the men to do their duty by the strangers who had brought them to serve on the mountain. " You are," he said, " nearly all of you my own parishioners. Year by year you come over the passes from Sola Khombu to seek my blessing. You have been well treated in the past by your employers and will I know be so treated again. Do not fail them, and I will pray for your safety and success." There was a dead silence for a moment and then, sharp and almost startling, came the promise from those 160 porters. Turning to us, the Lama said that he felt now that our motives were good, and that we had his support. He renewed his injunction to treat his people well, and to kill nothing in the valley where all life is sacred; he added a request that we should not cut any of the sparse brushwood round the Base Camp as that was needed for hermits; and that we would not go over to the Kharta or Karma valleys direct from the Rongbuk glacier as this might establish a frequented route and he wanted peace. Then he gave Karma Paul and me copies, printed in the monastery, of a little

78

pamphlet he had written on the subject of Mount Everest. A translation of this is given elsewhere.

We were now given a meal of mutton and macaroni with some particularly good sauces; and tea but no *chang*. Ceremony over, the Head Lama completely unbent, and applauded our now quite reasonable proficiency with chopsticks. I gave him, to his great pleasure, two photographs taken of him in 1933, and he then consented to be photographed again, stipulating shrewdly that we should not press the button when he was not looking. Lastly, he gave permission to visit the inner shrine of the monastery, and with a few final words of good wishes retired.

Karma Paul stated emphatically that there had never been anything like this at the Rongbuk monastery before and that the men were tremendously elated. We all left about noon for the last four miles to the Base Camp in the happiest frame of mind, past the nunnery, past the little caves in the hillsides or excavations in the tumbled heaps of old moraine boulders where hermits spend a life of what is called meditation but must closely resemble hibernation. One is forced to admire the strength which can keep them alive in those bitter solitudes where the rock faces are grooved by sand-blast from the driving wind. We think ourselves hardy when we approach these regions in the spring, with our tents and windproof clothing and swandown sleeping bags and pressure cookers. What have these men in the depth of winter but perhaps an old woollen rug and a smouldering branch of juniper, with a pittance of food just sufficient to ward off starvation ? " Our religion," they would probably reply, and the answer must suffice. The most wonderful thing is that they retain mental normality; I have conversed with a hermit who had just emerged after fifteen years' incarceration, and could observe no difference between him and an ordinary lama. We do not know everything in the West; is it possible that we have everything to learn ?

In 1933 the approach to the Base Camp was over the ice of a little lake formed from an overflow of the Rongbuk glacier stream. The porters used to toboggan on this ice, and we had to bore through to obtain our water supply; it was bitterly cold: men working among the store boxes had to put on windproof and even then would retreat from time to time to the Mess-tent, to thaw out their frozen fingers. Now there was no ice; we skirted the shores of the lake, revelling in the bright, warm sun. A good afternoon's work could be done without any discomfort, bearing in mind, however, that we were now at 16,800 feet and could not run about with the same abandon that was possible at Kalimpong. Certainly we were now within the " gates of altitude," as Norton has called them, but as yet unstrained.

Camp drill was now so good that the tents were up at the old spot and the expedition boxes all arranged within a very short time; and the animal transport was able to leave us before evening. So far as we were able to tell from a hasty check, the only things missing were five tins of soup, one of which was brought in later by a Tibetan; clearly these tins had fallen out of one of the many boxes which were by now in a rather dilapidated condition. So we were all " present and correct," on the best possible terms with each other, and ready for work.

Chapter V

AT CLOSE QUARTERS

ALTHOUGH we were well up to time on the programme settled at Gangtok, the party was so fit, and the weather so good, there was no possible reason or excuse for delay. Schedules of work up the glacier had already been prepared, and the advance was begun without confusion. On the morning after our arrival Smijth-Windham and Gavin started up to Camp I to establish the wireless base. It was found that the wireless equipment alone made up into no less than fifty-eight heavy loads, some of them over 80 lb. and indivisible, but 132 men made the carry and even those with the heavy loads (these included Neanderthal) made no sort of complaint. The second Dzongpen of Shekar, now quite recovered and happy, had accompanied us to the Base Camp, organising on the way a supply of shing, the local fuel of the country, and of 50 maunds of *tsampa* for the porters. Shing fuel would be used as far as Camp I, after which we would come on to a strictly rationed supply of kerosene oil. When the Dzongpen left his place was taken by the useful old Chonzay, or steward, who has helped two previous expeditions. The glacier ration and fuel schemes having been worked out, Shipton and I completed those for the actual assaults. On the next two days 260 loads were sent up, so that Camp I now became the real base of the expedition. The

G

magnificent weather continued; parties were out on the surrounding hills acclimatising themselves, oxygen was again tried out, and Smythe and Shipton, who were expected to form the first assault party, made a little expedition to 20,000 feet on a shoulder of the mountains to the west, which showed a number of jagged, rocky pinnacles. To this they vulgarly assigned the name of " Pyorrhœa Ridge." Warren was busy taking blood-counts and testing blood-pressure and vital capacity. At odd moments we examined the mountain with a telescope, seeking to decide the best line up the final pyramid. It was not, of course, possible to observe much detail at a range of 12 miles, and the final slopes looked completely different at different times of the day, according to the direction from which the sun's rays struck them.

At this point I think it will be as well, for the benefit of those who have not read any of the previous expedition books, to embark upon a general description of Mount Everest, and I venture to quote from *Everest, 1933* :

" The summit of Mount Everest, 29,002 feet, looked at from the north is a triangular pyramid, resting on the western end of the structure. From this, a great arête or ridge runs down to the north-west at a considerable angle. It is, perhaps, not completely unclimbable, but Mallory examined it in 1921 and formed the opinion that, if an easier way existed, it would be preferable. The ridge is exposed to the west wind, and great difficulty would be experienced in getting porters and camps up it.

" To the north-east descends a still longer arête, falling at a much easier angle for a distance of about two-thirds of a mile to a shoulder, beyond which it drops steeply to the Rapiu La on the east. On this arête, between the summit and the shoulder, are the first and second steps to which reference has so often been made. They are formed by the ends of two horizontal bands of dark-grey limestone rock, which run westwards across the face of the mountain and constitute the chief climbing difficulty.

"Just below the shoulder, a blunt ridge descends to the north, at an average angle of between 35 and 40 degrees, to the Chang La or North Col, a narrow neck of ice connecting Mount Everest with the North Peak.

"Near the upper western end of the north-east arête, at the eastern foot of the final pyramid, is a great snow couloir or gully. This is crossed high up by the two dark bands of rock above mentioned. At this point they are still continuous and precipitous ; but slightly to the west, where they emerge on to the north face of the pyramid, they are a little broken, and it is here only that followers of Norton's route, after traversing a few hundred feet below the crest of the north-east arête and below the two steps, and after crossing the great couloir, may hope to storm the defences and ascend towards the summit. Mallory preferred to take to the crest of the north-east arête and pursue it westwards, whatever the difficulties of the steps. Many mountaineers prefer the crest of a ridge to the traverse of a mountain face ; but circumstances alter cases, and it may well be that the second step in particular is utterly unclimbable. Could it be climbed or turned, the ridge beyond it, and the final pyramid, do not look too difficult. That the arête is for the most part very narrow was shown by a photograph which Air-Commodore P. F. M. Fellowes, leader of the Houston Mount Everest flight, most kindly sent me.

"The north face of the mountain, of which the top edge is the north-east arête, is composed of a series of highly altered limestones, mostly of a grey colour. The strata dip northwards at an angle of, for the most part, 35 degrees, but just below the lower of the two dark bands there is a stratum of yellowish limestone, about 1,000 feet thick, which forms a very marked feature. This is a good deal steeper than anything except the dark bands, but is fortunately composed of

83

a rougher kind of rock weathered into narrow ledges and offering better support to the feet.

"The general outward, downward dip of the strata produces an effect like the tiles on a steep roof, with the result that handholds and belays are practically non-existent, and careful, balanced climbing is necessary. A slip is likely to have fatal results. The upper western wall of the great couloir will always be dangerous to negotiate, for the dip of the slabs increases here. When powder snow lies on them to any depth, they are impassable.

"The eastern slopes of the North Col are formed by what is, in fact, a steeply falling glacier. This presents the first serious obstacle. The place looks, from the east, like an almost vertical wall of snow and ice, some 1,200 feet high, seamed by crevasses and broken into great ice-cliffs. As the glacier is continually on the move, these features change from year to year, and each expedition has been obliged to choose its own route of ascent. Below, the East Rongbuk glacier runs first east, then north, then west, on its way towards the main Rongbuk glacier and the Base Camp."

This year, owing to its exceptionally good condition at this time, the mountain looked possibly less formidable than before, and the more or less reassuring weather forecast we had brought with us from Calcutta was reinforced by the confident assertion of local Tibetans that we could now count on at least another month and a half of fine weather. Little did we think how soon this optimism was to be upset.

At the Base Camp I had to harden my heart and send away the inoffensive but sadly inefficient Chun-Chun. He had done quite well in a subordinate capacity in 1933, when possibly the example of a better man, Tencheddar, had galvanised him into some show of activity. As chief cook, however, he showed no initiative and no energy, and Smythe had a most difficult time with him. Wishing him no harm, for he is amiable and willing enough, I wrote him a very carefully worded certificate of conduct which I hope will enable him to obtain employment in less strenuous surroundings. We now had to rely on our second and third strings : Lhakpa, who was formerly a porter, but had taken up cooking when he found himself insufficiently strong for this rôle, and Pasang, who had taken to cooking *con amore.* The former, poor fellow, became progressively more feeble as the campaign advanced and unhappily took to drink to buck himself up ; the latter though timid and somewhat temperamental did his duty to the best of his powers throughout. But good food is so important a consideration in maintaining the health and spirits of a party that I hope future expeditions will make a point of having satisfactory cooks selected long before they arrive in India and properly trained in their duties, which should include the baking of bread.

In our Mess we sadly missed the services of Lhakpa Chhedi, the " tiger " of 1924 and head messman of 1933. I did not take him this time because he had lost some fingers from frost-bite and was also getting on in years ; and we had to pick out a few likely porters and train them as best we could. They were devoted fellows, who always did their best even in the most trying circumstances. I remember that the sturdy little Ang Tsering collapsed at the Base Camp with a severe intestinal pain which the doctors feared might indicate appendicitis. I sent three porters galloping off to Camp I late in the evening for the surgical instruments which had been already despatched there. They made a great effort and returned after dark, by which time poor Ang Tsering had recovered, and he escaped an operation. The very next day he insisted on turning up for duty and on working as hard as before.

Smijth-Windham had his wireless up and was in communication with Darjeeling on April 30. Almost the first message he received gave warning of the approach of a western disturbance, and that same afternoon, with startling suddenness, we had quite a heavy fall of snow, unaccompanied by any wind. The morning had been lovely; at about 3 p.m. a cloud developed suddenly out of a clear sky, obscuring Everest and our surrounding hills, and silently the rocks began to turn white. The barometer showed no change, but that evening and the night were cold (the ink froze in my pen), and on the morning of May 1, the cloud having dispersed, we saw a new Everest, glittering with an almost unbearable brilliance. Little did we think that never again should we see her as she should be if a party is to have a reasonable chance of success. But yesterday's snow did not lie long at the Base, and western disturbances were to be expected at this time—indeed they had been foretold; the normal north-west wind would certainly remove all the surface snow from the mountain. We carried on without a moment's delay, and on this day the whole expedition moved up to Camp I, leaving only Karma Paul to hold the Base and form a link with the Tibetan authorities. I see in my diary that in the morning I commented on the fact that there was a slight easterly wind.

Even at the first time of asking, the walk up to Camp I at 17,700 feet caused no distress whatever. From the corner where one turns away from the main glacier to the moraines of the East Rongbuk, Camp I looked much as usual, and it was not until we reached it that we observed the fertile resource of Smijth-Windham and Gavin. They had spent their scant leisure in providing the amenities of civilisation. At the entrance to the " Main Street " was a large boulder on which was inscribed in black paint " Slow through the village "; by its side an orange-coloured bandalasta plate on a bamboo which it was possible to identify as a Belisha beacon. Close by, pointing along the way we had come, was a road sign " A.1. Scotland and the North." Near my tent we were instructed to " keep left "; and at the end of the village was a notice " To the Mountain." Lastly, one of the Mess-tents bore the notice " TEAS." The place bristled with wireless masts—there were six or seven of them—and Smijth-Windham had even constructed a rockery. As this was in the Main Street and was trampled over by everybody, perhaps it is not to be wondered at that no single flower ever made its appearance. There was complete shelter for everybody; full use having been made of the old sangars, or stone walls, which also housed the kitchen. Smijth-Windham was having some difficulty in making himself intelligible to the Darjeeling operators, though their messages came through quite well. It seems, from subsequent experience, that the position of Camp I is not really suitable for a wireless station.

Wyn Harris and I now began to be a little worried by a complaint which was diagnosed as " migraine," to which we are not normally subject. It seemed to come on irrespective of weather or of work or food, and to cause double vision and other discomforts. My attacks usually lasted only half an hour or so, and arrived when I was walking up the glacier. Wyn Harris was not let off so easily. As we were well enough in other respects, it was difficult to account for this visitation.

Camp I has a good site, protected on the north by the enormous pinnacles of the ridge which descends from " Kellas' Peak," and on the south by the outliers of the North Peak, which hide Everest from us. Since the valley of the East Rongbuk glacier here lies east and west, we have the sun nearly all day, and it is appreciably warmer than at the Base Camp. Near by is the blunt snout of the glacier, from which issues a stream smaller than one would expect considering the great expanses of snow higher up. Mallory was misled by this during the Reconnaissance of 1921, concluding that this insignificant stream indicated a cul-de-sac, affording no way to Everest. At times there is a great surge of muddy brown water, where some ice-dam above has broken down; but even after the monsoon has arrived there is not much difficulty in crossing.

87

Next morning the disturbance had cleared away and the sun shone brightly. Losing no time, Shipton and Humphreys set off with 120 men to establish Camp II at a place in the medial trough observed in 1935—an admirable situation. This ascent took three hours. When they returned in the evening it was found that Shipton had achieved a record : he had succeeded in tiring out Humphreys, who after all had never been to over 19,000 feet before ; and Humphreys very honestly admitted it. In some ways our transport successes were becoming almost embarrassing : Shipton was aghast at the number of boxes which had to be moved and confessed to Morris that he had confidently expected at least a proportion to be stolen on the way across Tibet. I may add that at this time Shipton was doing an enormous amount of work, thus facilitating rapid progress up the glacier. Things were not always easy for him ; for instance, at this camp the rivalry between Ang Tarkey and Ang Tsering was brought out into the open by the discovery that during an issue of kit to porters a number of pairs of breeches had disappeared. Ang Tarkey instantly came to me and said that he would go home unless Ang Tsering was dismissed, he being the culprit. It was necessary to call in Nursang for some detective work, at which by the way he is not very good. Things sorted themselves out somehow, chiefly because it was found that Ang Tsering, strong though he looks, is a poor acclimatiser and a poor performer at altitudes. Accordingly we were able to keep the two men separate.

It would be difficult to speak too highly of the fine spirit prevailing in the party ; I am proud to be able to say that neither now nor later did a single member ask for anything on his own account. Indeed Kempson, who had been detailed with Wyn Harris to form the second assault party, volunteered to stand down in favour of Warren if the latter should be required to make oxygen tests on and above the North Col. I shall always remember Smijth-Windham's

answer when I remarked upon this happy state of affairs :
" Yes," he replied, " they *are* a fine lot ; so fine, that I believe
they would even take a licking well."

The mornings were now extraordinarily hot—on May 3
we recorded no less than 97 degrees at midday in one of the
Mess-tents. This, of course, made things pretty hard for the
men who were carrying up day by day to Camp II, accompanied sometimes by European members, sometimes by
Jemadar Lachiman Singh. They did not seem to mind,
however, provided they were given an occasional rest, and at
least they had not to stumble through snow on the moraines.
Incidentally the new route, which crossed over into the medial
trough close to where the ice pinnacles began, was a good deal
easier than anything used before. Just when the carries had
been completed there was a considerable snowfall, on the
evening of May 4 ; and some of us spent a day working out a
system of visual signalling, in case the wireless sets should fail
on the mountain. Oliver and Gavin made an ascent to 20,000
feet on the ridge to the south, while Smythe and Wigram over-
hauled the food boxes. Karma Paul came up for a few hours
from the Base Camp, where the solitary life was anything but
congenial. My last evening in this camp was ruined by
Morris and Warren, who induced me to submit to what they
called, I believe, a " reversion test." It consisted of writing
down alternately direct and reversed the letter S, at the
highest possible speed. Full marks from the examiners were
poor compensation for so degrading an exercise.

On May 6 we all moved up to Camp II except Smijth-
Windham, who could not, of course, leave his wireless base.
Morris was confident that he had recovered from his severe
attack of malaria, but Wyn Harris and I, who made the ascent
with him, soon saw that something was wrong, and in fact he
was only just able to drag himself into Camp II after 6½ hours
of painful struggle. Mount Everest is invisible from Camp I,
but comes into sight again at the corner about half-way to

Camp II. We observed that the queer weather of the past two days had considerably added to the snow on the North Face.

At the new Camp II, at about 19,900 feet, I observed for the first time some slight psychological effects of altitude. When first occupied, the camp was not very comfortable as it was difficult to find level space for the tents among the rough boulders. The cooks were not functioning well ; the machine-like efficiency of the transport during the last few weeks was not quite so regular, and just at first some of us felt the beginnings of a spirit of criticism. These changes are perhaps too subtle for analysis by the layman, but they must be observed and even anticipated by the leader, who has to watch himself no less than the others. Some very small incident, such as delay in the arrival of tea, or a smoky lamp, assumes an unnatural importance. The first instinct is to damn somebody else instead of quietly putting things straight oneself. Then two people will start an argument ; after a few minutes of this each thinks the other an obstinate idiot, and loses no time in telling him so. It all seems trivial enough, but we have to live together, in very close proximity and at altitudes of 20,000 feet and over, for another month and more, so everything must be done, and quickly, to smooth out nerves frayed by the effort of adaptation to oxygen-lack. Relaxation may come as suddenly, and from as slight a cause, as the strain it relieves. Anti-climax will do it—for instance, the mess-porter stubbing his toe on a rock outside the tent and dissipating in one glorious smash that tea whose late arrival we have been grumbling about ; or some unusually pungent insult from one of the disputants in the corner ; or a quiet but happy turn of phrase, of which so many in this team were capable. Then Smythe and Wigram had an infallible remedy : they would silently disappear into the cold and darkness outside, and find something exceptionally good for dinner, on the general and excellent principle of " feed the brute." Could Harley Street do more ? Perhaps I have

90

made too much of this question of adjustment to altitude ; but experience shows the danger of ignoring it. At Camp II a single evening's effort sufficed, and things went on as smoothly as before, except that poor Morris was entirely unable to eat and was out of action for the time being.

The site of this new camp was extraordinarily fine. The tents were pitched in the central trough which affords so good a route to the upper part of the East Rongbuk glacier, at about the place where in 1933 we used to get into this trough across the ice from the old Camp II. Except after a snowstorm, the rocks were dry and warm during the day, though chilly bed-fellows after sunset. On either side of the trough rose rank upon rank of ice séracs, changing hourly from white to blue or green or even mother-of-pearl, as their innumerable little prisms caught the light. Under a full moon they were incredibly beautiful in the silence of a windless night—a silence intensified rather than broken by the murmur of a little stream burrowing through the ice, or the occasional abrupt crack of glacier movement. Far above rose the great shoulders of Everest, lovely in their mantle of new snow but unapproachable. Sunset was the time to come out and watch the northern sky changing from azure to the dark blue of shaded steel, and the warm glow of the séracs fading into grey. In stormy weather, it was a very different landscape : each sérac a little Eddystone smothered in the flying spray of rollers from the Atlantic ; the brown tents shaking under the stroke of the wind, and snow bursting up into the air as it drove against the ice-barriers. No horizons then, but a suddenly small world a few yards wide and very desolate.

Just before leaving Camp I, Smythe, Shipton and I had come to the conclusion that we could allow ourselves to advance our programme by one week. This meant that we could aim at establishing Camp IV on the North Col by May 15 instead of May 22. In furtherance of this plan, no time was lost in pushing on towards Camp III, and on May 7

Smythe and Shipton took a strong body of porters up the glacier and made Camp III at a place about half a mile nearer the slopes of the North Col than before, and at 21,500 feet. Most of the porters returned that night, with a note from Shipton that the carry had gone well ; that the new site was excellent in every way, and that the North Col slopes appeared not to have changed since last year. Meanwhile Warren, Wigram, Oliver and Gavin gave themselves a little exercise cutting fancy routes up the surrounding ice-pinnacles. Oliver in particular made a sensational ascent up a very steep one about a hundred feet high, on which he must have spent something like four hours. It was evident that altitude was not at present affecting any of them ; indeed, porters rather than Europeans were showing the effects—quite a number of them at this camp suffered from mountain sickness and throat complaints and required medical help.

Warren, Wigram and Gavin went up to Camp III on the 8th with a second strong carry of porters in quiet weather, and were followed by Wyn Harris, Kempson, Oliver and myself next day. Morris protested that he was all right and would be able to come on soon ; and he remained with Jemadar Lachiman Singh for company.

Neither familiarity nor altitude seems to be able to blunt the fine edge of romance as one walks up the central trough of the East Rongbuk glacier between the serried ranks of gleaming ice-pinnacles, whose extraordinary formation reveals fresh beauty at every step. To attempt their portrayal in words is beyond me ; and, alas ! we had no great landscape painter to record their loveliness. Smythe's colour film has at least gone some distance in that direction. The main trough comes to an end about a third of the way to Camp III, after which one emerges on to the great open face of the upper glacier, where there are only a few crevasses to be avoided and where, on such a morning as this, there is not even wind to cause any distress. Nobody feels inclined for conversation

92

as the party moves forward in single file along the tracks made a day or two before. The slopes seem absolutely endless, for there is no immediate broken foreground, and the shoulder of the North Peak which we must turn to reach Camp III seems infinitely distant. But just when time itself seems to be drawing to a close, and one is convinced that one is on a treadmill which never advances, the last corner is turned and there is the great north-east shoulder of Mount Everest, and there the gleaming 1,200-foot wall of the North Col—the first real mountaineering difficulty, and the first challenge. We get off the ice on to the boulders where the old Camp III was situated, that bleak mound harried by incessant gales and the scene of so much misery in the past ; and we clamber on up steeper ground which is apt to take its toll of the new arrival, till over the brow of a rise appear the green and brown of tents. Camp III at last, amid scenery which banishes all fatigue. The site is admirably chosen, at a place which I believe has more shelter from wind than the exposed corner lower down. Immediately above rise the precipices of the North Peak, and at first sight one is inclined to suspect danger from falling stones ; but there is a trough in the moraine here which should catch them all. The glacier on our left is about half a mile wide, unbroken and gleaming in the sun. On the other side, Everest springs up 6,000 feet to the enormous pinnacles of the north-east shoulder beyond which, on the right, is the snowy cone of the summit. The North Face is concealed by the arête descending from the shoulder to the North Col, the effect being to bring that summit, in appearance, very much closer than it really is. In addition, the angle of the North arête deceives the observer into supposing that the general angle of this side of Everest is easy. Not till one reaches the North Col can one realise how steeply the face of the mountain falls away to the Main Rongbuk glacier ; and that face has got to be crossed high up. On the other hand the wall of the North Col, seen from Camp III, assumes an exaggerated appearance of difficulty. The danger there lies, not in steep ice, though that is sufficiently formidable in places, but in the ever-changing condition of the snow. This side of the Col faces east and is in full sunshine a great part of the day; it is immediately affected by the arrival of the comparatively warm air-currents from the south-east which herald the monsoon; and during north-westerly gales an enormous amount of dry powder snow is blown over the crest and down on to the slopes, there to form that most insidious peril—windslab.

Just before reaching Camp III, Kempson pointed out to me the spot where Maurice Wilson's body was found last year. When we arrived, Smythe, Shipton and Warren were already away and at work on the lower portion of the North Col slopes, cutting steps and fixing ropes. Gavin had begun his wireless telephone exchange.

Although the slopes had not changed much in character since the year before, they were quite different from what they were in 1933. In that year we forced a route up to the crest more or less along the line followed in 1922, and it will be remembered that an ice-wall about a third of the way up gave Smythe and Shipton a tremendous amount of trouble. It was soon obvious that we should not be able to use this route again. The ice-wall seemed to have doubled in height, and avalanche débris lay below it, possibly the remains of the great avalanche which fell last year across the line of ascent while Shipton and his companions were camped on the crest. On the same route seven porters were killed by an avalanche in 1922. It was plain that an attempt to renew the attack by this line was unjustifiable; the slopes to the south are entirely impracticable, and the only thing to be done was to find a route somewhat to the north, where the first 500 feet looked fairly easy, but would have to be followed by a long traverse southwards, inevitably dangerous on slopes of this character, ending in a steep ascent direct to the crest up snow lying on ice which

94

might have as much as 50 degrees of angle. On their return to camp, the reconnoitring party reported that this new route was fairly safe and would in any case have to be attempted, because there was no other.

So far, all had gone well, indeed perhaps better than might have been expected. With the exception of Morris, everybody was very fit, in good training, and unaffected by altitude. The porters, especially those selected by Shipton for establishing the high camps, were in great fettle, and there were to be seen signs of healthy rivalry between the Sherpas and Bhutias which was sure to result in a fine performance up the North Ridge. Two more carries from Camp II, and Camp III was completely stocked for the period of the campaign, as our advance base ; and this had been accomplished without a breakdown of any sort—a just reward for the united exertions of the party. The only thing that gave any cause for anxiety was the weather ; not that we were receiving any warnings from Alipore of serious disturbances or other calamities on the way, but the days were too warm and the nights not really cold enough. There was no north-west wind. Occasionally there was a gentle breeze from the east, which could do nothing to remove the snow from the mountain but seemed to introduce some dampness into the atmosphere which made us feel cold at night despite the evidence of the thermometer.

I am sorry to say that my first impression of Camp III was, not so much the feeling that we were nearly ready to make the assaults, but dismay at the frightful disorder of our Mess-tent. This induced me to get up at an unearthly hour next morning, and pull the Mess porters out of their tents to tidy up. Things had not been too comfortable the previous evening apart from the disorder, for our two remaining cooks were still down the glacier with Smijth-Windham and Morris respectively. Here my servant Tewang, who did such good work as mess-man in 1933, willingly undertook to do his best, and Gavin contrived to make some excellent omelettes over

95

a Primus stove.   I think the first night at all camps above the Base is invariably somewhat of a strain.   I think too that this year we rather overdid the Spartan life at Camp III, leaving there only one small arctic tent, which had to be appropriated for the wireless, and taking all the others up to the North Col. The Mess-tents used on the march across Tibet were not suitable at this altitude.   For sleeping purposes the little 16-pounder allotted to each man was admirable, but for the day we should have had at least two of the bigger pattern of Arctic tent, in which men can rest in warmth and comfort without getting in each other's way.

On May 10 the weather began to turn definitely against us, for there was a fairly heavy fall of snow.   It did not matter for the moment as this was a day of rest for the porters, but it made things difficult for Gavin, who was struggling to get into wireless communication with Camp I.   He had to change the position of his exchange to a tent as far away as possible from the shoulder of the North Peak, and to carry his masts out on to the glacier.   Then came news that Morris had developed a high temperature at Camp II, so I was obliged next morning to ask both Humphreys and Warren to go down. They found a recurrence of the malaria and he had to be carried down to Camp I with Humphreys in attendance. Heavy snow fell on this day.   Meanwhile one could do nothing but examine over and over again the plans for the assaults. Smythe and Shipton were to be the first party; Wyn Harris and Kempson the second; Warren and Oliver the third, using the oxygen apparatus.   The fourth would be Wigram and Gavin.

No more snow fell on the 12th, and although the mountain was still quite white we judged that it was justifiable to go for the North Col inasmuch as there was no sign of monsoon currents and the slopes should be safe.   Accordingly on the morning of the 13th Smythe and Gavin led off, followed by Wigram and Oliver, taking with them the under-sardars

96

Rinzing and Da Tsering, and Smythe's servant Da Tendrup, who gained snow experience on Nanga Parbat. Kempson, Warren and I brought up the rear, not intending to go far on this occasion, but to see the climbing party on its way and form some estimate of the conditions. The climbers ignored a sufficiently unpleasant spell of mist, snow and wind, and were rewarded by an improvement in the weather. They found all the steps cut on May 9 obliterated by the recent snow. Smythe had been asked to do as little step-cutting as possible himself, so that he might be fresh for the assaults. He now chose a new but good route up the first 500 feet, with the special object of avoiding danger from any avalanche that might fall from the North Peak on the right. Instead of ascending diagonally, he traversed below the slope on a safe ice-ledge and then went straight up on a part where little snow lay and protection was afforded by an ice-cliff and a crevasse above. Rinzing was given the honour of cutting the steps up this slope; Oliver, from whose notes this part of the narrative is taken, reported that the work was done in the tireless manner of a first-class Alpine guide. Some idea of the labour of making a route at this altitude may be gained from the fact that the ascent of these first 500 feet, and the fixing of ropes to long pitons driven far into the ice, took three hours.

After a rest on the edge of the crevasse, Smythe and Gavin led along the traverse southwards towards a shelf, passing above the wall of the 1933 route between the upper and lower tiers of ice-cliffs and having to do some hard step-cutting round two awkward corners. Along this line a hand-rail of rope was fixed by the supporting party, till a second crevasse was reached above which there was a 300-foot climb up steep ice to the crest of the Col. Oliver now changed places with Gavin and took it in turns with Smythe to lead up the final section; and at 3.30 p.m. Smythe pulled himself over the top. Watching him through the telescope from below, I felt

H

I could almost hear his grunt of relief as he did so. Oliver followed a minute behind. The party had been at it for five and a half hours with only twenty minutes' rest, and Wigram and Gavin were perilously near exhaustion. Smythe himself admitted that this was one of the hardest days' work he had ever done. The strain was probably even greater on the men who had to stand on one foot in an ice-step for perhaps ten minutes at a time in the worst places, hammering in pitons and attaching ropes. It was a fine effort, and meant that a reasonably safe route had been made to the North Col within four days, of which two were too bad for an advance. In 1933, owing to the gales, the same work took a fortnight.

Rinzing and Da Tendrup fixed the last ropes and then Smythe gave the word to descend. From the crest nothing could be seen over the Main Rongbuk glacier but a mass of yellow clouds, but distant mountains were clear to the north-east and south-east. It was a weary little party that tramped into Camp III that evening. After hearing their story, and congratulating them, I had particular pleasure in remitting the fine inflicted upon Rinzing after his Shekar escapade. He has now joined that growing company of Sherpa and Bhutia porters who are fit to go anywhere in any company.

A cold night was followed by a splendid morning. Wyn Harris and Kempson were able to take forty-six porters up to the crest and begin the establishment of Camp IV. In the absence of wind they felt the hot sun very much on the lower slopes but made good time. The under-sardar Ondi greatly distinguished himself. This is the man who nearly died of double pneumonia at the Base Camp in 1933, but after four weeks of so-called convalescence, during which he was sent down to the Kharta valley, turned up at the Base Camp with a heavy load on his back and demanded inclusion in the assault parties. I could have no hesitation in making a man like that an N.C.O. in 1936. On this day he was the first man to reach the crest (in three hours), and the first man home.

Up to this time Wyn Harris had not been at the very top of his form, being troubled at times with his migraine ; but I was glad to see that neither he nor Kempson appeared at all exhausted on their return. The porters looked as if they had just been for an afternoon stroll, yet half of them were recruits from Sola Khombu who had never in their lives been on an ice-slope. The day had not been altogether without incident : one man slipped from his step half-way up the final 300 feet and hung desperately from the fixed rope, scrabbling with his boots and in great danger of falling. Had he let go at this place, he must have dropped over cliff after cliff of ice, to the bottom of the Col ; but he was quickly pulled to safety by the nearest men. Another porter collapsed exhausted at the top of the first 500-foot slope. Watching through the telescope from below we could see a man who had already carried nearly to the crest hastily belay his load to the fixed rope and hurry down the steps and along the traverse. He was identifiable as Wyn Harris's servant Kusang Pagla, an eccentric (as his second name implies) but most loyal worker. As Oliver said, Kusang was not going to allow any stigma to spoil the record of the porter-corps. He took on the second load, and struggled infinitely slowly back up the line. No man could stand a double carry like this for long, and we were intensely relieved to see the load grabbed at the bottom of the last pitch and passed from hand to hand up to the crest. Kusang looked as unconcerned as the others when he came back to camp, going straight to Wyn Harris's tent for his duties as batman and saying nothing about his gallant performance ; and was quite astonished when told that the telescope had found him out. Can you wonder at our feelings of respect and admiration for these men ?

May 15 was another good day. Smythe and Shipton were now to go up and occupy Camp IV with fifty porters, of whom thirty-six picked men would remain with them to establish the higher camps. It had been a very cold night, so the slopes were sure to be in good order. The only fly in the ointment was that Shipton's throat was sore and he was beginning to lose his voice. All except Shipton were off at about 10.15, Smythe taking with him a little note from me which gave a general outline of what I should like done higher up, but naturally gave him a very wide discretion as to details. I ventured on a short address to the men, which was very well received, and shook hands with the under-sardars, all of whom except one were going up. They were showing tremendous keenness, assuring me of their determination to place a Camp VII at 27,800 feet. Shipton followed them up the glacier after attending to a few last details.

Still there was no wind. One could only hope that there was not enough snow on the mountain to prevent the establishment of the higher camps, and that during this process the north-west wind might arrive and blow everything off the slabs. The high-altitude tents had of course been specially designed to withstand a battering, and the double-skinned arctics intended for Camp V should be able to give the assault party ample protection. Meanwhile, it was quite hot at Camp III, and the rest of us lounged about on the rocks watching the ascent. Humphreys turned up just after lunch, having seen Morris down to Camp I. He was reported to be better, but still almost unable to eat anything. It was pretty clear that he would have to stay down with Smijth-Windham. Humphreys himself was a little the worse for wear, with a bad throat. Gavin was hard at work in his wireless exchange, preparing to send up to the North Col weather reports received by Smijth-Windham from Alipore and instantly forwarded to Camp III. There were fixed times for communication with Camp I, and Smythe had taken up with him one of the light high-altitude sets, by means of which he was to communicate with me three times a day, at 11.30 a.m. and at 5 and 7 p.m. Another light set would, it was hoped, be installed at Camp V, and possibly a third at Camp VII. This

100

would ensure efficient communication along the whole line of camps ; the assaulting parties could keep in touch with each other and with me, could receive support in case of trouble, and could have early warning of the rapid approach of bad weather.

The climbing party ascended with extraordinary speed. Ondi, though carrying a load, was the first man on the crest, in only two hours from Camp III ; and shortly afterwards we saw one of the pyramid tents go up and then the small wireless mast. Camp IV was in full occupation, on exactly the same date that it had been established in 1933, when it was placed on the little ice-ledge 240 feet farther down. That ledge had now disappeared, but in any case it was far better to have the camp right up on the crest in spite of the exposed position, thereby giving the men a less strenuous carry to Camp V at 25,700 feet. At 5 p.m. the first wireless message came through from Smythe. He reported that all was well in camp, but that there was a fair amount of snow on the ridge above. He thought that it might be possible to establish the three higher camps, but that the slabs on Norton's route beyond the first step were still impracticable. The faint easterly breezes continued with maddening regularity.

May 16 and 17 were days of anxious waiting. There was no sign of activity on the North Col. Gavin, resourceful as ever, furnished his dome tent with an armchair made from packing cases. We used to foregather there in the evenings to hear the Empire broadcast. Wyn Harris, casting about for amusement, set himself to the concoction of a marvellous lobster pie, co-opting me for the final stages, which demanded a nauseating admixture of condensed milk. I thought of Norton's famous ice-cream (made from strawberry jam and ice) on the North Col in 1922, and shuddered. After all, Norton's party had nothing else. But Wyn Harris likes " body " in his food ; and the others, who had not seen the

101

preparations, consumed the pie with a horrible avidity. Snow fell in the afternoon, increasing heavily as darkness came on. Smythe 'phoned down that conditions were getting worse and that it would not be worth while prematurely to exhaust the porters by attempting to make even Camp V.

The morning light on May 18 showed snow lying thickly everywhere, and I was not at all surprised by Smythe's forenoon message that there were from 18 inches to 2 feet of new snow lying even on that very exposed crest, and that both he and Shipton were of opinion that it was no good staying up while this lasted. We knew very well, from our experience in 1933, that a party deteriorates rapidly being kept inactive for any length of time at 23,000 feet ; and as there was not the slightest chance of the mountain clearing for several days they would be very much better off down at Camp III. Moreover, although the older porters were accustomed to this kind of life, and prepared to stick it out to any extent, some of the new men found it trying and were beginning to show signs of strain. I therefore agreed to a descent, but suggested that they might remain till next morning in the hope that a cold night would render the North Col slopes safer. Smythe, however, considered that as another fall of snow seemed likely, and the only real danger on the slopes was windslab, they had better risk the descent that afternoon. No doubt he was perfectly right, but I shall not soon forget the anxiety with which we watched those distant little figures coming down as it seemed with incredible slowness. Smythe went first, to test the condition of the snow, which varied from place to place, and at one point emitted a most intimidating crack. Undoubtedly there was a windslab here, but most fortunately it held. The situation, though dangerous, was not without its little touch of humour : Smythe was under the firm impression that he had tied himself on to Ondi, and when the rope ran out to its full length and Smythe found himself unable to advance, he turned round and cursed

102

poor Ondi for holding him up. He then found that he had inadvertently tied himself on to one of the fixed ropes. Altogether the descent was conducted with the utmost mountaineering skill and judgment. The men were at times up to their hips in new snow, and I think that only the fact that the monsoon air currents had not yet attacked the surface prevented a disaster. Several of the party looked a good deal shaken on their arrival at Camp III at tea time. When congratulating Ondi on his own performance, I explained the peculiar dangers of the North Col, adding that we did not want another Nanga Parbat disaster. I think he and his fellows appreciated the great care that had been taken of them by their climbing leaders. Even so, indications were observable that some of the more daring men, such as Rinzing and Ang Tarkey, thought that excessive precautions were being taken. The spirit of attack was very strong in them, and they had never been up the North Face when it was under heavy snow, nor seen the slabs in the great couloir; and they still lacked the finer knowledge of snowcraft which inculcated singularly delicate handling of the North Col slopes. They were to be undeceived before many days had passed. Even the best of these men are slow to foresee danger, and nothing but an accident, or a very narrow escape from one, will ram a lesson into their heads. As movers on steep ground, and as route-finders, they are magnificent. Judgment of snow will come with more experience, and then they will rank among the finest mountaineers in the world.

It was now time to consider carefully the next move. Mount Everest could not possibly be in a climbable condition for at least a week, the snow lying so thick that even the steeper parts of the north-east arête were masked and one could not pick out the broken rocks where Camp V was sited. Nothing but a prolonged north-wester could put things right, and that showed no signs of coming; the wind blew gently from the east, bringing more snow in the evenings. Weather reports said nothing about the monsoon ; presumably we had time in hand. The whole climbing party had now been for eleven days at or above Camp III. It seemed to me that perhaps already they had passed their peak of acclimatisation ; Shipton's throat was becoming really troublesome, Wigram was bothered by a cough, Gavin had a head-cold, and Wyn Harris, Kempson and Warren, though capable of work for which the opportunity was denied us, looked distinctly fine-drawn. As for those of us who were not intended to go high, it did not matter—we could carry on if necessary ; but it was of course vital to anticipate staleness in the climbers. Serious work being out of the question for some time, the whole party would obviously be better down at Camp I. Again, the psychological aspect of the question was important : the 1933 party worked for a more prolonged spell at Camps III and IIIa, in conditions of great hardship from gales and cold. But this kept them busy and interested. In 1936 we had to contend with that deadly foe—monotony, which seems to tell on men's spirits more fatally than any hardship. Having once enjoyed the satisfaction of knowing that the North Col was made, with European stores for four weeks, porter-food for six days, and fuel for both for fifteen days, and that everything was ready for the assaults, we were depressed by the succession of still, warm days which could be put to such good use but for that abominable factor—snow. It was my business to study the men's reactions, and I could see that they were threatened, in varying degrees, by what the French call *cafard*. A little talk with the porters also showed that, although perfectly willing to resume work on the mountain, they were bored at Camp III.

After an anxious night's thought, I gave orders on the morning of the 19th for a retirement to Camp I. Wyn Harris alone received them with dismay, but I think the result convinced even him. Men do not always know when they are tired. The morning was so hot that we could not even remain in our tents. Smythe, Shipton, Wigram and Humphreys were off before lunch. Gavin followed, after making himself an ingenious pair of ski, tipped with pieces of kerosene oil tins. These, if they held together, would take him as far as the entrance to the trough. The rest of us waited one more day ; I remember we invited Nursang into the Mess-tent in the evening, when over a glass of Navy rum he delivered himself of an opinion : he said, " I can't understand the way things are going this year : you have the most competent mountaineering party I have seen, and by far the best porters. The latter only ask for an opportunity—they will carry anywhere you like, and go to the summit if you want them to. But Everest is not willing. She has lured us on with false encouragement, and now closes the door. Always hitherto we have been beaten by wind and cold, never by this warmth and vile snow. I don't like it at all—we shan't get up unless the north wind comes." Next morning, when the rearguard left, the wind had veered to the south-east and was making a pitiful pretence of blowing snow off the mountain—not, of course, from the North Face. Nursang shook his fist at it.

The trough seemed like a hot-house. Beyond it we were surprised to come up with Humphreys and Wigram, and found that Humphreys' throat was so bad that he could scarcely breathe, and had taken six hours the day before to descend to Camp II, where he was obliged to spend the night. He protested that he was perfectly able to come on alone, but Wigram stayed with him, and we finished the course down the long moraines to Camp I together.

The effect of this descent to a lower altitude was immediate and very good. Morris and Smijth-Windham thought everyone the worse for wear on arrival, but appetites and powers of sleep returned almost at once, and I have never since doubted the wisdom of the move. One thing only retracted from the pleasure of seeing everyone brighten up—a telegram which arrived on the evening of the 19th. This was a message from

Alipore to the effect that conditions favourable for the formation of the monsoon had been observed off the coast of
Ceylon. Here was the very first intimation we received that
the monsoon was to be anything but normal in the time of its
arrival, and it was a frightful shock to us all. We knew, only
too well, the deadly, corrosive effect of the comparatively
warm south-east air currents on the slopes of the North Col,
and the practical certainty of continuous further snowfall on
the slabs of the North Face. However, it was no use crying
out before we were hurt ; one might reasonably hope that the
monsoon would take at least a fortnight in its passage from
Ceylon to the Everest region ; it might even split up in Orissa
and pass us by on either side ; it might exhaust its first fury
on the foothills of the Himalaya. There was always the
chance, too, of an onset of north-west winds which would
keep the monsoon currents back for a considerable period.
All things considered, and we did consider them at a meeting
of the staff, it seemed advisable to go back up the glacier
without delay and make ourselves ready at Camp III to take
advantage of any improvement in the situation.

Before this plan could be carried through, there was much
work to be done, organising the new advance. On the
morning of the 21st Smythe and Shipton went down on to
the Main Rongbuk glacier to a point from which they could
have a good view of the mountain. They returned with the
report that there were slight signs of evaporation of snow,
but no wind to blow it away. Several porters asked for permission to go down for a few hours to Rongbuk, where the
old Lama was celebrating a new moon ceremony. The rest
of us occupied ourselves with overhauling stores. Next
morning, which was fine enough, Smythe, Shipton, Gavin
and I went right out into the middle of the Main Rongbuk
glacier, determined to make the best of things. What *would*
Everest look like from that corner ? The answer was almost
a foregone conclusion in this warm stillness, yet we made an

impatient way through the ice in the pathetic hope that some hitherto unknown agency might come to our help in this year of contradictions. Our view-point reached, there was the mountain much the same as she had been since the end of April, lovely but—out of condition. The eye of faith, unnaturally stimulated, seemed to detect just the faintest sign of rock-strata appearing through the snow ; Shipton promptly argued that melting, or evaporation, or sublimation would have laid those rocks bare by the time we reached Camp III again. Smythe, with an air of inspired prophecy, remarked upon the likelihood of a turn in our fortunes, which was certainly due. In our heart of hearts we knew, of course, that one thing—and one thing only—could bring us to those far-off slopes : the north-west wind. On such a morning the Rongbuk glacier was superb ; we would rather have been driven off it by a gale.

In the afternoon Warren made a general medical examination, and I was obliged to persuade Humphreys to stay down a little longer to get his throat into working condition again. Apart from that he was very strong, and most anxious to do his share of the work. Snow fell heavily in the evening, with rather high temperatures and no wind, and we had news that it was raining hard at Darjeeling. Shipton and I finished the day going through the lists of porters, and food and equipment, for the nth time.

It was arranged that Smythe, Shipton, Gavin and I should occupy Camp II on the 23rd, with the high-altitude porters. We waited for the midday weather report, which conveyed yet another shock : the monsoon had already reached the Darjeeling hills, that is to say, it had travelled up the whole length of the continent from Ceylon to the Himalaya in four days. I believe I am right in saying that such a phenomenon has never occurred within living memory. Whatever the news, we could not blow hot and cold about going up again, so started according to plan in very quiet weather. The

107

Gurkha N.C.O.'s came with us to take charge of Camp II, as it seemed not improbable that in these conditions this camp would be used a good deal. There was a certain amount of wind during the night, and next morning Everest seemed just a little darker and more promising, so we carried on to Camp III just in time to get well snowed upon during the second half of the ascent. The camp looked frightfully dreary and forlorn, and Smythe was being bothered by ear-ache. I could not help reflecting that, with a little luck, Everest might have already been climbed; and that we should now have been packing up here, in complete happiness, instead of morosely peering through the tent door at a landscape which became whiter as the hours dragged by.

On the morning of May 25 I very nearly sent a porter down to Camp II to stop the second half of the party, who were following up one day behind us. Then I thought that the psychological effect of this would not be very good, and at any rate they might as well come up and see for themselves what was going on—that would prevent any unnecessary argument about a further advance. It was perfectly obvious that any attempt to meddle with the North Col was out of the question.

From now till the 28th was a miserable period of enforced idleness. Snow fell heavily every afternoon and evening, and the only subject of conversation was, "What *can* one do in a year like this?" We knew that by now the southerly air currents were eating into those dangerous snow slopes and producing conditions favourable for the kind of avalanche which fell in 1935 when Shipton's party was on the North Col; and we were not going to invite disaster by tackling them. One morning Shipton, Oliver and Gavin strolled across the glacier to the Rapiu La and went a short distance up the great south-east ridge. For lack of anything better to do, there was even some suggestion of attempting to make a route up this way; but it is very long, there is a difficult pitch about half-way up, and at the top are a series of gigantic gendarmes. In any case, all our high-altitude kit and stores were on the North Col. I see from my diary that I now threw out a tentative proposal to go round and have a look at the west side of the North Col. The suggestion was really but a peg upon which to hang argument, not a serious contribution to our plans. We knew that Mallory rejected this line of approach in 1921, and those members of the Reconnaissance party of 1935 who saw it thought there was nothing to be done there. One of them had retained the impression of a 3,000-foot ice-slope. So the matter was dropped for the present. Then I sent off a long wireless message to Dr. Roy, the meteorologist at Alipore, almost begging him to assure us that this was only the " chhoti barsat " or first burst of the monsoon, and that there would be a fine interval before the real monsoon arrived. Needless to say, Dr. Roy's answer devoted itself to scientific fact rather than to specious encouragement. This was the real monsoon all right, and we might expect a particularly severe storm on the night of the 27th. Certainly everything pointed to this, and heavy avalanches were beginning to fall, usually at night, from the shoulder of Everest. At last there was nothing for it but to order a second retirement to Camp I on the morning of the 28th. The storm had arrived, and although it was not of exceptional severity, it produced a blizzard which made the descent anything but comfortable.

Mount Everest had not yet finished amusing herself at our expense. On the morning of the 29th we awoke at Camp I to find a splendid north-west wind blowing strongly. Smythe and Shipton were at once asked to go off down to the main glacier and observe the mountain. They returned jubilantly with the information that a really genuine north-wester of the old type was blowing the snow in enormous sheets off the North Face. Then Smijth-Windham emerged with delight from his wireless tent with news that the monsoon depression had weakened, and was moving off towards Assam. It really did seem that at last our chance had come, and everyone brightened up tremendously. The thought of boulder-hopping all those weary miles up the glacier was as nothing to the hope that at long last we could make an assault. Incidentally I may say that the general physical condition of the party was by now distinctly better than it had been, and I think we should have had no difficulty in making at least two, and probably three, assaults on the summit, had the improvement in the weather been maintained. But even as we left Camp I on the morning of May 30 the north-west wind seemed to hesitate, and by the time we reached Camp II snow was coming down heavily once more. It continued to do so with very little intermission till the morning of June 3. This was a life of mere vegetation, if such an expression can be used of an existence in a wilderness of ice and snow. For the most part we could only lie in our tents, talk and read, and curse the weather. I except Wigram, whom I was obliged to ask to go up to Camp III on the 2nd with some good porters to bring down some badly needed provisions. This mission he carried out very gallantly through a blizzard. That same blizzard was from the north-west, and it continued through the night ; so it seemed worth while on the morning of June 3 to go on up to Camp III, to find out whether the wind had blown any snow off the North Col. It was not encouraging to start off with a wireless message from Dr. Roy in my pocket which said that not only was the Bay of Bengal monsoon strengthening again, but that we must now expect a further contribution from the Arabian Sea, bringing moist south-west winds. Camp III certainly did look most depressing when we arrived there in the afternoon. However, next morning Smythe, Shipton and Kempson were determined to go and have a look at the lower slopes of the Col. We could see that quite a lot of snow had been blown off them, for here and there were shining patches of ice. On the other hand, one knew that the north-west wind must have brought a lot of snow over from the western side on to the eastern, where it would form the exact conditions favourable to windslab avalanches. Again, practically the whole route would have to be remade, as all the steps would long ago have been filled up, and all the fixed ropes buried. With glasses one could just see a few traces of the old track near the crest. The crucial part, of course, would be the long and always treacherous traverse.

The party returned with a moderately favourable report ; they had only been a short distance up the lower slopes, and found these considerably better than they expected. They thought that, if the very greatest precautions were taken, and if the wind continued to clear the slopes, it might be justifiable to attempt to reoccupy Camp IV next day. I spent a very busy afternoon working out operation orders which should ensure the maximum safety possible for what we knew to be a difficult undertaking. As the whole of the route had to be remade, the full strength of the climbing party would be required. A very early start would be made, and Wyn Harris and Kempson would lead off and work for one hour, hoping in that time to complete the first 500 feet straight up towards the crevasse from which the traverse took off. They would then be replaced by Warren and Kempson, who would work cautiously along the traverse for one and a half hours, handing over in their turn to Oliver and Gavin for a similar period. Smythe would accompany both these parties on the rope, doing no step-cutting himself but forming a judgment from time to time as to whether further progress was justifiable. Finally Ang Tarkey and Rinzing, accompanied by Smythe, would cut up the final stretch to the crest. Shipton would be in charge of the forty-two porters who were to do the carry. These men were divided into four batches, each under a good under-sardar. The first batch would leave Camp III two hours after the leading pair of climbers, and

III

the remaining batches would start at forty-minute intervals. The men would not rope up, as large numbers of men on a rope are not in any way safer if the snow slips. As each buried fixed rope was followed up to its head, a long stick would be pushed into the snow to mark the point. If the ascent succeeded, Smythe and Shipton would remain at Camp IV with their forty-two men and proceed up the North Ridge next day or as soon as possible. Once the operation was launched, Smythe had full discretion to continue or break off as he saw fit.

The north-west wind blew strongly through the evening, and the North Face looked extremely grim as the snow clouds were whirled up into the air. But at least this snow *was* going and hopes began to mount. The porters were in terrific form ; under-sardars were invariably consulted in making up the batches, and the result was a fair subdivision among Sherpas and Bhutias, with a fine sporting rivalry between them.

The night was cold and clear, the wind continuing throughout. An early weather report said that a strong westerly wind had driven off the Bay of Bengal monsoon towards Assam. I was up at 3.30 a.m., and soon had the porters busy and the cooks preparing a hot meal all round for both climbers and porters. Wyn Harris and Kempson were off by themselves at 6 a.m. Unhappily they found that even that night of cold and wind had not materially improved their 500-foot section. They had a hard time recutting steps and tracing the ropes under the frozen snow. Worse than that, they presently came upon the débris of a small avalanche which had fallen from the southern shoulder of the North Peak, right across the line of ascent. They halted among the blocks of ice to consult with Smythe, who was following not far behind. Smythe agreed that the snow was not to be trusted, but he decided that some further advance was possible, and passed on with Warren and Wigram, followed by

Ang Tarkey and Rinzing. In their turn the leading batch of porters came up with Oliver and Gavin and were halted at a point where the traverse begins. Shipton, with memories of the previous year's avalanche, was manifesting great anxiety, and he halted the remainder of the porters at a point farther down.

Almost at once examination showed that it would be suicidal to proceed along the traverse, and this explains what I now observed through my glasses from Camp III : Smythe's party beginning to cut straight up towards the crest, up frightfully steep ice, from a point not far from the crevasse at the beginning of the traverse. The ice was part of a great band, above which was an evil-looking snow-slope, beyond that another band of ice equally steep, and then more bad snow to the crest. Altogether I should say 400 to 500 feet of really difficult climbing, and an impossible route anyhow for laden porters. I suspected what ultimately turned out to be the truth, that the men on the slope could not exactly see what lay ahead of them, as they were too directly underneath. This was really just an effort to escape from that horrible traverse ; and Smythe has frankly told me since that he realised that if they were turned back at this point now we were very unlikely ever to reach the North Col again. He was therefore prepared to make a somewhat desperate decision and try the lesser of two evils.

Presently I could see the main body of porters beginning to come down, and found afterwards that Shipton, convinced that they were in great danger, had anticipated Smythe's order to commence the descent. But once he had made up his mind that further ascent was out of the question, Smythe used every turn of his great skill and experience to get his party off safely. Conditions had already changed for the worse since the morning : the wind had veered to the south-east temporarily, producing an instant effect on the slopes. Where these had been at least reasonably safe, they were now

I

almost visibly rotting, and it was evident that the utmost care was necessary to prevent the whole upper layer from peeling off and crashing down on to the glacier below. Men were allowed to move only at long intervals and singly, so the descent naturally took a very long time and was a great strain. It was a huge relief to have the entire party down safe.

There could be no doubt that on this day fifty men had been in great danger on those treacherous slopes ; and I spent the evening trying to sum up the situation correctly. Some believed that excessive risks had been taken ; others that they had remained just within the safety factor, and that it was worth while persevering now that the wind had again gone round to the north-west and was blowing great guns. The evening weather report was on the whole favourable, indicating that we might expect a temporary continuance of this wind. Certainly the North Face was clearing rapidly.

On the morning of June 6 a full gale was raging, and the tents shook and trembled as the gusts tore at them. Inside, the debate whirled and eddied between the poles of advance and retreat, while for the time being I remained apart in my own tent, striving to maintain some balance of judgment. At last Wyn Harris came in and suggested that, if the gale moderated, he and Shipton might go some little distance up the slopes to see how they were getting on. Again those patches of ice were beginning to appear, but again I knew that snow was coming over from the north-west to settle on that abominable traverse. However, I felt that the experience of these two men could be trusted not to carry them too far, and I agreed to what they promised would be a very cautious piece of prospecting. They set out into the gale immediately after lunch.

Smythe, who had borne the burden of a great responsibility the day before, came and sat in my little tent, whence we watched the progress of the climbers so far as the flying clouds of snow permitted. We were both terribly anxious, but

Smythe hoped that this great wind would by now have whipped practically the whole of the upper surface from the snow, and that the slopes would rapidly become negotiable. We went over together to Gavin's wireless tent, from which a better view could be obtained, without discomfort, through the mica window. The party seemed to go very fast, and we saw the two tiny distant figures reach the crevasse 500 feet up and halt below a little ice-cliff. Evidently they were considering the position, and probably they were roping up. We looked away for a minute or two and then somebody outside—I think it was Nursang—shouted that there had been an avalanche. With our hearts in our boots, we rushed out of the tent, and there, sure enough, was the track of an avalanche below and a little to the left of the crevasse, and the track of yet another avalanche farther to the south. A single figure could be seen in the middle of the first one, and the other figure was close to the crevasse, but then slowly made its way down to join the first. Then very slowly both men started traversing away to the right and coming down the line of steps. I immediately had some hot tea made ready in a thermos and taken up by two porters, and followed them after hastily putting on my climbing boots. My servant Tewang caught me up just as I reached the ice-slope below the foot of the Col. We met Wyn Harris and Shipton on this slope, coming along steadily and well, though it was very evident that they had had a bad shaking.

It appeared that they found the snow on the lower slopes much better than it had been yesterday, and ascended the first 500 feet with an increasing confidence. Much encouraged, they roped up close to the crevasse and decided to test the traverse and if all went well continue right up to the crest. They were now on a moderate slope, and standing on what seemed to be a good sound snow. Shipton led out, his tricouni boot-nails biting well into the hard surface. He was about twelve yards out along the traverse, and Wyn Harris

115

had just begun to move in his turn, when there came a sudden horrible crunching sound some 200 feet higher up. A moment's silence, and the slope began to travel slowly but steadily down, breaking up as it did so into blocks of ice. Shipton was immediately upset on to his back and buried almost to his neck among the moving blocks. Wyn Harris made a terrific effort and sprang back out of the moving mass, which he was able to do owing to his being so near the edge of it. He dashed the pick of his axe into the hard snow on the lip of the crevasse and hitched the rope round it, but the flying coils of rope crushed his left hand against the axe head and he was obliged to let the rope run out free while struggling to regain his balance. He dashed the haft of his axe deep into the snow, with the rope round it, and threw his whole weight on to the steel head. He remembers how the rope hummed as the strain came on it ; but it held firm and Shipton was slowly pulled sideways from among the sliding blocks. This could not last long ; slowly but surely the axe was being pulled from the snow, and Wyn Harris with it, when a miracle happened : the avalanche seemed to hesitate and then quite gently came to rest, only a few feet above the lip of a 400-foot precipice of ice. Shipton was completely winded and could do nothing for some minutes but stand and gasp. Wyn Harris climbed carefully down to him and they then managed to edge their way along to the line of steps by which they had ascended, and get down safely to the glacier.

It had, of course, been a very close shave indeed. Wyn Harris could not possibly, by his unaided effort, have arrested the fall of several hundred tons of ice ; but I shall always think that, by instantly getting his own weight and to some extent that of Shipton and the surrounding ice-blocks off the sliding mass, he contributed to slow it down at a point where in all probability there was a slight easing off of the slope just before the final drop. Anyhow he did the right thing at the critical moment, as he always does.

At this point I cannot do better than quote Smythe's opinion (written for the *Geographical Journal*) of snow conditions on the North Col :

" From the point of view of danger the ascent of the North Col from the head of the East Rongbuk Glacier presents considerable problems, and a study of the history of this route shows how diverse are the conditions with which climbers must contend.

" In 1921 the Col was reached without incident towards the end of the monsoon season, though Mallory in his account mentions frozen avalanche snow. In the light of subsequent experience however it is probable that the party exposed themselves unknowingly to considerable risk.

" In 1922, shortly after the monsoon had broken, seven porters lost their lives in an avalanche.

" In 1924 no avalanche occurred except for a minor snow slip during the rescue of some porters who were marooned by pre-monsoon snowstorms on the Col.

" In 1933 the party on one occasion retreated owing to a snow formation resembling a windslab, and Camp IV which was on a ledge some 300 feet below the crest of the Col had to be moved on to the Col owing to the risk of an avalanche overwhelming it from above. A reconnaissance after the monsoon had broken disclosed dangerous conditions.

" In 1935 a large avalanche occurred shortly after the establishing of Camp IV which involved a considerable portion of the route.

" In 1936 after the abandonment of Camp IV prior to the monsoon the slope was heard to crack at one place. The same thing was heard later on another part of the slope after the monsoon had broken when an attempt was made to re-occupy Camp IV, and finally Wyn Harris and Shipton narrowly escaped disaster when an avalanche was detached during a reconnaissance of the route.

" All the major avalanches so far observed on the North Col have been of the slab type. The upper stratum of snow has slid off *en bloc*, breaking up into minor blocks as it did so. This is characteristic of the windslab, for the formation of which the east face of the North Col is peculiarly suited. The prevailing wind is from the west or north-west, and even during the monsoon when the prevailing air current is from the south it would appear that it passes over the 19,000-feet Col known as the Lho La to the west of Everest and is then deflected against the west slope of the Col. Thus the snow is blown over the crest of the Col and settles on the lee side. This, though one of the conditions necessary in the formation of windslabs, is not the only condition. It has been established by scientific experiments in the Alps that a certain percentage of humidity is also necessary. Mr. G. Seligman gives this as about 85 per cent. No measurements of humidity have been taken at or above 22,000 feet on Mount Everest, but the available evidence points to the fact that whereas before the monsoon air current reaches Everest the percentage of humidity is less than 85 per cent., after it reaches Everest it exceeds 85 per cent. during the greater part of the monsoon. From this, and the evidence already known, it would appear certain that whereas it is justifiable to ascend the North Col from the east prior to the incidence of the monsoon current, it is unjustifiable to ascend it after its arrival.

" The problem however is not so simple as it sounds. By ' arrival of the monsoon ' expeditions in the past have assumed this to mean the first heavy precipitation of snow on Everest which is not quickly removed by the north-west wind and which is accompanied by a marked rise of air temperature. From the point of view of safety or danger on the slopes of the North Col such an assumption is wrong. Monsoon precipitation may be preceded by a rise of air temperature and humidity slight enough not to be noticed by a party unequipped with measuring instruments yet sufficient to induce avalanches.

Thus, a party might continue the ascent in good conditions on the upper part of the mountain yet be overwhelmed by an avalanche on their descent of the North Col. Such a possibility makes careful observation essential, and if the same route to the North Col is to be followed by future expeditions I would strongly recommend the taking of instruments which should be under the charge of some competent person.

" In 1936 I believe such conditions as already described did actually occur, as when Shipton and I made the descent of the North Col after abandoning Camp IV the snow was in a dangerous condition and on one occasion cracked ominously beneath me as I was exploring it ahead on a rope. As even a small avalanche is likely to involve a party in disaster owing to ice-cliffs which are almost everywhere below the route, no precaution to avoid such danger can be too elaborate.

" A windslab is the most difficult of all snow conditions to detect. The climber is lulled into a sense of false security by apparently firm snow which may be so hard on the surface as to necessitate step cutting. Such a condition obtained when Wyn Harris and Shipton made their reconnaissance which nearly ended in disaster, and the avalanche which occurred was a typical windslab. For the past few days, and particularly during the morning before this incident, a strong north-west wind had been blowing. This was sweeping the face of the North Col almost horizontally, and I for one had no fears for the party and was of the opinion that the wind so far from forming windslab was consolidating the snow into a safe crust. In this I was mistaken.

" It cannot be too strongly urged that Everest climbers should visit the Alps during winter whenever possible so as to gain experience in windslab avalanches. Only through such experience is it possible to detect a windslab. A windslab can be detected both visually and by the feel of the snow. In appearance the snow is smooth but rippled by wind at the edges of the slab. In feel, though it may as already noted be

119

hard, it possesses a curiously velvety texture which is **par-ticularly** noticeable when ski-ing.

"Though it may be safely assumed that the avalanche which nearly overwhelmed Wyn Harris and Shipton was an ordinary windslab such as is common during winter in the Alps, the far larger avalanche which occurred in 1935 was a more complex affair. The monsoon then was well advanced and air temperatures and humidity had been high for some weeks. The slab was fully 6 feet thick and covered a considerable area ; the avalanche must have weighed tens of thousands of tons. During their ascent the party found the snow reasonably firm and apparently safe. The night temperature at Camp IV was low, yet the avalanche occurred, it is thought, early the following morning. Had the snow been wet and sticky the party would have turned back, for wet snow avalanches such as are common in the Alps during spring and summer are easy to detect, and the party was a competent one, and one member at least, Kempson, had had considerable experience of Alpine winter snow conditions.

" Shipton's theory is that weeks of monsoon weather had rotted the snow, but this is not a sufficient explanation. It may be that the avalanche was a combination of windslab and waterlogged snow. It cannot have been formed of purely waterlogged snow, otherwise, as already mentioned, it would have been detectable and the low overnight temperature would have held it *in situ*. There is the possibility that it was detached by an abrupt movement of the ice-fall on which it rested—a possibility that deserves consideration when ascending the east side of the North Col and one which militates against this route. From the available evidence it would appear to have been of a similar type of avalanche to that which overwhelmed the seven porters in 1922, though on that occasion the snow was considerably softer and the climbers were sinking several inches into it.

" It is possible that the avalanche was a windslab which

120

formed some time previously, but that it was not one which readily avalanched of its own accord. Subsequently it was covered by monsoon snow and the weight of this plus a movement of the ice-fall eventually dislodged it. I have on one occasion seen such a condition in the Alps when climbing on ski the Schilthorn above Murren. In this case a windslab had become covered by several inches of new powdery snow. The latter appeared quite safe as it was loose and crystalline in texture. Nevertheless the hidden windslab beneath cracked, but fortunately did not come away. It is difficult to imagine any more treacherous and incalculable form of avalanche than this. Neither visually nor by feel was it detectable, and the only possible clue in dealing with such an avalanche is previous knowledge that a windslab has formed coupled with knowledge of the direction of the wind during the snowfall which resulted in the formation of the slab. Neither in my case nor Shipton's was such knowledge available, and this in itself is sufficient proof that the North Col is very dangerous during the monsoon season and should be left severely alone.

" To sum up, there is no doubt that a route should be made if possible up the west face of the North Col. This face being on the windward side of the Col is certain to have safer and more easily calculable snow. Windslabs are unlikely, though it is not impossible for them to occur on a windward face. If a rock rib is followed the climber need ascend no more than 300 feet of snow, and if the worst came to the worst and an avalanche occurred he has a better chance of escape as there are no ice-cliffs below him.

" It is probably more difficult than the east face and may take a longer time to force. If the next expedition arrives a month earlier at the base camp there will be ample time for this, and the ascents and descents in making the route will serve to acclimatise the party, for it is certain that acclimatisation is better gained through a number of ascents and descents than through residence at any particular altitude.

"This does not rule out the possibility of the eastern route. This may be assumed safe in pre-monsoon conditions except after a heavy snowfall, but a route on the west side of the Col, even if not used to the exclusion of the eastern route, would serve as an alternative route in the event of the arrival of the monsoon air current finding the climbing party on the upper part of the mountain or in position to attack at Camp III. In 1936, when much of the snow was swept from the mountain by a north-west gale after the first monsoon precipitation and the party was in the unfortunate predicament of being unable to attempt the summit owing to dangerous conditions on the east face of the North Col, it is probable that the west side of the Col was practicable.

"Finally, it should be emphasised that Himalayan snow cannot obey different laws to Alpine snow, but that its study is complicated by swiftly changing and more varied conditions in which a greater range of solar temperature and changing air temperatures and humidity due to the monsoon play the principal part. And allied to these factors high winds and heavy snowfalls must be added.

"I have dealt only with the practical aspects of snow conditions on the North Col and have endeavoured to outline the problem as seen from the mountaineer's standpoint. I leave those more expert than I to add to our theoretical knowledge of an intricate subject. There is a considerable literature, and I would especially bring to the attention Mr. G. Seligman's book, *Snow Structure and Ski Fields*."

The avalanche was decisive; the climbers had pushed their attempts on the North Col to the very limit, and never again can there be any doubt that the North Col slopes must be left severely alone once the monsoon has really arrived. Many will think that those attempts were carried too far, but allowance must be made for the very difficult situation in which we found ourselves. After weeks of waiting, the mountain had at last shown signs of getting into some sort of condition for climbing. There were all our tents and equipment ready on the North Col; could we but reach them, at least one assault might be made. Shipton and Wyn Harris' courageous experiment probably saved the expedition from a major disaster, for had a large party tried to reach the North Col next day the entire slope might well have gone down. The weight of fifty odd laden men strung out along the traverse would have been a very different matter from that of two climbers.

The game was now up and I had no hesitation in wiring down to Morris at Camp I to call up the transport from Shekar Dzong. We evacuated Camp III on June 7, all the porters heavily laden. At this moment of departure Everest seemed to fling at us a gesture of derision: the upper slopes looked almost clear. Only for the moment, however—by next day the mountain was as white as ever. It made no real difference: those upper slopes might be negotiable, but never again would I allow any party for which I was responsible to climb those North Col slopes during the monsoon. Any attack from this side must be made before that. Had I then known what I now know, I would have moved the expedition round to the western side after May 19. It is extremely improbable that a serious attempt on the mountain could have been made at *any* time after April 30, but the climbers would at least have been saved the very dangerous work they so gallantly did in the full knowledge of the risks involved. The plan so carefully laid was wrecked by weather conditions to which there is no known parallel. To the snow of 1936 there is no answer.

Chapter VI

THE WEST FACE OF THE NORTH COL, AND THE RETURN

THE transport could not be expected to arrive from Shekar Dzong for some days; it seemed worth while to spend the interval in a little piece of exploration which might conceivably be of use to future expeditions. We already knew that it was easily possible to ascend the Main Rongbuk glacier and to approach at least the foot of the western side of the North Col. Should this side be found less formidable than had been supposed, we might be able to make a way up it, thereby providing an alternative route to the crest. Looked at from above, the final slope, though undoubtedly steep, does not appear by any means impossible, and one seems to have a choice of rock ribs by which to ascend. A closer examination of the lower part might reveal unexpected opportunities; so often a climb that looks impossible from a distance resolves itself into a negotiable route.

The party received with enthusiasm a proposal to start next day. Smijth-Windham, who had been tied down to weeks of unrelieved effort at Camp I, sending out during that period upwards of five hundred wireless messages, accepted gladly a suggestion that he should now have a little holiday and accompany us up the glacier; but he was not going to lose the opportunity of further experiment and brought with him a

124

light receiving and transmitting apparatus. Morris, now much better, was prepared to come at least part of the way. In the evening, while the others were busy with preparations, I wrote a careful analysis of the situation for the Mount Everest Committee, explaining exactly why our chances of success were now *nil*, with the monsoon in full force over the Indian peninsula ; and warning them that the projected move could not be regarded as preliminary to an assault, though it might be a contribution to the future.

It was a lovely morning when we turned the southern corner below Camp I and walked along the shelf above the right bank of the Main Rongbuk glacier, on June 8. Before starting we breakfasted in the open, and now I must make a confession : I am *always* rude to poor Frank Smythe at Camp I. Here in 1933 I called him a sybarite, because he had, quite reasonably, suggested that each climber should have a small tent to himself. On this occasion he, undismayed by the dangers of the last week, enlarged upon the value of a bold, optimistic outlook towards climbing Mount Everest. I took him up in quite the wrong way, and made some academic, even pedantic, remarks about a sense of responsibility. But he is far too good a fellow to let anything rankle, and by evening we were the very best of friends again. I should like to pay tribute to the way in which Smythe, in face of the exceptional difficulties of this year, maintained throughout the ardent spirit of attack. It is that spirit which will, I sincerely hope, some day take him to the summit.

The right bank of the Main Rongbuk glacier provides the most extensive course of boulder-hopping in my experience, but there is no difficulty whatever even for laden porters. In the afternoon we reached a corner of the moraine beyond which there suddenly appeared a marvellous little green oasis, called by last year's Reconnaissance " Lake Camp." It was strange in that great wilderness to find, at 18,000 feet, green grass, a few little flowers pushing their way through, and in the midst a lark's nest with two eggs in it. The hen was sitting and she hatched out those two eggs while we were farther up the glacier. A pleasant little lake was formed by water trickling from beneath the enormous masses of moraine rubbish higher up. We could not see round the next corner and up the Main glacier, but opposite stretched away the broad stream of the West Rongbuk glacier, above which towered Pumori and the Lingtren peaks. We experienced a feeling of freedom which was not to be had in the narrower valley of the East Rongbuk. The eye travelled across to distant peaks away in the west, to unknown country and a paradise for future explorers. Mount Everest from this point looked exceedingly grim—we were beginning to see the whole of the North Face, again covered deep in snow. Morris, in his weakened state, had some difficulty in reaching this camp, and decided to stay on for the present with Humphreys, collecting plants and insects.

Next morning began with a bad weather report, but for the moment the sun was shining and we resumed our boulder-hopping. Round the corner from Lake Camp, the right bank of the glacier is one gigantic rubbish-heap, boulders being poised in the wildest confusion and often in a very uncertain state of equilibrium. Indeed at one point Oliver started a regular slide of big blocks and narrowly escaped being crushed. Wigram and Warren in their turn took minor tosses which excited ribaldry rather than commiseration. We halted for lunch on a magnificent spur of the moraine, where Michael Spender fixed one of his survey camps in 1935; and then pushed on for about an hour till we found an excellent camp site at 19,000 feet, close to the edge of the ice and under the western ridge of the North Peak. From here we could see the whole expanse of the upper Main Rongbuk glacier and part of the North Face of Everest, but the south-west shoulder of the North Peak still hid from sight the western side of the North Col. This place was given the tentative name of " North

126

Face Camp." Across the glacier rose the enormous northwest ridge of the mountain; a good deal foreshortened, of course. Hazard drew my particular attention to this ridge before we left in 1933, because he had formed a theory that it might provide a good line of assault, especially as its average angle is not very steep. But the average moderation of this angle is due really to the great length of the ridge; the ascent of the lower portion would probably require prolonged step-cutting, and there are rock pitches of considerable severity at two or three points higher up. Again, the ridge is completely exposed throughout to the north-west wind, and I think that a party which committed itself with porters to this climb might have a terrible experience.

Smijth-Windham was taking advantage of his " holiday " to make sundry wireless experiments. He moved his mast to various places and set it up at various angles. He then disported himself for a considerable time on a large ice sérac, possibly with a view to planting a mast on the top of *that*. In doing so he cut his steps rather far apart, and had a difficult time getting down again.

In the evening it came on to snow heavily once more. I was looking out from my tent when I suddenly saw Smijth-Windham emerge from his tent as if propelled by some mysterious but powerful agency. He rushed across to me and explained that he had had quite a severe shock from his wireless set; that sparks several inches long were flying about in all directions, and that the falling snow must have become electrically charged. Shortly afterwards we ventured into his tent and watched this impromptu display of fireworks till the storm abated. In spite of this little setback the Marconi set was a very great success : its maximum transmission range was stated to be five miles, yet at his very first attempt Smijth-Windham got into immediate touch with Serjeant Frawley at Darjeeling, although the distance as the crow flies must be about a hundred miles and we were right under the lee of the

26,400-foot North Peak. Reception, too, was admirable; we received the Empire broadcast at full strength. Big Ben in the midst of this wilderness was thrilling enough, but it seemed extraordinary to be able to listen in to the polo match between England and America.

The morning of June 10 was splendid. We roped up immediately after breakfast in small parties to go out on to the glacier towards the Lho La and have a look from there at the western slopes of the North Col. Wigram led the first rope. About half-way across we were able to see round the south-west buttress of the North Peak and were suddenly brought up all standing by a spectacle which at once banished the Lho La from our minds. There, away to the left, were the western slopes of the North Col. But where were the difficulties we had anticipated ? In the foreground lay the almost level and obviously easy glacier ; beyond that a broken ice-fall which seemed to be by no means unduly complicated ; then a berg-schrund which looked as if it were at least partially filled with snow, and lastly perhaps 800 feet of very broad snow couloir, flanked on the right or southern side by rock ribs which did not look impracticable. All this was very encouraging, and the climbers lost no time in preparing for a closer inspection ; all except Warren, who was not feeling very fit on this day. The rest of us stayed where we were for a considerable time examining the slopes with glasses and photographing them ; but then had to start back for camp as the clouds began to roll up over the Lho La and gradually to obscure the North Face and the Col itself. These same clouds, of course, brought heavy snow again in the evening, through which the tired climbers fought their way back to camp with the report that they had been able to find a way up the ice-fall to the bergschrund, but being unable to see more than a few yards beyond that had not proceeded with the climb. The weather reports were now continuously discouraging ; the monsoon was in full force, and the evidence of our own eyes showed what it was doing to the

128

mountain, which was deep under snow. It was useless to employ the whole strength of the party in what could only be a reconnaissance of the western slopes not to be followed by a definite assault. Shipton was most anxious to have one more try for the North Peak itself, on which he and his men had been stopped by impossible snow conditions the year before. Perhaps at this earlier period of the monsoon he might be able to make better progress. It was therefore arranged that Smythe and Wyn Harris should take up a light camp with a few porters and establish themselves close to the bergschrund, with a view to pushing up to the North Col if conditions permitted ; that Smijth-Windham and I should remain with a few more men at North Face Camp, and that the rest should go down the main glacier, picking up Humphreys on their way, and reascend the East Rongbuk glacier to Camp II, from which the north-east shoulder of the North Peak could be attained. If he felt well enough, Warren would make a full-dress trial of the oxygen apparatus on this climb. We would all rendezvous at the Base Camp on the 16th, in time to meet the transport.

Next morning Smythe did not feel energetic, so decided to postpone his reconnaissance for a day. The North Peak party set off down the glacier, except Kempson and Gavin, who were full of zeal and went off across the glacier to have a look over the Lho La into Nepal before they started down. They called in at North Face Camp on their way back to explain that they had had a clear view of the western slopes of the North Col, and were of opinion that the final steep slopes were not more than 700 feet in height. They were convinced that a way up would readily be found.

In the afternoon Smythe happened to be sitting in Smijth-Windham's wireless tent when a weather forecast came through, the first lines of which appeared to promise better things. Optimistic as ever, and not worrying about the context or the concluding paragraphs of the message, Smythe rushed over

K

to me with a magnificent plan for an assault on the mountain from this side, in which he and Wyn Harris would endeavour to rush the peak, while Smijth-Windham and I acted in the rôle of supporters at Camp IV. Alas for poor Smythe's splendid enthusiasm ; he found me, I fear, a sceptical and blasé person who insisted, firstly on finding out exactly what the weather report had been (its general purport was anything but reassuring) ; secondly, on pointing out that Everest was most thoroughly snowed up and that we had only a few porters remaining to us, although some of them were of the best. I suggested, however, that the proposed light camp should be taken up next day and that we should first have a report on whether the ascent to the North Col from this side was in fact practicable. Coming down to earth at once, Smythe readily agreed to this, and the previous plan was duly carried out. He and Wyn Harris went off on the morning of the 12th with eight good porters led by Rinzing, who was to bring down five of them in the evening ; he being by now perfectly capable of conducting them on the glacier and spotting crevasses. The frightful heat of the morning sun made the ascent extremely trying, but by nightfall Rinzing was back with his party, bringing a note from Wyn Harris to the effect that after great labours in the soft snow the camp had been established close to the bergschrund yet out of the way of the avalanches which were now falling steadily both from Everest and from the North Peak. The note included a very sound appreciation of the general features on this side. Rinzing and the other porters were absolutely wet through, having fallen into various water-holes in the rapidly melting surface of the glacier. All that evening and night it again snowed heavily.

The wireless weather forecasts now became, if possible, more vicious than before, and I was anxious lest Smythe and Wyn Harris should get themselves into trouble in all this new snow ; and on the morning of the 13th Smijth-Windham and I with Rinzing and four other porters set out to see how they were getting on. The heat in the early part of the day was again terrific. Rinzing was allowed to lead the rope as he knew the way, and was obviously very proud to act in the capacity of guide. On the whole, he was successful in dealing with the many masked crevasses on the way, but was rather puzzled when we got on to a sort of little plateau at about 20,000 feet where these crevasses radiated like the spokes of an invisible wheel. Here the surface snow emitted terrifying groans as the weight of the party came upon it, but was safe enough if one took the usual precautions. Infinitely more trying was the heat of the sun, which was rapidly grilling our faces and hands in spite of layers of " Antilux." But the view-point was superb : in the foreground rose the tangled masses of the ice-fall, easily turned on the left by a shelf running up below the tremendous precipices of the North Peak—a place, however, that demands a watchful eye for falls of rock or snow ; on the right one looked up and up at the North Face—9,000 feet of outward-shelving slabs scored by gullies down which snow hissed incessantly. No way here for human moun-taineers. In front, beyond the ice-fall, were the slopes we had come to see, and the Col so long denied to us by the rotten snow on the other side. The climb would certainly " go," given the right weather. The expected avalanche débris were not to be seen, and alternative routes of ascent, on snow or rock, could be traced all the way up. After fruitless shouting, which was heard in the camp above but did not disclose our position against this background of confused ice, Smijth-Windham and I descended with Pasang " Picture " while the rest of the porters went on to bring the camp down. I did not take a single photograph because we were so close under the mountain walls that only the widest of wide-angle lenses could have embraced the scene, and even then dis-tortion would have given a wholly wrong impression.

In the prevailing conditions there was not the slightest chance of reaching the crest ; Smythe and Wyn Harris quickly realised this and came down through the snow of the evening, but they had had a pretty good view from where they were camped, and that evening Smythe sat down immediately after arrival and wrote out a very good report, the substance of which is given here :

" On June 11 a camp, known as the North Face Camp, was established at about 18,500 feet on the east side moraine of the Rongbuk glacier. The following day the party ascended the glacier into its almost level bay under the North Face of Everest, until a view was obtained of the easternmost branch of the glacier which is enclosed between the North Peak and Everest. At the head of this branch is the North Col which on this, the west, side falls from its lowest point in a continuous ice-slope, a wide tongue between the steep buttresses of the North Peak and an indeterminate rock face ending in the crest of the North Ridge of Everest.

" Mallory reported adversely on this approach to the North Col as a result of a reconnaissance in 1921, and it was somewhat surprising to note an obvious route up the ice-fall of the glacier to the foot of the final slope which optimistic estimates placed as being only 600 feet high—from the bergschrund—but which is probably 800–1,000 feet.

" Encouraged by this view a party mounted the ice-fall to reconnoitre the route. No difficulties other than soft fatiguing snow were encountered, and a zigzag tongue of snow led easily through crevasses and séracs. The route then ascended beneath the slopes of the North Peak, which are so steep and icy that any avalanches that fall must necessarily be small, though care would be necessary in certain conditions, particularly during or immediately after a heavy snowfall.

" Mist obscured our view of the final slope, whilst dangerously soft, wet snow prevented an advance beyond a well-bridged schrund at the foot of the slope.

132

" On June 12 Wyn Harris and I, with some porters carrying a light camp and food for two or three days, left the North Face Camp, intending to complete the reconnaissance and to reach, if possible, the North Col, where several hundred pounds' worth of material had been abandoned during the previous bad weather and avalanche conditions.

" The weather was typical of the monsoon : clear early mornings quickly clouding up, and snowstorms during the afternoons and evenings. The air was steamy and breathless and the snow soft and disagreeable to tread. We agreed, however, that the snow so far encountered on the west side of the North Col was more calculable than the windslabs which put the East Face out of court during the monsoon season.

" Camp was pitched at a height of about 21,500 feet well out on the glacier some 300–400 yards from the slopes of the North Peak, which were almost downhill relative to the camp owing to the convexity of the glacier. Snow fell heavily for the rest of the day. By nightfall nearly a foot had accumulated, and small avalanches, rushing down the North Peak one after the other, were making so suggestive a noise that we half regretted not having camped even farther out on the glacier. As the snow accumulated so did the avalanches increase in volume, and sleep proved impossible. Towards midnight an extra-large one descended, displacing a blast of air which nearly blew the camp into a large crevasse. Our tents were pitched entrance to entrance, and as Wyn Harris's tent was to windward it had the benefit of the blast, which poured powdery snow through the ventilator. This was the only long shot and presently the avalanches ceased and we were able to sleep.

" June 14 dawned magnificently on Pumori and the tangle of peaks to the north-west. Further reconnaissance, however, was out of the question with a foot or more of freshly fallen snow on the North Col slopes, and the narrow track of a pow-der-snow avalanche at one point was sufficient indication that

133

nothing was to be gained by prolonging our stay. Before descending we carefully noted the possibilities of a route up this side and came to the following conclusions :

" 1. The North Col is practicable from the west but though its difficulties should be confined to the final slope—estimated at 800–1,000 feet high—unless the ice-fall proves troublesome in some years, the technical difficulties are probably greater than the route via the East Rongbuk glacier.

" 2. In doubtful conditions, i.e. monsoon conditions, or the period prior to monsoon precipitation when the monsoon air current penetrates the Everest region, it is a safer route than the East Rongbuk glacier route, due to the fact that windslab is less likely to form, owing to its situation.

" 3. Prior to the monsoon it will be a very cold route as no shelter will be possible from the north-west gales : there is little on the other side until the actual slopes of the North Col are reached.

" 4. My own final conclusions are that it is inadvisable to forsake the East Rongbuk glacier route as this will almost certainly be practicable in all years unless some radical change takes place in the ice-formations. It has been established that Everest is impracticable by the only known route during the monsoon season ; also that the east slope of the North Col is not dangerous until the monsoon air current arrives. It is possible that a party might be trapped on the mountain by the onset of monsoon conditions. In this case the west side of the North Col offers a valuable bolt hole. Such a party could either descend more or less directly using fixed ropes—over 1,000 feet of rope would be needed—kicking avalanches in front of them, or descend indeterminate rocks from a point on the North Ridge some hundreds of feet above the North Col. As already mentioned no windslabs are likely to be encountered, and descent should be practicable within two or at the most three days after a snowfall provided it is made in the early morning."

The avalanches had given Smythe and Wyn Harris plenty to think about during their short stay in the high camp. The site of this was selected with care, and was really safe, but the wind of one avalanche from the North Peak nearly flattened out their tents, to the horror of one porter who was unaccustomed to this sort of thing. I think that this effort may be of real service to future expeditions, for it proved beyond reasonable doubt that we have on the west side of the North Col a fair alternative route to the treacherous uncertainties of the eastern face. All evidence goes to show that the latter is safely negotiable before the monsoon; but the moment the south-easterly wind currents begin it should be abandoned. Yet there may be time to bring off an assault or two before the monsoon puts down a heavy blanket of snow on the mountain, and this is where the western side may be used with profit. Early in the season these western slopes might be very troublesome, for they are completely exposed to the north-west wind, and it is not at all unlikely that when this is blowing parties may find the entire approach and the final slopes swept completely clear of snow and presenting long, steep stretches of hard blue ice. That would, of course, involve very heavy labour in step-cutting, great exposure, and probable difficulty with porters. But later on the ascent should become less difficult, and if adequate steps can be cut and ropes fixed in difficult pitches, the route should not be too exacting. At the worst, a party caught up on the mountain by the monsoon could probably find its way down on the western side, in almost complete safety from avalanches. Thus I think that one of the weakest links in the chain has been materially strengthened.

We had now done all that was humanly possible in such a year. On the morning of June 14 we were away down the glacier, hoping to have good news of the North Peak party at Camp I. There we found Morris and Warren—the latter had after all not felt equal to taking the oxygen up with the other climbers. No news had come down from them, but Shipton knew what he was about and was unlikely to push the attack beyond reasonable limits. So we set about packing everything for the descent to the Base Camp, Morris having already sent off a great deal of it with his usual foresight; and on the 15th the old Base Camp was seen again for the first time since April 30; looking of course completely different with its green grass and total absence of snow, and flowers beginning to blow everywhere.

That same evening, to my surprise, Wigram looked into my tent, closely followed by the rest of the North Peak party. They had had a frightful time on their mountain, finding the snow every bit as bad as it was in August the previous year. Having made one camp at about 22,500 feet, they had pushed on up the North-east ridge, the snow getting steadily softer and deeper. The ridge becomes narrower towards the summit, and it soon became clear that further progress would be not only excessively laborious but extremely dangerous, as avalanches might break away at any moment. At about 23,400 feet the order was wisely given for retreat. It was very creditable that Humphreys, at the age of 52, should have gone as high as the others. This climb proved once more that in the Everest region monsoon snow conditions above 23,000 feet are absolutely hopeless. The snow is powdery and incoherent almost immediately after the 23,000-foot line is reached. Up to that height it is safely negotiable except on that treacherous eastern wall of the North Col, which obeys no law but its own.

The North Peak party were tremendously fit, as was shown by the fact that they descended in one day from their 22,500-foot camp to the Base Camp. Meanwhile Smijth-Windham and Gavin packed up all the wireless equipment at Camp I and came down with it. This equipment and some of the oxygen was all that we were able to bring home for possible future use. All our beautiful high-altitude tents and sleeping bags (four hundred pounds' worth) were perforce left on the

136

North Col, where now they are doubtless slowly sinking into the ice. It would be most unwise to count upon them for a future expedition, for although a few things might be found intact the majority would almost certainly be ruined.

Our friend the second Dzongpen now turned up from Shekar with the promised transport, bringing all sorts of kind messages from the senior Dzongpen who, however, strongly advised me to travel back to India exactly by the regular route laid down in the passport, as this would be in accordance with the expressed wishes of the Lhasa Government, who might then be prepared to give favourable consideration in case we applied for a permit to go once more. This was a grievous disappointment to Shipton, who greatly hoped to put in some time on the way home in completing the surveys in the Nyönno Ri range, which his party had begun the year before. He pressed his case strongly, but I felt obliged in the interests of our successors to do as I was asked by the Tibetan authorities. Moreover, Mr. Gould had specially asked me to abide by the terms of the passport. Knowing, as we do, the hesitation with which the Tibetans admit strangers to their country, and remembering the very courteous hospitality which they extend to us when they have once overcome that hesitation, both good manners and common sense demand that we observe scrupulously any conditions they may lay down.

On the morning of June 17, after making many photographic studies of various groups of porters, especially those who were now going to leave us direct for their homes in Sola Khombu, we left the Base Camp for the last time. There was a great deal of cloud about, but we were able to see, at intervals, the massive snowy summit of Mount Everest which we had striven so hard to approach. We spent the night at Rongbuk, where it was arranged to leave a certain amount of gear which might be useful on some future occasion. The march home was to be conducted with as little transport as possible. We left our remaining supplies of kerosene with the old Lama, who has now enough to illumine his monastery for a considerable time to come. He went out of his way to bid us farewell in the courtyard of the monastery, condoling with us on our lack of good fortune but expressing the utmost satisfaction that no lives had been lost. In 1933 he told me that though he was not prepared to do anything which would prejudice our chance of getting permission again, he could not actively assist us, because he did not approve of these attempts to climb Mount Everest. This time, however, he actually volunteered a cordial invitation to return. He expressed great gratification when I thanked him and said that although I was too old to climb the mountain, I might instead come and sit at his feet and learn wisdom. Smythe and I had a short private interview with him after the others had left, finding it very difficult to say good-bye to the saintly and charming old gentleman. It was impossible to doubt now the absolute sincerity of his good wishes.

One parting gift of ours merits perhaps special mention, for it was much appreciated : a small cask of rum, supplied by His Majesty's Navy through the good offices of Admiral Sir William Goodenough, had brought comfort to both climbers and porters on many a cold night. It was now empty, and I coveted it as a water-cask for my small yacht, but could not resist the entreaties of a lama whose need seemed to be greater than mine. Now, provided with a spindle and filled with written prayers, it is daily turned as a prayer wheel by the faithful at the Rongbuk monastery. So even on the Roof of the World the Navy has left its mark.

Morris, Shipton, Wyn Harris and I, the evening before, wrote out character rolls for those porters who wished now to leave us for Sola Khombu, and settled up their accounts. They crowded round us as we left for Chödzong, thanking us warmly for the treatment they had received and begging to be taken on again as soon as the enterprise was renewed. They had served so well and so faithfully that I was more than sorry to see the last of them.

138

We had a fine sunny morning for the march to Chödzong, in the course of which Smythe and Humphreys displayed the utmost energy in digging up specimens of every flower we passed—and there were many. From now on these two devoted themselves to making a really representative collection. The last thing at night and the first in the morning they were to be observed poring over their precious flowers and arranging them to their satisfaction, and they took endless trouble to get them all home safely. There is every reason to hope that at least some have survived the heat of the Indian plains and of the voyage home, and the radical change of climate and soil. We had a night of torrential rain at Chödzong, which seemed to indicate that the sooner we were out and away from the Everest region the better. With the permission of the Shekar Dzongpen we allowed ourselves a deviation on the homeward route, crossing the Doya La and passing very close to Kharta. The Doya La might almost be described as one gigantic rubbish heap, for the rocks everywhere are in the last stages of disintegration ; but among the innumerable boulders and stones we found large numbers of the most lovely pin-cushion flowers, and the river valley on the other side was ablaze with dog roses and azaleas. Lower down, too, the valley was very fertile, and each little village was growing splendid crops of barley. It was pleasant to see and hear blackbirds again.

The following day's march was illustrative of the very sudden changes in Tibetan scenery. Instead of flowers and grass, arid stones and dust were our portion for fourteen miles during which we passed along the right bank of the Arun river, sometimes by very narrow and difficult tracks where the safety of the transport animals was more than once in doubt. A strong southerly wind seems always to prevail in this valley and it lashed us unmercifully all the way to Lungme. The dog Tendrup was in his best form at the beginning of this march, when the drivers were tying the loads on to their animals. We watched as he stalked through the lines, seeking oppor-

tunity and audience.   Both happening to coincide, he
silently approached, from behind, a Tibetan who was bending
over a box—a patent target.   It was a perfect piece of slap-
stick comedy : no savage, slashing attack, just a gentle pinch
at the right place ; the Tibetan leaped into the air, and Tendrup walked off with his tail well up, and laughing all over
his face.

On the way we passed the home of Pasang Bhutia, the
" tiger " of 1933 whose heart had been suspect at Darjeeling.
Like most Tibetans he is extremely hospitable, and did his best
to overwhelm Shipton and Humphreys, who were rash enough
to stay behind while the rest of us pushed on.   At Lungme,
Wyn Harris and the Gurkhas actually contrived to catch a few
small fish in a butterfly net, while Karma Paul, after a great
deal of negotiation, secured two sheep.   For some reason the
local Tibetans were not anxious to sell, alleging that it was a
sin to dispose of their flocks while they were in poor condition.
They said that the grazing had not been good this year.

June 23 was a black day for the expedition, for a tragedy
occurred.   We reached the rope bridge near Kharkhun, to
find the river running very strongly after the recent rains.
The bridge is just an affair of four ropes made out of twisted
yak hair ; tied between old tree trunks set up at a point where
the rocky walls converge.   Just above is a series of rapids,
after which the river is confined between these rocky walls
and pours through with tremendous force, to crash over
another series of rapids about 200 yards farther down.
Crossing is effected by means of a sort of wooden crutch which
slides along one of the ropes.   A passenger is securely attached to this crutch with leather thongs, and is then pulled
across to the other side by means of an attached line.   Tibetans
who are accustomed to this kind of thing just support themselves by the crutch, cock one leg over the rope, and pull
themselves across backwards by sheer strength of arm and by
a sort of technique of kicking with the legs.   When we arrived

140

the Tibetans responsible for the bridge were not ready, and Kusang Seti, a good porter who had recently been carrying my cameras and leading my pony, expressed the desire to cross by the unorthodox Tibetan method. I pointed out to him that there was as yet nobody on the other side to help ; that he was unaccustomed to this method, and that his brother had nearly drowned himself the year before trying this very thing ; and I told him not to be so foolish. My attention was then distracted, and the next thing I saw was Kusang Seti attempting to cross. Once he was fairly on to the rope it was practically impossible for him to get back, and I doubt if he ever heard our shouts in the roar of the waters. The sag of the rope took him speedily down to the centre, only a foot or two above the racing torrent, and then he began the struggle to pull himself up the sloping rope beyond. He had perhaps 30 yards to go in all. It was soon evident that he was feeling the strain on his arms, for his progress was slow and painful. Gavin had himself well tied on to another crutch with stirrup leathers and followed. Kusang seemed just to have succeeded, for we saw him unhitch his leg from the ropes and touch the rocks on the other side with both feet. Then his feet slipped on the damp rock and he had no strength left to pull himself up another foot or so to safety. He dropped into the water like a log. At this point there was a fairly strong eddy which set up the left bank of the river, and had Kusang been able to swim one single stroke he could doubtless have grasped the rocks and have got ashore. He was out of his depth, but there seemed to be an uprush of water from below which kept his head and shoulders free, and we were amazed to observe that he made no effort whatever to get to the bank. Instead he was very slowly borne up stream by the eddy to a corner where it seemed that he had only to turn and wade ashore. He seemed absolutely paralysed and unable to help himself, and gradually the eddy began to draw away from the bank towards the frightful race of waters in the centre. Gavin was making

141

most desperate efforts to detach himself from his crutch and drop into the eddy, where he could probably have pulled Kusang out without much difficulty. Failing in this, he just contrived to reach the rocks—a few seconds too late, for as he rushed up to the corner Kusang suddenly disappeared and the next thing we saw was his head twenty yards down stream and going faster than a man could run. I think he was already unconscious. It would have been certain death for anybody to jump in to his assistance at this point, but Wigram flung off his clothes and raced along as fast as the boulders would allow to a place farther down where he hoped to be able to grab Kusang as he passed. But poor Kusang was out of reach and already in the grip of the rapids. L. V. Bryant of New Zealand contrived to swim this river the year before, but he admitted to Shipton that it could only be done by a very strong swimmer using the crawl stroke. Anyone who got well down into the water would be sucked below and absolutely helpless. It was very sad that this porter, who had shown good abilities on the mountain, should thus lose his life for a whim. I heard afterwards that several of his porter friends advised him to obey orders and not risk the passage.

The brother who was so nearly drowned attempting this same thing in 1935 arrived with his load while this tragedy was being enacted, and it was pitiful to see his distress and the attempts of the kindly Tsering Tarkey (who was himself to die after the return to Darjeeling) to comfort him.

Now that it was too late the Tibetan bridge keepers turned up, and we all crossed. The transference of the baggage from one bank to the other took till noon the following day. From Kharkhun village, far up above the left bank of the river, it was hard to realise that that apparently insignificant stream had destroyed a man's life. This was the only one lost throughout the campaign, though there had been many occasions when the North Col might have claimed several.

The rest of our march back to India was entirely uneventful. In mild sunny weather we travelled by double marches across the plain of the Yaru river, where a little assistance had occasionally to be rendered by means of our ponies to old Tibetan ladies bent on pilgrimage ; and across the Tengkye La, rejoining our outward route at Tengkye Dzong. At Lingga we were privileged to receive telegrams of sympathy from His Majesty the King, the Viceroy, the Governor of the United Provinces, and from Sir Percy Cox on behalf of the Mount Everest Committee ; and a letter from the Governor of Bengal. It was encouraging to read these, as well as many kind messages from friends ; and to feel that people understood that we had after all done our best in difficult circumstances. Kampa Dzong offered none of the brisk argument about transport rates which was so amusing in 1933. Our needs were now very modest and we were able to cross over the Sebu La and Kongra La to Tangu with no delay whatever. The acclimatisation resulting from three months in Tibet made the passage of a couple of 17,000-foot passes seem an easy matter—too easy and too rapid for me, as I reflected that I was probably bidding a last farewell to that country of strong, self-sufficing people, to Lama and Dzongpen and wild yak-driver, all of whom had taught me many things. How I should miss those camps on the open plains, however dust-swept and pungent ; the stately surge forward of the yaks with their deep-toned bells ; the splashing and fun at the river-fords ; the snow-lashed tents up the glaciers, and Everest. What mattered success or failure ? The life and the game were the thing.

On the southern side of the Kongra La sheep were feeding, attended, it seemed, by a couple of sheep-dogs. On closer inspection it was startling to find that these " dogs," which allowed us to approach quite close, were wolves busily engaged in stalking the flock. Doubtless we ruined a long morning's work.

At Gayokang just above Tangu, Shipton, Kempson, Warren and Wigram branched off eastwards to do a little

143

climbing on their own account, while the rest carried on steadily down the northern Sikkim Valley, beautiful with its blue poppies, cowslips and grass. Lower down we were fortunate to travel through a break in the rains. The bridges which had been so carefully repaired by Rai Fakir Chand Sahib, the State Engineer of Sikkim, were still in good order, and there were very few landslides on the road. Even the leeches seemed to have agreed to a self-denying ordinance, for they seemed less aggressive than usual. A last double march of twenty-four miles brought us to Gangtok on July 6. The 250 miles from Rongbuk had been covered in eighteen days.

For a very long time past it had been evident that the majority of the letters despatched by us from the expedition were not reaching their destinations. I had already reported this fact to the Postmaster-General of Bengal, from Kharkhun. After Kempson had made a careful analysis of dates of despatch and other details, we put two and two together and came to the conclusion that everything pointed to something wrong in the post office at Gangtok. On arrival there we closely questioned the sub-postmaster, who protested his innocence but could not account for the loss of letters. Morris and I found several in his office which had not been posted but he explained this by alleging a temporary shortage of stamps. To make a long story short, the investigations of the Postmaster-General, combined with those of the Bengal police, resulted in the prosecution and ultimate conviction of this sub-postmaster, whose abominable conduct caused great distress to our respective families at home. We must have lost in all five or six hundred letters. Since our arrival in England, the Postmaster-General of Bengal has been kind enough to forward a total of 494 letters which were found hidden in an outhouse attached to the post office.

We were sorry not to be able to say good-bye to Mr. Gould at Gangtok, as he was away in Simla preparing for his mission to Lhasa; but Morris and I, who stayed behind to deal with various business matters and to see the transport off to Darjeeling while the others went on to catch their respective ships for home, were most hospitably entertained by the Maharaja, at whose house we spent a delightful evening. We could not stay long anywhere as there was an immense amount of work awaiting us in Darjeeling, where porters would have to be paid off and their character rolls written up; but we paid a farewell call on Mr. and Mrs. Odling, whose never-failing sympathy and kindness are one of my abiding memories. At Kalimpong Tendrup, that original and amusing character, found a good home with Raja Topgye Dorjé, into whose house he walked with an air of finality which there was no mistaking. Clearly he foresaw that life with Oliver in the hot valleys of Jandola would not suit his constitution, while here were good quarters and an excellent climate. That dog is a practical philosopher.

I shall not soon forget the journey by road from Kalimpong to Darjeeling across the valley of the Tista. Heavy rain had converted the great slopes into a mudslide, and I was unable to procure wheel-chains in the Kalimpong bazaar. How the little 9-h.p. Ford contrived to reach Darjeeling without falling off the road or sliding backwards is more than I can say.

At Darjeeling, Morris, Mr. Kydd, Lachiman Singh, Karma Paul and I had a tremendous week of it. The porters maintained their splendid discipline right up to the last, so at least we were able to find them as required, and there was no rioting. But each man sets great store by having his little character book (something like an Alpine guide's book) written up by the leader in person, and a similar entry had to be made in the Expedition roll. This, and the exact payments of sums due, took a considerable time, in spite of the fact that Wyn Harris and Lachiman Singh had kept the accounts with the utmost care. A dispute between that hard case Nursang and one of the porters wasted many hours. The

L

porter, incoherent but tenacious, contended that money placed in Nursang's care at Camp I had not been restored to him. Nursang, with a face of wood, emulated the pleas in the famous case of the damaged jar : " (1) we never had the jar ; (2) it was cracked when delivered to us ; (3) we returned it whole." A little rattled by cumulative evidence on the porter's side, he then offered to pay in full if the latter would swear, with a holy book on his head, that the sum was due. The porter accepted this challenge with an alacrity for which Nursang was clearly unprepared ; but he procured the book, thumped it heavily down on the porter's head and called on him, in a third-degree voice, to swear. The porter swore, with immense conviction. Judgment for the plaintiff, without costs (irrecoverable).

Then poor Kusang Seti's mother turned up, a pathetic little woman grieving for her lost son. We did what was possible, and hope that she will live in some comfort for the rest of her life.

We gave a dinner to the men, which they seemed greatly to appreciate, and they gave us a great send-off when we started down the hill for Siliguri and Calcutta, pressing round us with pleasant little offerings of flowers, and saying they looked forward to our early return. The friendship of these men is something really worth having. Independent by nature, they are capable of an immense loyalty.

At Calcutta our welcome was as warm as that which had greeted us on the outward journey, and we were shown very clearly that our friends there attached greater value to the game itself than to success. Had we reached the summit of Everest two or three times over, we could not have been received with greater kindness.

So the expedition came to an end, with the summit of Mount Everest still untrodden. In a recently published book it is said " Man was ignominiously beaten this time." I have a great respect for the author, but feel that in justice to my comrades and to the Committee to which I was responsible I cannot let that statement pass unchallenged. Men who are knocked down but rise again to continue a battle are not ignominiously beaten. Nature is stronger than Man, and in her moods of 1933 and 1936 she must win. But the last round has not been fought. Next year another expedition goes out, and if necessary there will be more. There is no surrender.

Chapter VII

(1) THE PARTY

THE days of empirical selection of personnel for expeditions to the greater Himalaya are past, for experience has taught us the essentials. Judging from many applications received when a new attempt on Mount Everest is announced, it would seem that some young men place their trust in general physical fitness and enthusiasm; and they have to be undeceived in the kindest manner possible. Mountaineering ability is, of course, the first essential; but that requires closer definition. This is the age of specialists, in sport no less than work; and although individuals can readily be found whose technical efficiency in one branch of mountaineering is enormously greater than that of a generation ago, it is perhaps much less easy nowadays to discover men who are really proficient in every branch. The latter are the true mountaineers, and the only material for Everest. There is some difficult rock on the mountain, but to take a man simply because he can lead " super severes " in the English Lake District is simply asking for trouble. The rock-expert may be at a complete loss on Himalayan snow and ice; and may be a failure as a route-finder on a great mountain face. He may also be unable to work at all at high altitudes. The general practitioner, though lacking specialised skill and

148

knowledge, will be sufficiently at home on rock and snow and ice to adapt himself to all conditions, provided that he has the necessary qualities of stamina and character, and—above all—experience.

There is really but one ideal way to select your party, and that is to test candidates in the Himalaya. This is of course a counsel of perfection, but in recent years much work has been done there and the number of experienced men is growing. I apply this term particularly to those climbers who have received their early technical training at home and in the Alps and are therefore prepared for work on the larger scale. It is most difficult for the novice to learn the game in the Himalaya because the physical adjustments which the trained mountaineer makes automatically take so much out of the beginner that he has little energy left for the struggle when altitude has him in its grip. On Mount Everest—weather apart—everything depends upon conservation of energy. This can be compassed only by men who have learnt, through years of experience, to climb rhythmically and in perfect balance. Watch Smythe and Shipton beginning a climb: they seem to be moving very slowly, but that pace will never vary from start to finish. Each succeeding foothold is subconsciously studied before the foot comes down upon it—there will be no shuffling and scraping, no effort to recover lost balance. The weight of the body will be slowly transferred from one point to the next without the slightest jerk, and the steps will be short. All movement will be unhurried but continuous. Such technique is not learnt in a day, and cannot be mastered by the impatient young athlete who rushes an Alpine peak in record time and thinks he will do as well in the Himalaya.

There is another type of man who is prima facie suitable but may fail at great altitudes. He has a strong constitution and exceptional physical energy; he has taken the trouble to make himself a good mountaineer; he prides himself on great endurance and powers of resistance to exposure. This perfectly harmless little vanity may be his undoing: he acquires a reputation for " bagging " an exceptional number of Alpine peaks in a season, for absolute tirelessness on the longest day, for indifference to lack of sleep or to cold and hunger. " Splendid," you say, " this is the very man for Everest " ; and the inference is natural. But I am convinced that Nature has endowed every man with a certain reserve of energy which has a definite limit. The man who draws upon that reserve with too prodigal a hand may find himself bankrupt just when he is called upon to make the greatest effort of his life. My choice will always be the man who has nursed his strength and avoided unnecessary strain. On the final pyramid of Everest he will have to give everything, once and for all, and to be given it must exist.

The Mount Everest Committee has always, in my experience, accepted the principle that the leader of an expedition should choose his party. As in 1933, so in 1936 I was given an unfettered discretion, and only those who have done this kind of work know the strain such autonomy imposes, for the mission of the irresponsible is to advise. But I had the great advantage of being able to select without hesitation Smythe, Shipton and Wyn Harris, all of whom had been to 28,000 feet or over in 1933. The former two and I kept in close touch and made every decision in harmony. At the outset we agreed that a smaller party than that of 1933 (sixteen) was advisable. It was now reduced to twelve. Shipton's Reconnaissance of 1935 proved that Kempson, Warren and Wigram were both good mountaineers and good " high altitude subjects." Smythe in the same year took parties to the Alps, where at least mountaineering competence and general adaptability to circumstances could be observed. Consideration of all factors, including medical examination, resulted in the choice of Oliver and Gavin from this source ; and the climbing personnel was then complete. Of these eight men, six already knew Everest—an incalculable advantage; Oliver climbed Trisul, in the Kumaun Himalaya, in 1933, showing thereby that he possessed initiative and powers of acclimatisation. Gavin alone lacked Himalayan experience.

From some points of view, to be discussed later, these eight climbers made up an expedition sufficient unto the day. But I have a weakness for a transport officer who is a specialist, more particularly when I can lay my hands on one like John Morris, who went to Everest in 1922 in this capacity and is a first-rate Nepali scholar. Nepali, by the way, is the Sherpa porter's second language. Then I prefer to have two doctors. The Base Camp is twelve miles from the mountain; anywhere in the camps along the glaciers there may be accident or fever cases, and during the assaults injured or exhausted men may be in urgent need of attention from the North Col upwards. It is gambling on your luck to take only one doctor. Warren, as one of the climbers, must be free for work on the North Ridge; Humphreys, our senior M.O., would in normal circumstances remain at lower altitudes, going if need be to the North Col. Thirdly, it was decided again to have both wireless transmission and reception; partly because our arrangements with the *Daily Telegraph* demanded them and partly because the Meteorological Department in India has always told me that their weather forecasts are facilitated if they can receive daily telegrams from the Base Camp informing them of existing weather conditions on Everest. We could afford but one wireless officer, and Smijth-Windham was again available. Lastly, there was myself: like the Duke of Plazo Toro, leading my regiment from behind. High altitudes are no respecters of persons, especially if they are 51, but as this was my eighth excursion to the Himalaya and my second to Everest I might be expected to understand the problem and take a detached view, from the Capuan luxury of Camp III or possibly the North Col; besides making a tolerably good buffer state. I think there is something to be

151

said for a non-climbing leader, especially in a large expedition : in no circumstances can he compete, even subconsciously, for a place in the climbing parties ; and at the advanced headquarters he is in the right position to deal with crises instead of being, as might well happen, isolated high up on the mountain or placed *hors de combat* by his own exertions.

This party owed its eventual composition to the Medical Board of the Royal Air Force, who again most kindly examined all candidates. Special acknowledgments are due to Group-Captain H. E. Whittingham, Group-Captain H. A. Treadgold and Wing-Commander R. W. Ryan for the trouble they took to see us through. As before, the examination was extremely severe, and caused us the loss of two very good mountaineers whose reaction to the test for resistance to oxygen-lack was reported to be unsatisfactory. The Board, which of course knows its own mind very well where Pilots are concerned, made no attempt to dogmatise over us ; but it would have been wholly illogical to consult the only authority in England on high-altitude work and then ignore its opinion. Wyn Harris, Morris and Oliver, who were abroad, underwent tests as closely approximating to this as possible.

Survival implied anything but freedom. The next port of call was the Royal Dental Hospital, where Dr. Fish and his colleagues generously devoted their time to us. They remarked, I remember, that all members of the expedition had phenomenally hard bone in their jaws—they were too polite to investigate our skulls. Then to St. Mary's Hospital, where Dr. MacLean vaccinated and also inoculated us against enteric fever. Smijth-Windham, having already undergone the regulation Army inoculations, was justly aggrieved by all this extra puncturing. Ears were left to private enterprise, and Shipton and I created a little consternation by sitting for twenty minutes in a Kensington chemist's shop with our heads on one side—the uppermost ear in each case being full of olive oil which must not be allowed to run out.

The question—much debated at the present time—of numbers in an Everest party will be discussed later. Here I would only say that the twelve men who formed the 1936 Expedition were a competent and homogeneous body which, by all known standards, was fit to grapple with Mount Everest.

(2) PORTERS

After the 1933 expedition I was able to praise very highly the conduct of this corps, which was recruited chiefly in Darjeeling. In 1936 a majority of the men joined us direct from Sola Khombu—an experiment deliberately made and justified by results. Comparisons, besides being odious, would be ineffective because the 1933 men went far higher and endured much greater hardships than those of 1936. I am, nevertheless, convinced that the morale of the Sherpas and Bhutias has advanced another step and that, had the weather permitted an assault, ample carrying power for the high camps would have been forthcoming.

I attribute this advance, in the main, to two causes : firstly, Shipton's explorations and careful training of the very best men, such as Ang Tarkey, and his judgment in choosing those who were to go high; secondly, Morris's admirable first selection at Darjeeling and his continual contact with and understanding of the men. Anyone who has experience of administration, especially perhaps in the East, knows the importance of the personal factor. It would be a great mistake to suppose that the Sherpa, or the Bhutia, is a thick-headed country bumpkin, wreathed in a perpetual smile. On the contrary, he is often a shrewd and highly intelligent person whose faculties have not been dulled by mass education. He will smile readily enough, being optimistic by nature, but he has a temperament which must be understood. I have seen him as obstinate and unresponsive as any mule under wrong handling, and openly mutinous when aggrieved. He sums

153

up each European member of an expedition with devastating acumen, labelling him with some nickname which may amuse but certainly does not spare. Yet he will give unswerving loyalty and even affection where it has been fairly earned, and his trust in good mountaineering leadership is complete. He likes to be encouraged to bring his troubles to headquarters, when he will usually accept a decision, provided that he has had a patient hearing. Two things bring out his worst side : sarcasm and softness.

It should not be forgotten that he does not yet share to the full the European mountaineer's ambitions and ideals. I have never yet seen him show any signs of wishing to climb a mountain on his own account ; he is satisfied if he can help his employer to reach the summit. When in a tight place he will often prospect on his own, showing remarkable skill and judgment, and a great objection to defeat. With all these qualities, however, he must be most carefully watched when things go badly wrong, especially when an accident occurs or a heavy storm blows up. Someone must then make decisions for him on the instant.

Although sometimes casual in manner and address, he resembles his Gurkha compatriot in appreciating a reasoned discipline, which is a very different thing from the methods of a stiff-necked martinet. I think it can be claimed that the system adopted in 1936 kept natural exuberance in bounds without producing an inanimate rigidity. What work was possible the men did with the greatest keenness, and their general conduct was above reproach. That they ignored the rewards offered for going high I do not suggest ; they are good husbands and fathers, and do their best for their families. But the mainsprings of their actions were genuine love of the sport and a very real pride in their association with their English comrades.

(3) Operations

Although the circumstance of weather prevented an assault on Mount Everest in 1936, it may be profitable to review the campaign, and to reflect whether a different strategy or tactics might have given better results.

The chief difficulty of framing plans beforehand consists in the absence of reliable data, and of static conditions. Six parties have visited Mount Everest, and each has had different experiences, with the result that one can only attempt to collate and to select what appear to be recurring phenomena on which to base decisions. The chief factor is of course the weather, and considering that its vagaries puzzle trained meteorologists, the simple mountaineer may be acquitted on a charge of lack of foresight if his plans are wrecked by forces over which he has no control.

The considered opinion of the most experienced men in the 1936 Expedition was that an early arrival at the Base Camp would be a mistake, because previous experience showed how exhausting is the effect of heavy work on the East Rongbuk glacier and the North Col before the normal spring storms are over. I speak of normality for lack of a better term—so far as our present knowledge goes, severe north-west winds usually prevail in the Everest region between the middle of March and the middle of May. If a party is taken to the Base Camp in such conditions by, say, April 1, the chances are that it will suffer great and even incapacitating hardship before it begins the assaults ; alternatively it will be able to do no constructive work at all, and will be forced to live in idleness in inhospitable surroundings, with the worst possible result on its morale ; waiting, like Mr. Micawber, for something to turn up. Our party was so fit and so well acclimatised that we anticipated a more rapid advance up the glacier than in 1933, without distress. Obviously all members would be better prepared for the assaults if they had comparatively warm weather in the early stages, of march and approach.

155

The reader may find it interesting, at this point, to study a comparative table showing the progress of expeditions up to date :

	1922	1924	1933	1936
Base Camp reached	May 1	April 29	April 17	April 26
Camp I established	May 4	April 30	April 21	April 27
Camp II „	May 5	May 4	April 26	May 2
Camp III „	May 6	May 5	May 2	May 7
Camp IV „	May 17–19	May 21	May 15	May 15
Camp V „	May 20	June 1	May 22	—
Camp VI „	—	June 7	May 29	—

In 1922 the first and second assaults were launched on May 20 and 24 respectively, from the North Col. In 1924 the relative dates were June 2 and 6 ; and Odell started up the North Ridge on June 7 and 9. In 1933 assaults began on May 28 and 30.

In all these previous years the parties concerned suffered severe hardships before they were able to begin the attack. Could they have been spared this their chances of course would have been proportionately greater. In every case their programme was delayed by the weather : Norton, for instance, in 1924, planned his first assault for May 17. With these facts in mind, we of the 1936 party budgeted for being in position to assault by May 23 ; it was not till the fitness of the party and the unusual mildness of the early spring were appreciated that we altered this date to May 16, and we were able to carry out that programme, so far as getting into position was concerned. Actually, though we did not know it at the time, the snowfall of April 30, which was never fully cleared away owing to the failure of the north-west winds, destroyed our chances at the very outset.

Had we been gifted with prophetic knowledge, no doubt we should have made a point of arriving at the Base Camp during the first half of April, and we might then have been able to assault before the snow came. But I must reiterate the miseries experienced by earlier arrivals, and the fact that bad weather was observed on the mountain during the march across Tibet. The calculable chances were that we should get the best conditions at the agreed time. In my opinion it is unwise to base future plans upon the experience of 1936, which should be regarded as a wholly abnormal year. Premature arrival and commencement of operations may exhaust and even destroy the climbers.

A theory which still obtains some measure of support should be mentioned here. It is that Mount Everest should be attempted after the monsoon, say in October or November. Many of us have observed that often in those months there is little wind ; and certain Himalayan peaks have been climbed then. The obvious objections are great cold and short days, but it is argued that improved tents and windproof clothing can counterbalance them. I think it unsafe to employ the analogy of these other peaks, because Everest is so much higher and has a different rock formation. The experience of the last few years has proved that in the Everest region snow above 23,000 feet is not negotiable, at any rate during the monsoon. Is it likely to be better in the cold months ? I very much doubt this, for it will not melt and re-freeze, and will therefore be more powdery than ever. We cannot expect it to be wind-impacted, for the very reason that October and November are comparatively windless. Again, the nature of the North Face of Everest is such that dry rock is needed for the ascent. Powdery snow on those outward-shelving slabs is an insuperable barrier. The Reconnaissances of 1921 and 1935 saw the mountain late in the season : it was always under deep snow, and local Tibetan evidence is all to the effect that it remains so throughout the winter, till the spring gales blow it away. I think that we must struggle on to do the climb in that usually short interval between the end of spring and the advent of the monsoon, hoping to meet with a season when the latter is delayed.

157

Two points in our tactical plan are worth further discussion : the number of camps to be placed above the North Col, and the question of allowing porters to descend from the highest camps unattended. To some extent these are interdependent. Both were most thoroughly discussed at the staff meeting at Gangtok in March.

The advantages of having three camps above the North Col are that climbers and porters have shorter carries to make between camps ; that there is perhaps a better chance of placing the highest camp under the First Step, or farther still if only a suitable platform could be found ; that porters descending unattended have shorter distances to go, can be seen the whole way, and can obtain shelter if a sudden storm comes up. The disadvantages are that more men have to be taken high, to carry the additional equipment and stores ; that the assaulting parties have to remain longer on the mountain, where they are always in danger ; and that deterioration may get a firmer hold.

As for the porters, we know since 1933 that they are perfectly capable of carrying from Camp V, at 25,700 feet, to 27,400 feet. The climbers who led them when this was done thought that they might have been able to reach 27,800, under the First Step ; but it is a very long carry. Still, in 1936 our men were confident that they could do it. On the whole, they are more to be depended upon for one very long carry than for two comparatively short ones with a night of severe cold and discomfort in between. Can they be trusted to come down from the First Step by themselves ? Shipton thinks that men like Ang Tarkey and Rinzing certainly can. From Camp V downwards there is no serious difficulty, nor from Norton's old Camp VI on the North Ridge. But the direct route to our Camp VI of 1933 and to the First Step is not so simple, especially in bad weather. Would *all* our " tigers " in 1933 have got down safely if Longland had not been there ?

158

I am inclined to think that in the interests of simplicity and speed we should revert to the old two-camp plan, and that the paramount obligation to safeguard our porters demands that one member of the climbing parties should accompany them down at least to Camp V.

(4) EQUIPMENT

Every expedition learns from its own experiences as well as from those of its predecessors ; and it is worth while to place on record what has been done in the way of improvement, or even of elimination. Equipment implies transport —that critical problem in Tibet—but for obvious reasons it must be ample and of suitable design. Shipton and I devoted four months to this work before the expedition started, with help from Smythe, Humphreys, Warren and Gavin. Although the list at the end of this section may seem startling I do not think that any item was redundant ; when you have to travel for months away from the world of shops and to attempt a great mountain, you do need a good many things, remembering that fond regrets are useless. Notes and lists of equipment are always useful to later travellers, who can then use their own discretion.

I do not propose to describe here the oxygen apparatus taken by our expedition, as Warren has undertaken that task. I would merely express our great indebtedness to Sir Leonard Hill and Sir Robert Davis, to whose help and generosity we owe our equipment.

In 1933 we were particularly pleased with a new kind of dome tent which saved us from much hardship during the gales at Camp III and on the North Col. It has been now improved and strengthened, and can be recommended to all high-altitude expeditions. For use at Camp V a pyramidal type was taken ; unfortunately we had no opportunity to give it a full test, but I think that some day it will make all the difference between misery and comfort at Camp V, and

159

enable parties to continue up the mountain in full strength
instead of being half-frozen, battered and weary from loss of
sleep on that wind-lashed platform at 25,700 feet. For the
march across Tibet and the lower camps we have standardised
an " A " pattern of large Meade tent, one to each man ; this
has a " Zip " fastening and weighs only 16 lb. It was a great
success. The tents for the highest camps also could not be
fully tested, but they promised well. So far as we were
able to see, the improved " Zip " fastener was satisfactory,
but tapes should always be in reserve. The principle of
having three Mess-tents for a party of twelve instead of one
general tent worked well, but the tents should be more
strongly built, and have higher side walls, and sewn-in
groundsheets. Bell tents for the porters were again made
by the Muir Mills of Cawnpore ; the others were mostly made
by Camp & Sports, Ltd.

A difficulty with sleeping-bags has hitherto been that
after much use the down was apt to bunch unevenly, and at the
points where stitching was placed to prevent this as far as
possible the cold could get through. We had interior cloth
walls built up between the compartments, with satisfactory
results.

Windproof suits were made up entirely from Grenfell
cloth presented by Messrs. Baxter, Woodhouse & Taylor,
Ltd. Mr. Eric Taylor of that firm and Mr. Williamson went
to great trouble personally to see that we had everything right,
and Mr. Taylor also made up a " surprise packet " which we
were not to open till we reached the Base Camp, when it was
found to contain two high-altitude tents of the same material,
dyed a brilliant colour which would show up well at a distance.
The suits, which wore extremely well, were dyed different
colours for Europeans, sardars and porters, to facilitate
identification during bad visibility. The tailoring, though
strong, I should like to see done on different lines, for our
suits were a trifle clumsy. For the eight climbers some special

160

light suits padded with eiderdown were made by Mr. Robert Burns. These are expensive but should afford protection against the very worst winds.

Special acknowledgments are due to Captain Llewellyn Amos, who on behalf of the Fifty Shilling Tailors volunteered to fit us all out with mufti. Times are hard, and it was entirely due to this kindness that we were able to defy sartorial criticism during our wanderings.

Boots were, as before, ordered from Mr. J. S. Carter and Mr. Robert Lawrie, both of whom have gone out of their way to turn out a good design—by no means an easy thing to do when strength, lightness and warmth have to be combined. The chief feature of these boots is a sheet of asbestos material between two leather soles. The lower leather sole has special light clinkers and hobs driven through it and turned over so that they do not penetrate the asbestos or the upper sole and thereby conduct cold to the feet. Lightness and strength involve a compromise, in that the boot will serve for the special purpose of the climb but cannot be guaranteed to last very long.

Humphreys contributed an idea from his arctic experience which was adopted to replace the ordinary woollen socks. Ours were made of sheepskin with the wool inside, and could be easily slipped into and out of a boot. Formerly the boots had this material stitched in, but it was found that after a climb ice was liable to form and the interior of the boot could not be dried. Now all that one had to do was to remove the sheepskin sock, turn it inside out and dry it over a Primus. This almost eliminated the risk of frost-bite. Messrs. Clark, Son & Morland again supplied lambskin camp boots, of excellent quality. I have already spoken of the marching boots supplied to porters by Messrs. Cooper Allen of Cawnpore. These were nailed by us at Kalimpong, and were very satisfactory.

The perfect mountaineering glove has not yet, I think, been designed—it is so difficult to find a material which is

M   161 warm enough yet allows of a sensitive grip of ice-axe or rope, and does not harden or slip when wet. We found that an under pair of thin silk gloves, then one of wool, and finally special ski-ing gloves of leather made by Messrs. Peal & Co. of Oxford Street, served our purpose well.

Most mountaineers are content with a simple form of goggle for use on the Swiss glaciers ; but something more elaborate is required in the Himalaya, where at midday the sun can be very hot and the climber is much worried by his goggles " steaming up." At the same time he must have protection from the wind. Consequently the problem of efficient ventilation is equally important with that of providing an adequate field of view. Mr. Hamblin of Wigmore Street again set up special machinery for the purpose and again generously presented a complete outfit of improved goggles for the expedition, adding a deeper orange glass than before. These goggles were a great success ; at an early date I found porters, with transparent villainy, contriving minor accidents in order to secure a fresh pair, and was obliged to pass an order that the price of a second issue would be deducted from their pay. The accidents then miraculously stopped.

Messrs. Melson Wingate of Wimpole Street also again presented a dozen pairs with mica fronts.

Messrs. Arthur Beale's Alpine rope and line was used for the roping of the North Col and for the climbing parties ; supplemented by 800 feet of ivory silk parachute cord supplied by the Irving Airchute Company. This very light yet strong cord was intended for roping the difficult section of the great couloir under the final pyramid.

Thanks to the enthusiasm and kindness of Mr. Oscar Condrup, I think we can say with confidence that the problem of using stoves at high altitudes has been mastered. As is well known, lack of oxygen has generally resulted in very poor combustion of kerosene fuel in the higher camps, and men have been obliged to use solidified fuel—quite good in its way (we took Meta as a reserve), but not so quick in its action as properly vaporised kerosene in a Primus. After many experiments in the decompression chamber at the Royal Air Force Establishment at Farnborough, the right type of burner was discovered, and Primus stoves worked to perfection in an atmosphere equivalent to that existing at 29,000 feet on Everest. This is a great advance, because I am sure that hitherto the assaults have been delivered by men who were virtually starving because they had not the means to cook adequate meals at Camp V or Camp VI.

Having mastered the Primus problem, we were emboldened to take another step in the direction of efficient yet economical cooking. In 1933 I lamented the absence of pressure-cookers, in which steam under pressure does the cooking while you turn off the tap and save your fuel. Shipton tried this system during his Reconnaissance with success, and now Messrs. Easiwork, Ltd., of Tottenham Court Road and Messrs. Pentecon, Ltd., of Southwick Street were good enough to offer various models for further experiment. Both makes gave excellent service, and I hope that Camp V will never be without one or two. Possibly a light model could even be made for use higher still. It is worth trying anything to " keep up the revolutions " in the summit party.

I have again to thank Messrs. N. C. Joseph, Ltd., of Stratford-on-Avon, for their gift of excellent aluminium cooking-pots, which disappear at the close of an expedition with a rapidity which shows what that practical economist the Sherpa porter thinks of them.

One more item connected with the commissariat remains to be mentioned—vacuum flasks. The kindness of Mr. J. E. Roy and his daughter secured us an ample supply of these most useful things. Not that they are essential to the real bull-dog breed : Humphreys, in a particularly cold camp on the hills above Kampa Dzong, shared his sleeping bag with one. The cork came out in the night and the contents of the flask froze solid, but Humphreys was heard to remark that he had been very comfortable.

Speaking of comfort reminds me of the difficulty of procuring a mattress which will keep one's back off the ice yet be light enough for transport up the mountain. In the past we have used, and some still use, light rubber pads, kapok mattresses, or even sheepskins—all useful in their way but not ideal. In 1936 Messrs. P. B. Cow & Co., Ltd., of Streatham Common, gave us a dozen special " Li-Lo " pneumatic mattresses, which defied the sharpest of rock splinters and were a splendid insulation against cold.

Ice-axes were procured from Messrs. Horeschowsky of Vienna—a good pattern, light and well-balanced. Also light crampons, which are an advantage on the East Rongbuk glacier, especially for the porters, when the ice has no covering of snow and is extremely hard and slippery.

I think more use should be made of pressure lamps; they will stand a lot of knocking about—even the mantles sometimes survive a day's march during which the lamp has been cheerfully swung about by a porter. They give, of course, infinitely better light than candles, and supply plenty of heat in a tent.

A particularly welcome gift was received from Mr. L. C. Letts, a fellow-member of the Alpine Club, who decided that each man should have one of those diaries which we all enjoy writing up when the sun has gone down, the thermometer shows 40 degrees of frost, and our ink is solid ice.

All equipment and stores were packed and forwarded by Messrs. R. G. England of Goswell Road. Mr. England and his staff took immense trouble to carry out our ideas about packing-cases and locks, and we owe them sincere gratitude. The system of consecutive numbering—black for equipment and red for food—made things very much easier for the transport officers than had been the case in 1933 ; and the comprehensive storebook was well arranged.

164

(5) Food

Expeditions to the Himalaya had not been thought of when Napoleon told the world that an army marches on its stomach; yet his aphorism applies to them as well as to the soldiers of the Little Corporal. But there is a difference: armies in the field need food, and are glad to get what they can; so also Arctic explorers, whose appetites appear to be unaffected by monotony. This cannot be said of Everest climbers; I do not suppose that they are, in private life, more capricious than other men, but their kaleidoscopic changes of inclination, and obstinate refusal to applaud the Messing Officer, once the first flush of enthusiasm over the carefully-thought-out menus has subsided, are the despair of everyone who has undertaken the thankless task of caterer. There is a simple reason for this—altitude. The men must march, and climb, on their stomachs; but when the whole metabolism of the body has been altered by lack of oxygen and by life in conditions where Nature denies life a time must come when all food, however good and however varied, is simply revolting and can be absorbed only as a duty. I have observed the contradiction that when, at high altitudes, appetites are most capricious, they are tempted less by exotic and highly flavoured foods than by a simple but fresh diet—eggs, lentils, even Tibetan mutton, and bread. Perhaps it is not a contradiction after all: artificial stimulation is all very well and may serve for a time, but the machine must be kept running on the fuel to which it is accustomed, and ultimately revolts against doping.

For this reason I find myself, generally speaking, in agreement with Shipton, the burden of whose song is " cut down your tinned food to a minimum and do everything in your power to obtain fresh." Indeed, I have adopted that policy in my own Himalayan wanderings. Of course, it is not easy to procure even the simplest of food for a large party in Tibet, especially in the spring, and that merely adds force to

Shipton's argument that large parties are a mistake. This is not the place to discuss numbers from a tactical point of view, but *if* a fairly large party is considered necessary for Everest you are faced with the problem of satisfying a community which is not homogeneous in its preferences. Some men, however hardy, crave for the flesh-pots, and it is not given to everyone to assimilate the flour of the country (which contains a high percentage of grit) without serious after-effects. Are you to turn down a first-class mountaineer because he likes good things, and substitute one less expert simply because he can live on the country ?

I suppose the middle way provides a solution : take a proportion of the best tinned foods, but do all you can (using perhaps the methods of Monsieur Coué) to persuade your men that fresh food is best ; and make sure beforehand that you can get it. For my part I have found that the Indian lentil (arhar ki dál) is a magnificent climbing ration ; and I never tire of it. For all his lack of mountain knowledge poor Maurice Wilson, who died at Camp III in 1934, travelled far on the simplest diet. Shipton and Tilman, exploring the Garhwal mountains in the same year, kept up their strength at times on one cup of " sattu " (ground and parched barley) a day. Our porters prefer it to anything else.

However, it was thought in 1936 that a Spartan régime was unlikely to produce the best results in a party of twelve, and the list at the end of this section will give some idea of the trouble that was taken to obtain everything of the best, and full variety. Whatever the principle, the practice of selection is hardly open to criticism, for no expedition has ever set out with a better commissariat. I think that even the lovers of the simple life would have had less to say but for the fact that our porter-cooks were incapable of dealing with this *embarras de richesses*. Nothing could survive unspoilt their ideas of cookery.

We did not lose sight of the scientific aspect : proteins,

carbohydrates, etc. etc., and the mysteries of vitamins were all explored under the guidance of Dr. S. S. Zilva and Dr. A. L. Bacharach. It remained to reconcile these essentials with gastronomic preference. Here Smythe worked out a good system of percentages calculated to include the vital ingredients ; and for the special purpose of keeping scurvy away Messrs. William Hay Ltd. took immense trouble to prepare some excellent fruit juices. Various compounds of fish-oil were also taken.

A particular debt of gratitude is owed to a fellow-member of the Alpine Club, Mr. C. Scott Lindsay, who not only placed his special knowledge of producers and of the canning industry at our disposal but threw himself heart and soul into the work of personal selection and provision. It was very hard work, and he never spared himself—or us. Smythe and I are not likely to forget the day when we accompanied him down to Messrs. Chivers' factory near Cambridge, where the firm had everything ready for inspection, and more than inspection. There was no escape—we had to taste, and to go on tasting, until that particular sense could function no more. Mr. Lindsay introduced me personally to all the best firms, with the most favourable results to our budget ; and conducted practically all the correspondence himself, at the cost of what disturbance to his own business he alone can tell. Nothing but the very best would satisfy him ; he even contrived to secure a consignment of " vintage " sardines—I did not know that such things existed—and other delicacies, of which only connoisseurs know the source. In my grateful thanks to him I must include a word for his most efficient and friendly staff.

It is impossible in this book to make sufficient acknowledgment of the kindness and consideration we received from various firms. I would specially mention my friend Mr. C. L. Hansen of the Danish Bacon Company Ltd., who not only supplied us with admirable tinned hams and sides of bacon preserved in special wrappings, but has given me many proofs of his friendly interest in our adventure. Again, Sir Harry Hague came to our help with a notable contribution in the shape of 3,900 preserved eggs, so efficiently packed that very few were broken during the march. Those eggs were a wonderful standby, and even Shipton refrained from comment on the extra burden they entailed on the transport. Messrs. Tate & Lyle Ltd. gave us an enormous supply of sugar—I believe it worked out at 12 oz. per man per day, yet it was all wanted, and perhaps this is the first expedition which has not had occasion to lament a shortage of this commodity. Messrs. Johnny Walker presented Black Label whisky, and Messrs. James Hawker & Co. Ltd. sloe gin, for which Dzongpens always express a special fondness.

In short, the expedition was extremely well found in the matter of food. Indeed, it is possible that Smythe and Wigram sometimes wished that there had been less variety, as they worked away on their store lists and boxes at the end of a long march. The Tibetans anyhow had no cause to grumble, for they consider tins of greater value than their contents.

(6) The Future

Six expeditions, including the Reconnaissances of 1921 and 1935, have now visited Mount Everest. Each has made its contribution to the common stock of experience, but not one has been able to place a climber on the final pyramid, and still the difficulties and dangers of the last thousand feet or so are matter for conjecture. Four men—Norton in 1924, Wyn Harris, Wager and Smythe in 1933—have reached a height of about 28,100 feet, when exhaustion and bad snow conditions forced a return ; the expedition of 1936, certainly not inferior in strength to any of its predecessors, and equipped with the hard-won experience of fifteen years, got no further than the first expedition of all.

In these circumstances it is natural that the public in

general, and mountaineers in particular, should ask themselves two questions : first, *is* the summit attainable at all ;
second, are our methods sound ?   I think that all men qualified to give an opinion will support me when I answer the first
question in the affirmative.   There is not one iota of evidence
to the contrary.   The four men who reached 28,100 feet were
all handicapped by circumstances which will not necessarily
recur : Norton was prematurely exhausted by the struggle to
establish Camp IV in very bad weather ; by the necessary
rescue of porters marooned there ; by the effort to get the
men to carry up to the higher camps ; and by the fact that
his highest camp could not be placed high enough to bring
the summit within reach on the final day.   Wyn Harris and
Wager and Smythe had equally bad weather on the glacier and
the North Col, but better protection through improved equipment.   Their assaults were delayed by events over which
they had no control, and when they were able to ascend
deterioration had already set in and the weather was unfavourable.   Again, Wyn Harris and Wager, unsure of the best
route to the summit, lost time in prospecting alternate ways.
Smythe in his turn had to climb alone, and to negotiate bad
snow on the higher slabs.   Lastly, all these four men were
inadequately equipped in respect of high-altitude tents and
food.   Therefore they were capable of still finer performance
and, with better resources and less previous strain, might
have reached the summit.

The psychological factor is all-important, and has definitely changed for the better.   Climbers and porters are
now perfectly sure that they can place a camp at about
27,800 feet, on the snowslope below the First Step.   The
worry of uncertainty about this has now gone for ever.
Equipment of every kind is now so good that the problems
of shelter and food are practically solved. The tactical
necessity of saving the climbers from excessive labour in the
early stages is appreciated, and the selection and training of

the assaulting parties are understood. The one still incalculable factor is the weather. Here the element of luck must come in—without luck I think that Everest cannot be climbed. In good weather I am certain it can. Whether oxygen must be used I do not know. Sir Leonard Hill and Captain G. I. Finch are convinced that it is both necessary and efficient. Some of our best climbers insist that the mountain can be climbed without it, and that the dangers from breakdown of apparatus and from carrying the weight across difficult slabs outweigh any possible benefit. The tests of the Royal Air Force on their pilots indicate that oxygen-lack at very high altitudes causes quite sudden insensibility. I advocate that oxygen be taken to the highest camps for use at the discretion of the climbers. Given all equipment, and the right weather, and sent up when they are at the top of their form, they should reach the summit.

Now for the second question: Are our methods sound? Controversy is focused chiefly on the season for operations, and on the numbers and composition of personnel. The former point I have already discussed, and would merely repeat here that I think the period between spring and summer is the best—indeed the only—one ; and that too early an arrival is fraught with danger. The matter of personnel requires full and dispassionate consideration. One difficulty is to dissociate the genuine needs of the enterprise from our personal preferences. I have so often heard men say: " But a small expedition is so much more easy and pleasant." Of course it is—my own happiest memories in the Himalaya are of small parties—but that is not the point. Pleasure and facility are not the criteria. An Everest expedition is not like a holiday climb in the Alps. We have to decide, not what we like, but what will give the greatest efficiency.

Many mountaineers, including some who have distinguished themselves on Mount Everest, believe sincerely that large expeditions are inherently inefficient. The chief reasons advanced in support of this belief are : unwieldy and slow transport ; the strain of contacts between too many climbers whose nervous systems are already affected by altitude ; overlapping of work, loss of speed and mobility ; adverse effect on the economic and social system of Tibet ; and an objectionable publicity. In some cases there is yet another reason which should be mentioned : a partly subconscious resentment at the inclusion in the party of men who are not potentially capable of reaching the summit. It is thought that their work, however useful and however essential in a large expedition, can be dispensed with in a small one. The holders of these views allege that not a single large expedition to the Himalaya has ever succeeded in achieving its purpose.

I should like to take the last assertion first, and to say that it is special pleading which begs the question. No expedition, large or small, has yet climbed a peak higher than 25,660 feet ; so the superior efficiency of a small party on one of the real giants remains to be proved. I yield to none in my admiration of the comparatively small expedition which climbed Nanda Devi last year—they were magnificently efficient for their purpose and they succeeded. But I submit that it is unsafe to infer that the same numbers and the same methods would succeed on Mount Everest, where the really serious difficulties only begin at an altitude greater than that of the summit of Nanda Devi. Again, on the latter mountain the climbers did their own carrying, their Sherpa porters having failed them. I am absolutely convinced that the European members of an Everest party should not—probably they could not—carry loads up to the highest camps.

So much for analogy ; let us now examine the other arguments. No one knows better than I do the difficulty of procuring and of expediting transport for a large expedition across Tibet. But this difficulty can be overcome, as it was in 1936 ; and it is not a brake on efficiency, because a party is unlikely to benefit from a very rapid march to Everest, and from arrival with indifferent acclimatisation. As for the effect on the economic and social system of Tibet, I can only refer to what I said in the chapter on the march.

The strain of contacts is and should be negligible in parties of twelve or so, especially where the men know each other well. There must, of course, be a certain amount of give and take, and there is no room for the egotist; but most Englishmen understand and can apply the team spirit which should survive such a test.

Overlapping of work does not occur where the leader knows his business—on the contrary, there is plenty of work for every man, even in a large party, with no occasion for him to trespass on his neighbours' domains.

The question of having none but potential summit men deserves a fuller treatment; and with it should be linked the question of leadership. It is only natural that men who are to face the dangers and endure the hardships of the assaults should consider themselves capable of framing their own tactics and working out their own salvation, especially when they already know most of the ground on which they will have to work. I have every sympathy for this view, and will only enter the caveat that tempers are short at high altitudes and men become critical of one another. Sometimes, therefore, a non-climbing leader may be able to take a more dispassionate view of a situation than the protagonists, and to help them to recover their lost equilibrium. It has been suggested that there should be no officially recognised leader, but that the Alpine precedent should be followed according to which decisions are informally arrived at and occasion produces the natural leader. I am afraid this would bring about chaos on Everest, where circumstances may often demand instant and authoritative orders.

Again, it must be sorrowfully admitted that our best high-altitude climbers do not include a single linguist. I wonder if they realise how often potential trouble has been averted

172

by, for instance, Morris's ability to discuss matters with porters in their own language. So long as things are working smoothly, a smattering may suffice ; but there is real danger in having no one within reach who can do better than that.

I have already ventured the opinion that two doctors should accompany an Everest expedition. It may be a positive advantage that one of these is unlikely to go higher than the North Col.

Lastly, if wireless reception and transmission are required you must have a specialist, who might well be trained also in the science of meteorology. He will have no leisure for climbing. Of course, several men think that wireless transmission is unnecessary and that the reception of weather reports from India—which can be done by anyone—is sufficient for all needs. Certainly transmitting apparatus increases transport difficulties. It would be easy to argue on either side ; for my part, I am inclined to think that contact with the outer world both ways is worth maintaining. A situation might easily occur in Tibet where it was necessary to invoke the assistance of the Government of India.

The question of publicity has been, so far, spliced to that of finance. Big expeditions cost a lot of money, and such is the outer darkness in which we live at home that wealthy individuals consider the climbing of Mount Everest unworthy of support. But newspapers require news, especially in the silly season, and there is reason to suppose that the general public takes more interest in these adventures than it used to do. If money is obtainable from newspapers and not from private subscription, we are forced into the limelight, however much we dislike it ; and, unhappily, exciting headlines and a tendency to " improve upon " sober despatches are a part of much modern journalism. This is where the advocate of a small party becomes really eloquent, knowing full well that his opponent is now in the same box with him—" Reduce your numbers," he says, " and your expenses drop at once to a figure which can be met by private subscription. You are aware that most people of taste object to sensationalism, as you do yourself; conduct your affairs in a respectable obscurity, and sufficient support will be forthcoming. Reject, if you must, all my other arguments; from this one you cannot escape with dignity."

It is, indeed, a strong argument—a shot between wind and water. Let us suppose that it has gone home, and consider the implications. Some, for instance, would like a party of six Europeans, all potential summit men. We can, undoubtedly, collect six of the very best; our budget will be extremely modest and we will probably be able to raise sufficient funds without bothering our heads about publicity. The transport organisation is easy. Perhaps thirty porters will suffice for the mountain. Progress across Tibet will be rapid, and immediate advantage can be taken of fine weather to establish the North Col. The six climbers, all supremely competent, able to rely upon one another, and well acclimatised by previous service, will be able to select their moment and deliver at least two, and probably three, formidable assaults, with the assistance of the very pick of the Sherpa and Bhutia porters. No one is redundant; perfect economy of effort has been achieved; the chances of success are good.

I readily admit the symmetry of this plan, and the possibility of success if all goes well; but it reminds me of Wellington's remark about the French Marshals' campaigns in the Peninsula: that they resembled a beautiful piece of leather harness, which served only so long as nothing broke, whereas his own could easily be repaired with rope. Things do not always go according to plan on Everest. What *might* happen to this party of six? We may assume that they all arrived fit at the Base Camp—larger parties have achieved that. At that point two might fall sick; this happened in 1933. Then four would have to go on and make the camps up the glacier and establish the North Col. If they met weather like that of 1924 and 1933 they would be tired men by the time this work was done. An interval for rest might be necessary, during which time the weather might be perfect for the ascent, only to break the moment the invalids rejoined and the others were ready again. With the menace of the approaching monsoon in their minds the party would make desperate efforts to establish the high camps and deliver the assaults; during this time two men might break down, and the survivors would have to carry on knowing that they had no supports on the North Col or elsewhere, in case of bad weather or of accident to themselves or to porters. In all probability no one could be spared to accompany porters down from the highest camp—they must fend for themselves, in fine weather or in foul. If a camp were cut off by a blizzard; if a man so much as sprained his ankle, no relief could come; each assault party must rely on its own resources to win through.

While accepting the possibility of a smaller expedition than has hitherto been thought necessary, I do plead for adequate reserves. The case for climbers only is perfectly rational, but I would never agree to less than eight; to take less seems to me an unjustified gamble. I should not envy the position of a leader who on returning home was obliged to report, "We had splendid weather in May and early June, but at that time I had not enough fit men available to carry out the assaults."

There is reason to believe that the Tibetan Government will not renew indefinitely their permits to enter the country. Next year's party, however composed, is sure to be a very good one; but I do hope it will not cut things too fine. If the future holds only one expedition for us, let us be sure that the means are sufficient to the end.

I have said little about the Mount Everest Committee which has from the very beginning presided over this enterprise. It consists of Fellows of the Royal Geographical

Society, members of the Alpine Club and one representative of the Himalayan Club. Its functions have been to obtain permission from the Tibetan Government through the Secretary of State for India ; to collect funds for each expedition ; to select the leader and supervise the composition of his party ; and to maintain an expedition in the field and conduct all business during its absence.

Some men of individualistic outlook are averse to committees on principle, arguing that they are slow in action, uncertain in policy, and generally inefficient. They hold that Mount Everest is much more likely to be climbed by a privately formed party which is completely independent, and can therefore adapt itself to circumstances. I am not of that opinion : Mount Everest is not in British territory, but is on the boundaries of two most jealously guarded countries— Tibet and Nepal. We have at present no hope whatever of being admitted to the latter, and the consent of the Tibetan Government is most difficult to obtain. For the sport of mountaineering they have neither understanding nor respect, and its most distinguished exponents are, in Tibetan eyes, of no importance whatever. Negotiations must be conducted by men of standing in the worlds of diplomacy and administration.

Again, in a foreign Eastern country events may occur, with startling suddenness, which might place an expedition in great difficulties, even in jeopardy. It is, I think, essential to have at home a body which is in a position to give and obtain support in times of emergency.

Then there is the question of finance. Assuming that permission is renewed, unless a succession of parties can be sent out privately financed, and it would be difficult to ensure that, a committee of this nature is the strongest possible guarantor.

I should like to place on record the fact that I have invariably received unstinted support, encouragement and trust from the Mount Everest Committee. In matters of organisation, selection and conduct of operations they have allowed me the greatest freedom of action, and no leader could have asked for a more generous acceptance of his decisions. The Committee has been a very good friend to all expeditions ; I sincerely hope that it will continue to direct the enterprise, till success is attained.

MOUNT EVEREST EXPEDITION, 1936

LIST OF FIRMS SUPPLYING FOOD

DANISH BACON CO., LTD. : Bacon, Ham, Lunch Tongue, Brawn, Butter.

KEARLEY & TONGE, LTD. : Brisket of Beef.

W. WEDDELL & CO., LTD. : Ox Tongues.

J. ALLMANN & SONS, LTD. : Sausages, Sauerkraut, Suet, Pumpernickel, Cerebos Salt, French Mustard, Colman's Mustard, Pepper, Gents Relish.

C. & E. MORTON, LTD. : Army Rations, Herrings in Tomato, Kippers, Cod Roe, Herring Roe, Bloaters.

BOVRIL, LTD. : Pemmican, Bovril.

BRAND & CO., LTD. : Chicken Breasts, Salmon, Pastes, Oxtail, Mock Turtle, and Cream of Chicken Soups, Sauce A1, Essence of Beef, Essence of Chicken.

J. SAINSBURY, LTD. : Peas, Sweet Corn, Sardines.

BRITISH SALES, LTD. : Spinach, Asparagus Tips, Tomato Juice, Pears, Peaches, Grapefruit, Figs, Apricots, Logan-berries, Dri-Pak Prunes, Grapefruit Juice.

CHIVERS & SONS, LTD. : Broad Beans, Leeks, Mushrooms, Celery Hearts, Carrots, Beetroot, Asparagus, Victoria Plums, Black Currants, Greengages, Golden Plums, Raspberries, Pineapple, Strawberry Jam, Plum Jam, Raspberry Jam, Black-currant Jam, Gooseberry Jam, Apricot Jam, Greengage Jam, Red-currant Jelly, Apple Jelly, Marmalade, Honey, Artichoke Purée, Celery Purée, Carrot Purée, Christmas Pudding, Jelly Creams.

PETTY WOOD & CO., LTD. : Tomatoes, Pilchards, Figs (dried), Crystallised Fruits, Crystallised Stem Ginger.

H. J. HEINZ CO., LTD. : Pork and Beans, Cream of Tomato, Cream of Pea, Cream of Mushroom Soups, Tomato Ketchup, Salad Cream, Spanish Olives, Spanish Olives Stuffed, Capers, Horse-radish Powder, Spanish Olive Oil, Pickles Ideal, Pickled Onions in brown Vinegar, Pickled Onions in white Vinegar, Pickled Walnuts, Mango Chutney.

GILBERT KIMPTON & CO., LTD. : Dried Vegetables.

THE AUSTRALIAN DRIED FRUITS BOARD : Sultanas.

GRAPE NUTS CO., LTD. : Grape Nuts.

BEMAX SALES, LTD. : Bemax.

A. & R. SCOTT, LTD. : Porage Oats.

GEO. HARKER & CO., LTD. : Macaroni.

APLIN & BARRETT, LTD. : Dripping, Cheeses (Stilton, Cheddar, Cheshire, Chedlet, Chedlet with Celery, Parmesan).

VAN DEN BERGHS, LTD. : Margarine.

CHARLES BROWN & CO., LTD. : Flour.

CADBURY BROS., LTD. : Bourn-Vita, Chocolate Wafer Biscuits, Peppermint Crêmes.

R. LEHMANN & CO., LTD. : Black Cherry Jam, Dilma Drinking Chocolate.

HORLICK'S MALTED MILK CO., LTD. : Horlick's Tablets, Horlick's Powder.

A. WANDER, LTD. : Ovaltine, Eggs.

FRANK COOPER, LTD. : Oxford Marmalade, Mint Jelly.

C. A. HARRISON, COM. AGENT PROVINCE OF QUEBEC : Maple Syrup, Maple Sugar.

GLAXO : Glucose, Ostermilk.

TATE & LYLE, LTD. : Golden Syrup, Sugar (granulated, cube).

FORTT'S : Biscuits (Bath Oliver, Bath Oliver with Chocolate, Beau Nash, Honey Ginger).

W. & R. JACOB & CO., LTD. : Biscuits (Cream Crackers, Digestive).

MACVITTIES GUEST & CO., LTD.: Shortbread Biscuits, Oat Cakes.

A. ROMARY & CO., LTD.: Ginger Nuts, Honey Bake, Chocolate Biscuits.

THOMAS MITCHELHALL: Healthy Life Biscuits.

HUNTLEY & PALMERS, LTD.: Petit Beurre, Ginger Nuts.

MUNCH BISCUIT CO.: Munch Biscuits.

CARR & CO., LTD.: Coffee Rusks.

WM. HAY, LTD.: Fruit Juices (Lemon, Lime, Orange, Ginger, Raspberry, Strawberry).

FULLERS, LTD.: Peppermint Lumps.

JOHN MACKINTOSH & CO., LTD.: Toffee Assorted, Toffee de Luxe.

S. PARKINSON & SON (DONCASTER), LTD.: Barley Sugar, Mixed Fruit Drops, Bull's-eye Mints, Old-fashioned Humbugs, Old-fashioned Butter Drops.

ROBERT WIPER: Kendall Mint.

CHARBONNEL & WALKER, LTD.: Mixed Chocolates.

JOSEPH TERRY & SONS, LTD.: Marching Chocolate.

A. J. CALEY & SON, LTD.: Chocolate.

NESTLÉ & ANGLO-SWISS CONDENSED MILK CO.: Full-cream Sweetened Milk, Full-cream Unsweetened Milk, Café au Lait, Milk Chocolate.

MARMITE FOOD EXTRACT CO., LTD.: Marmite.

CROSSE & BLACKWELL, LTD.: Vinegar (Malt, French Wine), Worcester Sauce (L. & P.), Harvey Sauce (Lazenby), Piccalilli, Mixed Pickles.

LIST OF FIRMS SUPPLYING EQUIPMENT

BAXTER, WOODHOUSE & TAYLOR, LTD., 17 Sackville Street, Manchester, 1: Grenfell cloth. Windproof suits for Europeans and porters. Cloth presented by firm—suits made up by: *European*—Howard Flint, 48 Maddox Street, W.1. *Porters*—G. Glanfield & Son, Ltd., 1 Brick Lane, E.C.1. High-altitude tents.

ARTHUR BEALE, 194 Shaftesbury Avenue, W.C.2 : Cashmere puttees. Alpine rope. Alpine line.

BERKEFELD FILTERS & WATER SOFTENERS, LTD., Town Mills, Tonbridge, Kent : Filters complete with accessories.

BOOTS CHEMISTS, LTD., Criterion Buildings, Piccadilly Circus, S.W.1 : Toilet requisites.

BROOKES & ADAMS, LTD., Barr Street, Hockley, Birmingham : Bandalasta ware.

BRYANT & MAY, LTD., Fairfield Works, Bow, E.3 : Matches.

ROBERT BURNS, Hanover Mill, Buxton Street, London Road, Manchester, 1 : Special sleeping bags. Special high-altitude sleeping bags. Special high-altitude tents, 7 ft. × 4 ft. ; ditto, 7 ft. × 4 ft. 6 in. Whymper type tent, 7 ft. × 7 ft. in Willesden proofed cotton duck. Lightweight rucksacks. Special mountain stretcher, complete with slings for four bearers, double Thomas leg splints and fittings. Eiderdown suits—for high climbers (padded double-breasted waistcoat and knee breeches).

CAMP & SPORTS CO-OPERATORS, LTD., 21 Newgate Street, E.C.1 : Ordinary camping equipment (rucksacks, rubber sheets and mats, kapok sleeping bags, mattresses, pillows). *Small dome tent*—outer 10 ft. to corners, 6 ft. 6 in. high, inner 9 ft. to corners, 6 ft. high. 2 *large dome tents*—outer 13 ft. across, 7 ft. high, inner 12 ft. across, 6 ft. 6 in. high. 4 *pyramid tents*—outer 7 ft. 6 in. × 9 ft. × 7 ft. high, inner 6 ft. 6 in. × 8 ft. × 6 ft. 6 in. high. 16 *small " A " pattern tents with eaves*— 6 ft. 6 in. × 3 ft. 9 in. × 3 ft. 9 in. high. 14 *large " A " pattern tents with eaves*—7 ft. × 5 ft. × 4 ft. 6 in. high. 3 *Mess tents*—7 ft. long+porches, 7 ft. 6 in. high × 8 ft. wide × 2 ft. 9 in. walls, 2 ft. 9 in. eave. *Camp furniture*— folding chairs, tables, canvas water buckets.

J. S. CARTER, 16 South Molton Street, W.1 : Climbing boots.

CLARK, SON & MORLAND, LTD., Glastonbury, Somerset :
Lambskin camp boots.

CONDRUP, LTD., 77 and 78 Fore Street, E.C.2 : Primus stoves.

MRS. CORFIELD, Stone Cross, Lexden Road, Colchester :
Ski socks—hand-made.

P. B. COW & CO., LTD., Rubber Manufacturers, Streatham
Common, S.W.16 : Pneumatic mattresses, " Li-Lo."

MRS. DUNCAN, New Road, Scalloway, Shetland : Shetland
wool underclothing (hand-made).

ROBERT DYAS, LTD., 53 High Street, Bloomsbury, W.C.2 :
Tools.

EASIWORK, LTD., 242 Tottenham Court Road, W.1 : Pressure
cookers.

BENJAMIN EDGINGTON (SILVER & EDGINGTON, LTD.), 69
Great Queen Street, Kingsway, W.C.2 : Heavy green
rotproof canvas kit bags, waterproof inner lining and
shoulder straps, 3 ft. 2 in. × 2 ft. 4 in.

ELMESAN (LONDON), LTD., 66 Victoria Street, S.W.1
(London Agents for Meta, Basle, Switzerland): Meta fuel.

EVER READY, LTD., Hercules Place, Holloway, N.7 : Torches
and batteries.

A. W. GAMAGE, LTD., Holborn, E.C.1 : Sports equipment,
games, etc.

HORESCHOWSKY, Austria : Ice-axes.

GEORGE IBBERSON & CO., 112–116 Rockingham Street,
Sheffield, 1 : Cutlery.

IRVING AIRCHUTE OF GT. BRITAIN, LTD., Icknield Way,
Letchworth, Herts : Ivory silk parachute cord, breaking
strain 800 lb.

JAEGER CO., LTD., 95 Milton Street, E.C.2 : Woollen underclothing, camel-hair mitts, etc.

N. C. JOSEPH, LTD., Aluminium Works, Stratford-on-Avon :
Aluminium culinary.

ROBERT LAWRIE, LTD., 38 Bryanston Street, Marble Arch,
W.1 : High climbing boots.

MILLETTS STORES (1928), LTD., 29–31 Oxford Street, W.1 : Porters' clothing.

PEAL & CO., 487 Oxford Street, W.1 : Special ski-ing gloves.

PENTECON, LTD., Southwick Street : Pressure-cookers.

PRICES PATENT CANDLE CO., Battersea, S.W.11 : Candles.

H. J. RYMAN, LTD., 6–10 Gt. Portland Street, W.1 : Stationery.

SYDNEY BROS., 190 Elthorne Road, Upper Holloway, N.19 : Mountaineering gloves.

TUCKER ARMOURED PLYWOOD CO., LTD. (successors to McGruer Hollow Spar Co.), Crayford, Kent : Hollow wooden snow pitons.

S. TYZACK & SON, LTD., 341–345 Old Street, E.C.1. : Tools.

BURROUGHS WELLCOME & CO., Snow Hill Buildings, E.C.1 : Medical stores and equipment.

THEODORE HAMBLIN, LTD., 15 Wigmore Street, W.1 : Goggles.

SIEBE GORMAN & CO., LTD., 187 Westminster Bridge Road, S.E.1 : Oxygen apparatus.

JOHN DICKINSON & CO., LTD., Apsley Mills, Hemel Hempstead, Herts : Notepaper and envelopes.

II
OBSERVATIONS

Weather

BY W. R. SMIJTH-WINDHAM

So much is now known of Mount Everest as a mountaineering problem that there can be little doubt that it is climbable in the right weather. On the other hand, no party, however competent, however fit, has the smallest chance of success if conditions be unfavourable at the time of making the final assault. In consequence, recent expeditions have paid increasing attention to the necessity, firstly, of making systematic observations in order to build up a local weather-lore, and secondly, of arranging to be supplied with meteorological bulletins.

What little is known about the weather in the Mount Everest region is confined to the experiences of previous expeditions. Mallory wrote a valuable general account of the conditions encountered by the 1921 Reconnaissance party, from June onwards. The 1922 and 1924 Expeditions recorded only disconnected observations. Ruttledge, therefore, set out with his party in 1933 without much definite weather knowledge to guide him, although, of course, he had based his plans on unwritten information given by those who had been before. He had two assets, one in Wager, who had made a study of meteorology, the other in wireless equipment, by means of which he was able to co-operate with Dr. Sen, Director of the Indian Meteorological Department's station at Alipore. Dr. Sen took great trouble over his arrangements, though as he himself wrote : " In the vast area of the Eastern Himalayan region there is only one high-level surface observatory, namely Darjeeling, which reports telegraphically to Calcutta. Vast regions, like Nepal, Bhutan and Tibet, are yet meteorologically unexplored and unrepresented. The difficulties in the way of forecasting weather over this region are therefore formidable." In order to help Dr. Sen it was agreed that an observatory should be set up at the Base Camp, whence twice-daily reports would be wirelessed to Calcutta where they would at least serve as a check on the accuracy of Dr. Sen's predictions. In spite of the well-known caprice of weather in mountainous regions, Wager was afterwards able to write: "Weather bulletins of the sort received in 1933 would be of great value to future expeditions now that some faith in their validity has been built up."

Ruttledge decided to take wireless in 1936 in order that the help of Alipore might be sought once more. He had no meteorologist this time, and allotted the task to me, my sole qualification being an apprenticeship under Wager in 1933. The instruments with which observations were to be made were confined to a 3-inch aneroid barometer, wet-bulb, dry-bulb, maximum and minimum thermometers.

When the 1936 Expedition set out, official meteorological data combined with the experiences of previous expeditions had shown that the weather in the Everest region is subject to predictable seasonal variations, which bear close relationship to similar changes taking place in north-east India. From November to mid-February Everest suffers from a wind remarkably constant in direction and severity. Broadly speaking, it blows from the west, though locally it is usually felt as a north-west wind, this being probably due to the effect of neighbouring mountain masses. It is uniformly strong, rising sometimes to gale or even hurricane force. In conjunction with short days and very low temperatures, such weather renders climbing impossible in spite of the likelihood of the North Face of Everest then being free from snow. During the months from mid-February to May, often termed the pre-monsoon months, the wind tends to be slightly less constant in direction, though it still blows predominantly from the west. Wind speeds are lower, but temporary gales must still be expected. Towards the end of the period days draw out, and air temperature rises, while any precipitation that occurs near the summit, being of powder snow, is rapidly blown away, constituting part of the well-known plume.

Precipitation in this region is normally due to moist air entering from the valleys to the south on account of a disturbance. Such disturbances are of two kinds :

1. *Western Disturbances*

Having their origin in the Mediterranean or south-east Europe, these cyclonic storms cross the North-West Frontier of India travelling eastwards. Their effect depends upon their strength, vertical thickness, and upon whether, as often happens, they split into two portions over the Punjab. In general, they may be expected to cause cloud or precipitation in the Everest area. Their average frequency is weekly, but as many as nine in a month have been known.

2. *Depressions in the Bay of Bengal*

Storms and depressions of this type have effects that can only be predicted by the expert, who has to take account of many factors, including the possible interaction between such a storm and the western disturbances already discussed. Their frequency is known to be 0·3 per month for April, 0·9 for May, and 1·3 for June. If they are of considerable strength, it is likely that the southerly or south-easterly humid current following in their wake will penetrate the Everest region.

To sum up, it may be expected that during late April or May Everest is experiencing periods of clear, sunny days, interspersed with weekly storms lasting for a day or two, and causing light snowfalls. The westerly wind, however, soon reasserts itself, and restores the North Face, in which we are interested, to a climbable condition.

THE MONSOON

All this time, however, a south-easterly current of air in the Bay of Bengal has been gaining strength. Suddenly a depression forms over the head of the Bay. Alipore announces : " Conditions are favourable for the formation of the monsoon." The Bay air, rapidly gathering momentum, invades Bengal. The monsoon has begun.

From Camp III a veritable battle of the giants may now be witnessed. Fleecy clouds, the vanguard of the monsoon, sail up behind the Rapiu La. As they approach the summit of Everest they are checked in their career, stopped, and hurled back at a higher level. But the north-west wind is fighting a losing battle. Inexorably the sea of clouds advances until Everest is surrounded, and henceforth wears a thick white mantle of snow. Not until October does the monsoon current weaken, abandoning the eastern Himalaya to the merciless westerlies of winter and spring.

Owing to the inclined slabs of which the North Face is composed, offering no handholds, and only a precarious grip for boot-nails, it has always been considered impossible to climb Everest while under snow during the monsoon period, a season that from a climatic point of view has great advantages. On the other hand, the climber, even if he did not contract serious frost-bite in the spring, would stand a very good chance of being blown to his death by a wind the speed of which amply makes up for its lack of weight. The only course open to a leader is to place his party so that they can take advantage of the brief lull which may be expected while

190

the north-west wind and the monsoon currents are fighting for mastery of the summit, and, in effect, are each cancelling out the other. So far, so good. The fly in the ointment has always been that there is no reliable method of forecasting the date of arrival of the monsoon. The leader must be prepared for an early monsoon, yet the twin evils of inactivity and deterioration are ready to sap the morale and physique of his party in the event of a late one.

Upon these data, then, the plan was based at a conference held early in the march. A normal or late monsoon had been predicted, that is to say, one that would not affect Everest until the first week in June or later. Keeping time in reserve, it was decided to reach the Base Camp on April 24, leading to an attempt during the last week in May, or earlier if conditions seemed favourable. What was not anticipated was that a succession of disturbances, more frequent than usual, would so retard operations as to leave us vulnerable to an early and exceptionally rapid onset of the monsoon.

THE MARCH

To those of us who had been with the 1933 Expedition a marked contrast was apparent during the march across Tibet. There were few hardships, and for the most part people could be seen marching in shirt-sleeves, whereas in 1933 windproofs and mufflers were worn. Between Kampa Dzong and Shekar Dzong the night minimum varied between 25° F. and 12° F., averaging 17° F. In 1933 between the same places, only a week earlier, it had varied between 23° F. and 6° F., averaging 15° F. These figures are insufficient to account for the change. In the daytime a westerly convection current springs up at about ten o'clock, reaches its maximum force early in the afternoon, and dies away at about five. It seemed this year that this daily wind had lost its sting. There was no apparent reason why this should have been the case, unless it was that it received less assistance than usual from the predominant westerlies of the upper air. Alipore sub-sequently confirmed that the westerly drift had been below average strength.

During the march no readings were taken of barometric pressures, or of daily temperature maxima. Towards the end, however, there were two remarkable phenomena. While we were encamped at Tashidzom on April 23 the air temperature in my tent rose to 104° F. at 3 p.m., and during the march from Chödzong to Rongbuk on April 25, just short of Rongbuk (16,000 feet), several members were distinctly heard to complain of the heat. Nevertheless, nobody had as yet suspected anything abnormal in the season. From Rongbuk, on the same day, Gavin and I independently estimated the wind velocity at the summit to be west or north-west, 40–50 m.p.h. Owing to the great height such a wind velocity would presumably have the weight of a 15-m.p.h. breeze at sea-level, so that, in the absence of an unduly low temperature, one can assume that reasonable climbing conditions existed.

Similar conditions persisted during the last few days of April. Wireless contact with Darjeeling was made on May 1, and the first weather forecast to be received predicted a western disturbance likely to affect the Everest region on the following day. From May 2 until June 8 weather observations were made at Camp I. Until May 11 they were made at noon; thereafter Alipore requested that they should be made at 9 a.m. and again at 5 p.m. Wireless conditions, however, were always so bad in the evening that it was found better to send a short general survey of the day's weather rather than detailed readings which might have been too complicated to transmit until the following morning. It may also be noted that Camp I, as a weather station, suffers from being too closed in; moreover, Everest is not visible.

Table I gives details of the weather conditions obtaining at Camp I on successive days from May 2 to June 8, and includes, for comparison, a précis of the weather forecasts issued from Alipore on the previous day. Table II is concerned only with temperature readings taken at Camp I, and should be read in conjunction with Table I.

SUMMARY

A study of the information given in Tables I and II shows that :

1. Weather in the Everest region was seriously affected by five western disturbances during the period May 2–22. Normally an average of four per month may be expected.

2. During May the normal strong westerly or north-westerly winds were conspicuously feeble and intermittent. The following two messages, quoted verbatim, show how puzzled we were by the abnormal season, and give Dr. Roy's explanation of its causes.

(*a*) To : WEATHER, ALIPORE.   CAMP III,
    From : RUTTLEDGE.   *May 25.*
                      16.30 hours.

Extremely puzzled by apparent arrival of monsoon so early and only five days after first report of conditions favourable for its formation in south Bay of Bengal stop Most grateful if you will give an opinion as to whether this may be " chhoti barsat " with consequent possibility of period of fine weather before real monsoon sets in stop Everest has been under snow practically whole of May with warm temperatures and gentle winds from all directions principally east stop Is there any chance re-establishment normal north-westerly wind ?

(*b*) To : RUTTLEDGE.   ALIPORE,
    From : DR. ROY.   *May 27.*
                      10.40 hours.

Reference your enquiry stop Throughout May this year winds in Bengal have been from south instead of south-west

o

and west favouring inflow of moisture towards Everest rather than to Assam stop Western disturbances have not been typical stop They have not been backed by strong westerly or north-westerly winds capable of blowing away the moisture stop Due to depression advancing up western half Bay conditions for continuation of southerly winds over Bay and Bengal have been remarkably favourable since last week when monsoon appeared near Ceylon stop Unfortunately depression now near Sandheads in head Bay seems likely increase supply of moisture towards Bengal and eastern Himalayas for a few days stop Regret cannot foresee behaviour monsoon after disappearance this depression stop At this moment chances seem against establishment of strong north-westerly winds after disappearance depression.

3. The monsoon reached Everest within five days of the first warning; a fortnight had been expected.

4. Previous expeditions had noted the establishment of the monsoon on Everest as follows :

1921.	July 7.
1922.	First week of June.
1924.	June 16.
1933.	May 30.
1935.	June 26.

This year it broke on May 25, that is, ten days earlier than usual. Students of the law of chance will notice that the only parties who have been favoured with a late monsoon have been reconnaissance expeditions.

TABLE I

SUMMARY OF WEATHER EXPERIENCED ON EVEREST (CAMP I) DURING PERIOD MAY 2, 1936, TO JUNE 8, 1936

Date.	Weather forecast by Alipore.	Barometer at 9.0 a.m. (Inches).	Cloud, description and amount.	Precipitation during past 24 hours.	Wind direction and force (Beaufort). On ground.	Wind direction and force (Beaufort). Upper air.	Remarks, including observations at Camp III at 8 a.m., if any.
May 2	Western disturbance	—	Cumulus 2	Nil	Nil	N.W.3	—
,, 3	Western disturbance	—	Cumulo-nimbus 7	Nil	Nil	W.2	—
,, 4	Western disturbance	—	Totally overcast	1 in. snow	Nil	Nil	Clear evening and night
,, 5	Western disturbance	—	Cumulo-nimbus 7	Slight	W.5	S.E.4	Unsettled
,, 6	Western disturbance	14·85	Fracto-cumulus 4	1 in. snow	W.3	W.3	Clear night
,, 7	Western disturbance	14·80	{ Cumulo-nimbus 3 / Cirrus 4	1 in. snow	Nil	S. (?)	Unsettled
,, 8	Western disturbance	14·80	Sky overcast	Brief snow showers	—	S.W.3	Unsettled
,, 9	Clearing sky, rising wind, falling temperature	14·80	Fracto-cumulus	Nil	—	N.W.3	Gusty but improved
,, 10	Feeble western disturbance unlikely affect Everest	14·78	Cumulo-nimbus 8	¼ in. snow	—	N.W.3	Disturbed thundery conditions during night
,, 11	Improvement	14·80	Fracto-cumulus 1	Blizzard 4–9 p.m.	—	N.W.3	Heavy snow at Camp III on previous day
,, 12	Strong W. or N.W. wind, low temperature	14·91	Nil	Snow blizzard during night	—	Not observable	Snow-flakes were electrically charged
,, 13	Western disturbance approaching Everest	14·89	Alto-stratus 2	Nil	—	N.W.2	Camp III report: Wind W.I and wind on Everest S.W.
,, 14	Western disturbance, weak winds, higher temperatures	14·90	Nil	Nil	Light, variable	Not observable	Cold night. Camp III report: Wind E.I. Wind on Everest nil
,, 15	Western disturbance persisting	14·90	Cumulus 2 / Cirrus 4	Nil	—	Appears S. light	Light S.E. wind previous evening. Camp III report: Wind E.I, wind on Everest W., cloud cirro-stratus 7
,, 16	Western disturbance, further precipitation	14·98	Nimbus 10	Light, intermittent snow since 3 p.m.	—	E.4	Camp III report: Wind nil, cloud nimbus 8, with slight snowfall

NOTE.—Brackets in Column 2 denote the limits of separate disturbances.

195

Date.	Weather forecast by Alipore.	Barometer at 9.0 a.m. (inches).	Cloud, description and amount.	Precipitation during past 24 hours.	Wind direction and force (Beaufort).		Remarks, including observations at Camp III at 8 a.m., if any.
					On ground.	Upper air.	
May 17	Western disturbance persisting, moderate precipitation	14·89	Fracto-cumulus 8	Continuous snowfall during previous day, fair night	—	S.2	Camp III report : Wind E.2, wind on Everest W., slight snow since morning, 4 in. snow on North Col yesterday
,, 18	Disturbance passing away, showers still likely	14·93	Low cloud in valleys, upper sky clear	Heavy snow 12–9 p.m.	—	N.W.4	Camp III report : Wind N.3, wind on Everest S., 2 in. snow, 15 in. on North Col
,, 19	Less cloud, rising wind, but fresh feeble western disturbance approaching. *Conditions becoming favourable for advance of monsoon in South Bay*	14·90	Fracto-cumulus 3	Slight during previous evening	—	E.3	Camp III report : Warm night, wind E.2, wind on Everest E., cumulus 2, 2 in. snow
,, 20	Western disturbance more marked. Precipitation possible	15·00	Fracto-cumulus 1	Nil	—	E.2	General improvement noticeable. Camp III evacuated, so no report
,, 21	Western disturbance, causing light to moderate precipitation. Advance of monsoon in South Bay maintained.	14·91	Nil	Nil	—	Not observable	—
,, 22	Western disturbance moving away. Moderate showers. Monsoon unlikely penetrate inland within three days	14·85	Almost nil	Nil	—	Appears S. very light	—
,, 23	Fair weather. Monsoon likely remain in south and Central Bay	14·77	Cirrus 6	Moderate snowfall during evening	—	Appears S.W., very light	Clear night
,, 24	Monsoon likely extend temporarily to Everest region within two days	14·79	Cumulo-nimbus 10	Nil	Nil	Nil	Heavy monsoon rain reported from Darjeeling during 23rd

Date	Forecast	Barometer	Cloud	Precipitation		Wind	Remarks
,, 25	Monsoon likely cause "unlucky" weather for at least two or three days	14·90	Nimbus 10	Almost continuous	—	Appears W.	Typical monsoon weather. Camp III report: No wind, cloud nimbus 4, snow.
,, 26	Monsoon strengthening in N.E. India	14·79	{ Cumulus 3 / Cirrus 1	Heavy snow during evening	—	S.E.2	Camp III report: Wind S.E.2, wind on Everest S.W.; cumulo-nimbus 3, slight snow
,, 27	Monsoon continuing for three or four days	14·78	Nimbus 9	Intermittent	—	S.1	Camp III report: Warm night, no wind, overcast sky, slight snow
,, 28	Vigorous monsoon, heavy precipitation for next three days	14·89	Nimbus 8	Snow during night and morning	—	N.3	Camp III report: Wind E.3, 2 in. snow since 2 p.m.
,, 29	Heavy precipitation	14·80	Nil	Nil	—	Unobservable, thought to be N.	On previous evening conditions improved, with fresh N.W. wind
,, 30	Monsoon conditions persisting for few days, but temporarily weak	14·77	Cirro-stratus 5	Nil	—	W.S.W. 3	Marked improvement noticed during previous day
,, 31	Monsoon likely to strengthen then again	14·80	Nimbus 10	Heavy snow since early hours	—	Nil	Previous afternoon showered improvement with fresh N.W. wind
June 1	Conflict of moist easterlies with land westerlies favour instability Everest region	14·71	Cumulo-nimbus 10	Frequent snowfalls during previous evening	—	S.W.2	—
,, 2	Further instability	14·75	Nimbus 10	Snow since early hours, and previous evening	—	Nil	—
,, 3	Monsoon strengthened and helped by Arabian Sea branch. Moist south-westerlies likely	14·65	Fracto-cumulus 8	Nil since previous evening	—	S.W.4	Unusually high ground winds in past 24 hours
,, 4	Strong W. or W.S.W. winds favouring showers	14·61	Cumulo-nimbus 5	3 in. snow during night	—	S.W.5	Camp III report: Strong ground winds, strong W. wind on Everest, 4 in. snow during night

NOTE.—Brackets in Column 2 denote the limits of separate disturbances.

Date.	Weather forecast by Alipore.	Barometer at 9.0 a.m. (Inches).	Cloud, description and amount.	Precipitation during past 24 hours.	Wind direction and force (Beaufort).		Remarks, including observations at Camp III at 8 a.m., if any.
					On ground.	Upper air.	
June 5	Monsoon active. Strong high-level westerlies	14·69	Nimbus 8	Nil	—	S.W.5	Conditions deteriorated slightly
,, 6	Monsoon weak owing strong westerlies	14·66	Nil	Nil	—	S.W.3	Best morning for some time. Camp III report: Wind N.W.6, wind on Everest W.
,, 7	Westerlies weakening. Monsoon too weak to affect Everest	14·80	Stratus 7	Nil	—	N.W.3	Improvement maintained. Camp III report: Wind W.4, stratus 3
,, 8	Monsoon reviving after two days	14·80	Nil	Nil	—	Unobservable	Very fair weather

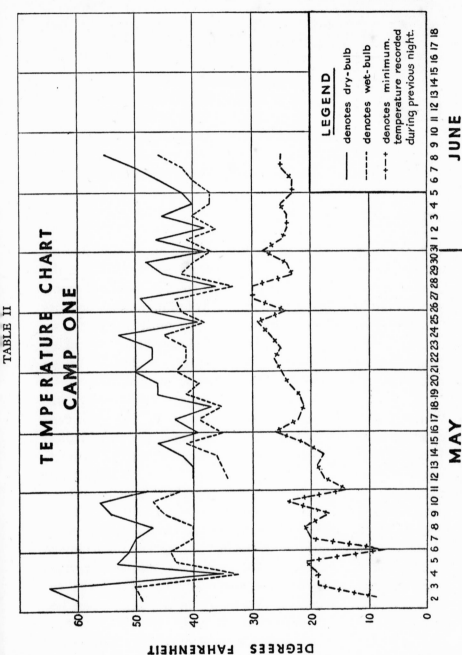

TABLE II

TEMPERATURE CHART
CAMP ONE

DEGREES FAHRENHEIT

LEGEND

—— denotes dry-bulb

---- denotes wet-bulb

–+–+ denotes minimum. temperature recorded during previous night.

MAY   JUNE

NOTE.—Up to May 11 wet-bulb and dry-bulb readings were taken at 12 noon ; from May 12, at 9.00 a.m.

Health

BY G. NOEL HUMPHREYS

THE responsibility of medical officers on Mount Everest expeditions is threefold. They must advise the leader in the selection of the personnel, they must treat the selected members prophylactically so as to reduce to a minimum the chances of sickness on the expedition, and they must deal with any illness as it arises. As regards the 1936 expedition : speaking broadly, the first two parts of our work were done for us so efficiently that the third responsibility scarcely arose.

As in the preparations for the 1933 expedition the preliminary testing of the physical fitness of the European candidates was done by the Royal Air Force Central Medical Establishment. The tests normally applied here for estimating the fitness of air pilots to fly at any height to which airplanes can reach are the most suitable which have as yet been devised for candidates for mountaineering expeditions. However the medical report is only one factor for consideration by the leader in making his team. There are the technical ability and experience of the candidate ; also his previous experience at high altitudes, especially his Himalayan experience, and his general experience in the field. Not less important is his temperament ; the leader must be something of a psychologist. Perhaps the most important factor is the reaction of a candidate to great height. This however is

200

difficult to estimate in advance. Recognising these facts the leader of the 1936 expedition adopted a system to which experience can as yet suggest little improvement. The first candidates to be appointed were those who had on previous Himalayan expeditions proved themselves exceptionally able to withstand the effects of altitude, while climbers who, however skilful technically and however good their physique, had on previous expeditions been unable to adapt themselves to great heights were not selected. The remainder of the climbing team was made up of first-class mountaineers with an outstanding medical report and, if possible, with Himalayan experience or, failing that, field experience which had shown them to be exceptionally good travellers.

For future expeditions it may be suggested that all candidates should join the expedition at home so as to be available for the searching tests of their physical fitness which cannot so well be applied abroad. At first it may be possible for the personnel of small expeditions to be made up entirely of members who have already shown their power of adaptability to great height; but if expeditions become frequent new Everesters will have to be found and candidates might well be tested in a decompression chamber, though the limit of the value of such test is obvious.

As regards prophylactic treatment we are under great obligation for help given us by the honorary staff of St. Mary's Hospital. Dr. I. H. Maclean vaccinated us, and inoculated us against typhoid. Dr. E. W. Fish advised us about our jaws and teeth. The advantage of having preliminary dental treatment lay in the fact that on previous expeditions it had been found that the reduced vitality due to living at a great height was liable to cause a flare up of latent abscesses at the apices of teeth. Mr. S. Blackman of the Royal Dental Hospital very kindly made the X-rays of our jaws and on his and Dr. Fish's advice a number of extractions were made and other work done. All these precautions were justified by results, as no European members of the expedition joining from England suffered in health except as the direct result of height.

The medical equipment of the expedition was based on Raymond Green's list for the 1933 expedition, modified slightly on his advice and on the experience of Warren on the Reconnaissance Expedition of 1935. A complete list of the equipment is given at the end of the chapter. The quantities of drugs were influenced by our intention of doing what work might be possible among the Tibetans, but as it turned out most of the amounts were enormously in excess of our requirements. There was no shortage except of linctus scillæ co., pastilles, and throat sprays, of which we could have used three times the amount, though their use was as a placebo, for we discovered no treatment which could relieve altitude throats. Most of our drugs were supplied by Messrs. Burroughs, Wellcome & Co., who also did for us the packing of all our medical stores and equipment. The medical supplies were satisfactory in every way and the packing was most efficiently done. We are moreover under great obligation to the following, who presented to the expedition stores or equipment : Messrs. British Colloids Ltd. (The Crookes Laboratories), Messrs. Bayer & Co., Messrs. Hoffman La Roche, Messrs. H. R. Napp Ltd., Messrs. Genatosan Ltd., Messrs. Smith & Nephew, and Mr. Eustace Thomas, who presented the expedition with one of our two stretchers. The oxygen apparatus, which was especially designed for us by Messrs. Siebe Gorman Ltd., was not ready when the advance party left England and was taken over by Warren, who came out with a later party, and it henceforth became his especial charge.

The next medical work of the expedition was the selection and prophylactic treatment of porters at Darjeeling. Here the greatest assistance was received from Major T. S. Thomas, I.M.S., and Dr. Yen Sing, at the Victoria Hospital. All candidates were physically examined and their medical report considered in conjunction with their general records on previous expeditions. The selected candidates were then vaccinated and treated for possible internal parasites. Just before we left Darjeeling one of the porters developed tetanus and had to be left in hospital. Luckily he was able to receive immediate treatment, and recovered.

The expedition was well equipped medically. Besides the two doctors, Wigram was a senior medical student who postponed taking his finals in order to come on the expedition. Morris had two sharp attacks of benign tertian malaria, for which he was successfully treated. There was the extraction of a tooth from a member of the expedition who had joined from abroad and so missed the careful dental examination given to members joining in England. There were slight alimentary disturbances, due perhaps to mica in the drinking-water. With the best intentions, however, we could find nothing really serious to treat.

It was not until April 29, at Base Camp, that it looked as though we should have a chance of showing our skill. A porter was found collapsed and groaning, doubled up with pain. His abdomen was rigid. There was pain in the umbilical region, extending to the right groin. He vomited blood. Later he passed into a state of coma. Unfortunately the surgical boxes had been sent to Camp I. It was dusk. We called for volunteers, and porters went off at 6 p.m. to bring the boxes back. They returned at 8.30. It was now too dark to operate. Nothing could be done until the morning. At the first light of dawn I went to the porter's tent. He was not there. Fearing that we might stop him, he had got up early to carry a load to Camp I and had already left camp.

In spite of the lack of serious illness there was, on both the outward and return journeys, plenty to occupy the medical officers. Before and after the day's march there was a large number of porters to be treated for cuts, abrasions, dysentery etc., and from Base Camp onwards for headaches and sore throats. The porters were especially pleased with elastoplast dressings, producing small scratches, weeks old, in the hope of receiving this adornment. Pastilles were in great demand, and twice a day there were parades for spraying or painting throats. It was difficult to get the sick parades assembled, as fixed times were impossible because all the sick porters could not be spared at the same time from their work. Tibetans often came into camp for treatment, sometimes from a great distance. This was always given to the best of our ability, though the time of their arrival was often inconvenient. As with the leader and the transport officer, the medical officers' day was never definitely finished.

During the 1936 expedition Camp I was used as our base camp, but the old names of camps were retained to avoid confusion. Up to the height of Camp I, 17,700 feet, members of the expedition had suffered little from the effect of height. There had been a little mountain sickness while crossing the passes, one or two sore throats, an occasional altitude head-ache, and two members had suffered from migraine. Before we had left Camp I on our ascent these symptoms had passed. There was no doubt as to our acclimatisation to the height of Camp I. At Camp III, 21,500 feet, we were all affected by the height in such ways as sore throats, headaches, sleepless-ness, loss of appetite, breathlessness, lassitude, a feeling of nausea or actual vomiting, hæmorrhoids, indigestion, diar-rhœa, and such visual disturbances as double vision and " blacking out," which was our term for the sudden temporary loss of vision, in fact the first stage of a fainting attack. This last occurred only during great physical exertion, as when steps were being cut up the North Col. On returning to Camp I we started to recover our normal health. On each return to Camp III we were able to adapt ourselves more quickly to the altitude. It was marked that members who

204

had been on previous Everest expeditions adapted more quickly than those who had had less or no previous experience at that height.

In spite however of the fact that adaption to a height of over 21,000 feet enabled one to stay at that height with less distress yet deterioration continued, and this was manifested by muscle wastage. The cause of this was probably the difficulty in eating. At over 21,000 feet even the thought of food caused nausea, and it was impossible to eat enough to keep up one's weight. Further deterioration must be caused by the toxic effect of ulcerated throats. As was pointed out by Hingston, this double process of adaption and deterioration is easily understood if one considers a drunkard who, while steadily going down hill physically as the result of his excess, is yet adapting himself to withstand the effects of amounts of alcohol which would kill a teetotaller.

From observations made during the expedition on the western slopes of the North Col it is suggested that this route to the crest of the col, though more difficult technically, might have advantage over the eastern slope of the col in that it might be climbable when the danger of avalanches would make the eastern slope impracticable. Should some expedition try this route a further advantage may be found. At a point near the Reconnaissance Expedition camp of 1935, where, travelling up the main Rongbuk glacier, west of Changtse, the first view of the North Col is obtained, is a site, at 19,370 feet, which would to some extent combine the functions of Camp I, the base camp of 1936, and of Camp III, the advanced base. The site would be at about the same distance as Camp III from the ultimate objective, would be in sight of the slopes of the North Col, and yet would be at a height at which acclimatisation is possible.

There was little to be learned from the use of oxygen on the 1936 expedition as we did not reach a height at which its use was necessary. The apparatus was tried experimentally

205

on the way to Everest and it worked perfectly. There was no discomfort from wearing it and one could move as rapidly up hill while using the apparatus as one could move at sea-level without it but carrying the same weight. It was however noticed that after the experimental use of oxygen we were more tired during the next day's march than we had been on previous marches. This might of course be expected from the increased metabolic rate during the inhalation of oxygen. Now that a Mount Everest expedition has had for the first time a really satisfactory oxygen apparatus it was particularly unfortunate that a height was not reached at which its help was needed.

Although the physiology of the use of oxygen, as well as the apparatus, is dealt with fully elsewhere it may be interesting here to restate the oxygen controversy. From experiments in decompression chambers, especially that used at Farnborough by the Royal Air Force for testing air pilots, it has been shown that at or before the reduction of atmospheric pressure to that corresponding to a height of 28,000 feet the victim of the experiment becomes unconscious. This happens quite suddenly and is not preceded by any great discomfort. The subject of the experiment who is recording his experiences as the pressure is being slowly reduced may, just before he has reached the critical pressure, write : " Am quite fit ; can easily do another two or three thousand feet." A few seconds later he becomes unconscious. On the pressure being increased so that consciousness is regained the subject of the experiment often does not know that he has been insensible.

On previous Mount Everest expeditions three climbing parties have reached 28,000 feet and each at that height has turned back without any sudden feeling of physical disability and without having encountered any overwhelming technical difficulty. It is possible that they were nearing the limiting level at which it is possible to remain conscious.

On the other hand it is pointed out that conditions in the

decompression chamber do not exactly reproduce those on the mountain, where climbers approach great heights slowly and only after having lived at a high level for weeks. Also, whereas some subjects in decompression-chamber experiments become unconscious at pressures corresponding to heights considerably below 28,000 feet, yet there is no case of an Everest climber becoming unconscious from height alone. The matter remains controversial, and even if there should be no great technical difficulty found above 28,000 feet, and even with ideal weather conditions, it is still unknown whether the mountain could be climbed without oxygen.

Now that such friendly relations have been established with the Tibetans, thanks largely to the fact that leaders of expeditions have been chosen partly for their experience of the East, it is likely that permission will be obtained for more frequent expeditions, and that for the sake of economy these will be small expeditions. The importance of the selection of the personnel of such expeditions will, if possible, be increased. Among other factors there will be the consideration of the candidate's probable speed of acclimatisation to the critical level, and of his speed of adaption to the heights above that level. Unfortunately there is no method of foretelling this. The excellence of the medical report is of little avail. Some climbers who have had a particularly good medical report have been unsurpassed in their power of adaption above the critical level. Other climbers with amazingly good medical reports have adapted slowly. This is as one might suppose, for the man perfectly designed to live at sea level would, *ipso facto*, be in a measure unsuited for life at very high altitudes. Another consideration is that some climbers who have adapted slowly on one expedition have retained their acquired adaptability better than others, and on the next expedition have adapted quickly.

The question of the rate of deterioration does not come up for consideration to the same degree. There is no evidence that it varies among individuals to any great extent. Loss of appetite above the critical level is inevitable. Sore throats are universal. However, as there must be muscular wastage it is clear that very unmuscular subjects will the more quickly reach a stage where loss of muscular strength will of itself stop further climbing.

As regards medical equipment for future expeditions this will probably be smaller. Where men of picked physique are marching through an exceptionally healthy country the amount of sickness to be dealt with should not be large. Climbing accidents, if they occur, will not be different from climbing accidents elsewhere. As for the effects of height : headaches and insomnia are easily relieved by the usual drugs, and other conditions scarcely yield to treatment except by a return to a lower level. Of these the most serious is the " altitude throat," due to auto-infection of mucous membrane desiccated by the inhalation of rarefied air, which was treated without definite effect with throat sprays, Mandl's paint and pastilles. The advent of the condition might be postponed by the use of the Matthews respirators, which were tried on the 1933 expedition. By breathing through copper gauze the moisture in exhaled air is condensed and reabsorbed by the inspired air. This must retard the process of desiccation of the throat. The use of this apparatus was discontinued as it gave a feeling of claustrophobia, but as some climbers were able to sleep while wearing the respirator it is possible that the habit of its use could be acquired.

The question of what food should be taken on Everest expeditions is another controversial matter. Some would have luxuries taken for use above the critical level, on the ground that anything which might tempt the climber to eat more is worth the transport. Against this it is pointed out that above 21,000 feet all food tastes the same and one's appetite is not affected by change of diet. On the march there was, on the early stages, a preference for tinned foods

208

because they were more palatable; but later on fresh food of any kind was preferred. Smaller expeditions will be able to live more on the country than has been possible with large expeditions, and where economy in transport is necessary dried food could replace tinned food almost entirely. Rations for Arctic expeditions have been worked out to give the necessary proportion of hydrocarbon, protein and fat; and essentially the requirements of a climbing expedition are the same. Moisture must be excluded as far as possible so as to reduce weight and in order to prevent food becoming frozen. On an Arctic expedition I have found that pemmican, Cabin biscuits and lump sugar formed a completely satisfactory diet. The biscuits were hermetically sealed and had been so carefully dehydrated that they were no harder at a temperature below zero than when warmed. It is axiomatic that staple foods such as rice, bread, plantain or potatoes are almost flavourless, and, in the Arctic, plain biscuits and lump sugar were preferable to fancy biscuits and sweets. However, for mountaineering above the critical level there is the additional factor of loss of appetite and with it the craving for strong flavours. At Camp III chicken breasts in aspic were refused with loathing by climbers who would with the help of a spoon consume the entire contents of a pot of jam, or have a craving for very strong bovril or marmite. In this connection I remember that, on returning from Camp III to the lavish opportunities of Camp I, I was quite unattracted by the ample fare provided, but poking about the Mess tent I discovered behind some empty bottles a half jar of chutney, most of which I consumed; only to discover too late that it was the last of its kind and had been carefully put on one side for private consumption. A year later, though time had changed the portion of chutney to a bottle of capers, this melancholy incident remained unforgiven.

The ideal system for feeding a Mount Everest expedition would appear, then, to be to live as far as possible on the country,

P

and to carry in addition a supply of food such as has so often and so carefully been worked out for Arctic and Antarctic expeditions, supplemented by such additional commodities, on the one hand, as jam, sweets and chocolate, and, on the other, oxo, bovril, marmite—and chutney.

List of Medical Supplies

Supplied by Messrs. Burroughs, Wellcome & Co. :

2×500 " Tabloid " Aspirin gr. 5.

1×500 " Tabloid " Aromatic Chalk Powder gr. 5.

1×500 " Tabloid " Aromatic Chalk with Opium gr. 5.

1×100 " Tabloid " Calomel gr. 1.

1 tube 20 " Tabloid " Hypodermic Cocaine Hydrochlor. gr. $\frac{1}{10}$.

150 " Tabloid " Chloral Hydrate gr. 5.

3×100 " Tabloid " Cascara Sagrada gr. 3.

12×100 " Tabloid " Cathartic, War Office No. 9.

2×100 " Tabloid " Dover Powder gr. 5.

6×36 " Tabloid " Emetine Bismuth Iodide gr. 1.

2 tubes 12 " Tabloid " Hypodermic Emetine Hydrochlor. gr. $\frac{1}{2}$.

1×100 " Tabloid " Potassium Bromide gr. 5.

1×500 " Tabloid " Quinine Dihydrochloride gr. 5.

1×500 " Tabloid " Potassium Chlorate gr. 5.

4×100 " Tabloid " Sodium Bicarbonate gr. 5.

2×500 " Tabloid " Soda Mint.

1×100 " Soloid " Boric Acid and Zinc Sulphate.

2×100 " Soloid " Potassium Permanganate gr. 5.

24 tubes 6 " Soloid " Sodium Chloride gr. 80.

2 tubes 12 " Soloid " Calcium Chloride Compound.

2×100 " Soloid " Naso-Pharyngeal Compound.

24 tubes 25 " Tabloid " Magnesium Sulphate Eff. gr. 60.

2 tubes 12 " Tabloid " Hypodermic Morphine Sulphate gr. $\frac{1}{4}$.

1 box of 10 " Hypoloid " Morphine Hydrochloride gr. $\frac{1}{6}$.

1 × 25 c.c. " Wellcome " Adrenalin Solution 1 in 1000.

12 × 10 c.c. " Wellcome " Adrenalin Solution 1 in 1000 with droppers.

2 × 12 " Vaporole " Amyl Nitrite min. 3.

2 × 12 " Vaporole " Aromatic Ammonia.

12 phials " Wellcome " Anti-dysentery Serum (Shiga) 10,000 units.

36 tubes " Hazeline " Cream.

24 tubes " Borofax."

2 × 2½ oz. Collodion.

2 × 4-oz. bottles " Wellcome " Chloroform.

6 " Vaporole " Ephedrine Spray Compound, 1-fl. oz. bottles.

1 × 16-oz. bottle " Paroleine " Spray Compound.

5,000 Eucalyptus Throat Pastilles in 1-lb. tins, and 12 empty boxes.

2 × 2 oz. Mandl's Paint in stoppered bottles.

6 × 2s. size Vapex

200 Acriflavine Tablets gr. 1·75.

2 × 2½ oz. Weak Solution Iodine.

12 × ¾ oz. Weak Solution Iodine in screw-stoppered bottles in metal containers.

2 oz. Tr. Opii.

1 box of Crooke's Tannic Acid 2·5 per cent. ampoules and Spray (1 complete set with spray in cardboard box ; 1 box of 6 spare ampoules).

4 oz. Aqueous Picric Acid.

200 Allonal.

3 lb. Sodium Sulphate Crystals (Pea Crystals) in lever-lid tin.

1 × 1 lb. Magnesium Sulphate Crystals in lever-lid tin.

4 oz. Magnesium Sulphate Paste in container.

1 lb. Castor Oil.

15 ampoules 1 c.c. Coramine.

72 tubes Vaseline.

2 × 4 oz. Ung. Hyd. Ammon. Dil. in gally pots with celluloid lids.

2 × $\frac{1}{2}$ lb. Alkaline Powder.

4 × 12 Novutox ampoules.

1 × 2 oz. Novutox.

1 box Light Percaine Solution.

1 box Heavy Percaine Solution.

1 × 1 oz. Tr. Aconite and Iodine B.P. Codex.

1 bottle Dentalone.

2 × 1-lb. lever-lid tins Dusting Powder (Starch, Zinc Oxide and Boric Acid).

1 × No. 10 " Tabloid " Hypodermic Case containing :

  1 tube " Tabloid " Hypodermic No. 3, Morphine Sulphate gr. $\frac{1}{4}$.

  1 tube " Tabloid " Hypodermic No. 23, Cocaine Hydrochloride gr. $\frac{1}{10}$.

  1 tube " Tabloid " Hypodermic No. 14, Atropine Sulph. gr. $\frac{1}{100}$.

  1 tube " Tabloid " Hypodermic No. 16, Strychnine Sulph. gr. $\frac{1}{60}$.

  1 tube " Tabloid " Hypodermic No. 100, Hyoscine Hydrobrom. gr. $\frac{1}{100}$.

  1 × 20-min. 1-c.c. " Agla " Syringe.

  1 × No. 205 " Agla " Surgical Needle.

  1 × No. 207 " Agla " Surgical Needle.

  1 Bundle of Wires.

  1 Finger Grip.

  1 Soft Leather Cover.

1 × 20-min. Nickel-plated Hypodermic Syringe (Burroughs, Wellcome & Co.) complete in metal case.

12 × No. 109 cases containing 6 empty corked tubes and 1 " Vaporole " Iodine Applicator (no dressings).

1 × No. 254 " Tabloid " Medicine Case.

1 drm. Ung. Cocaine 4 per cent. B.P.C.

1 pint Olive Oil.

2 bottles Lysol, 8-oz. bottles.

2 soft red rubber Catheters, very fine, for nasal transfusion.

2 of each Gum Elastic Catheters Nos. 6, 7, 9 and 10.

1 × 2 oz. Glass Measure in leatherette case (cylindrical).

3 Eye Baths.

1 × No. 93 " Tabloid " Ophthalmic Case containing :

    2 tubes " Tabloid " Ophthalmic " C," Cocaine Hydro-
chloride gr. $\frac{1}{20}$.

    3 tubes " Tabloid " Ophthalmic " A," Atropine Sulph.
gr. $\frac{1}{200}$.

    1 tube " Tabloid " Ophthalmic " Z," Fluorescein
gr. $\frac{1}{250}$.

    1 tube " Tabloid " Ophthalmic " F," Physostigmine
Salicylate gr. $\frac{1}{600}$.

    1 tube " Tabloid " Ophthalmic " H," Homatropine
Hydrochloride gr. $\frac{1}{400}$.

    1 tube " Tabloid " Ophthalmic " R," Zinc Sulphate
gr. $\frac{1}{250}$.

    1 Mortar and Pestle.

    1 Vulcanite Rod.

    2 Camel-hair Brushes.

    1 Liquid Dropper.

    1 Nickel-plated Eye Spud.

1 Parker's Knife (Handle only).

6 Spencer Wells Artery Forceps.

1 pair Dissecting Forceps Mouse-toothed.

3 boxes of 12 Safety-pins—large and medium.

1 Thomas's Collapsible Splint.

24 × 4-in. Plaster of Paris bandages.

12 × 3-in. Plaster of Paris Bandages.

3 × $\frac{1}{2}$-min. Clinical Thermometers.

3 tubes Catgut Suture 50 × 12 in.

3 tubes Fishing Gut Suture 50 × 12 in.

1 tube Horsehair Suture.

6 tubes Fishing Gut Suture 6 × 14 in.

6 Arm Slings.

5 spools 3-in. × 10-yd. Zinc Oxide Plaster.

6 spools 2-in. × 10-yd. Zinc Oxide Plaster.

30 × 2-oz. pkts. Absorbent Gauze uncompressed.

3 sq. yd. Oiled Silk.

48 × 3-in. × 6-yd. Uncompressed Bandages.

48 × 2½-in. × 6-yd. Uncompressed Bandages.

1 pair Dental Forceps—Universal.

2 sheets Corrugated Rubber.

1 tube Drainage Tubing assorted sizes.

1 × 1 lb. Cotton Wool uncompressed.

36 × 2 oz. Cotton Wool uncompressed.

1 × 20 oz. Enamel Iron Measure graduated in c.c.

24 × 1 oz. " Tabloid " Compressed Boric Lint.

1 tube extra-long Mountless Needles.

6 spare regular Dental Needles No. 201.

1 " Tabloid " All-metal Dental Syringe min. 30 complete in cardboard box.

2 bottles of 200 " Tabloid " Sodium Salicylate gr. 5.

1 doz. tubes " Menthofax " Compound Methyl Salicylate Ointment.

4 × 30 c.c. " Wellcome " Concentrated Streptococcus Antitoxin (Scarlatina)—globulins.

1 × 25 c.c. " Agla " Syringe in metal case with 2 adapters, and 2 each " Agla " Surgical Needles Nos. 209, 210 and 242.

2 × 1 pint Linctus Scillæ Co. B.P.C.

2 doz. Anusol Suppositories.

1 set of Ash's Oxyphosphate of Zinc Tooth Stopping.

2 oz. Glycerine and Carbolic Acid Ear Drops.

1 doz. sticks Gutta-percha Stopping.

2 Czerny's Double-ended Retractors.

Stethoscope.

Presented by MESSRS. BRITISH COLLOIDS LTD. (THE CROOKES LABORATORIES) :

144 × 25 Halibut Oil Capsules.

36 × 5 c.c. Halibut Oil.

1 × 560 c.c. Transfusion Amp. Glucose 5 per cent. Normal.

1 × 560 c.c. Transfusion Amp. Glucose 5 per cent. with Saline 0·9 per cent. Normal.

1 complete set Accessories including Screw Clip and Count Drop Regulator.

1 box 3 × 50 c.c. Conc. Trans. Amp. Hypertonic Saline (1·7 per cent.).

1 box 3 × 50 c.c. Conc. Trans. Amp. Normal Saline (0·9 per cent.).

1 Tannic Acid Spray in metal case.

2 boxes 3 Tannic Acid Amps.

2 × 1-oz. Iodine Oil.

6 Vest Pocket Mercurochrome.

6 × 6 oz. Kaolin.

2 × 2½ lb. Kaolin.

4 × 8 oz. Colloplasma.

2 × 3 oz. Calamine Lotion.

2 × 1 oz. Lactocalamine Cream.

2 × ½ oz. Argentum Ophthalmic.

12 × 10 oz. Swing-stoppered Sterilised Bottles (empty).

2 *Contemporary Transfusion Practice.*

2 Tannic Acid Spray Leaflets.

Presented by MESSRS. BAYER & Co. :

8 × 5 c.c. Tetanus Antitoxin globulins " E. v. Behring."

1 doz. boxes of 15 Plasmoquine.

6 boxes of 15 Atebrin.

4 boxes of 5 sets Evipan Sodium Intravenous Anæsthetic.

2 boxes of 5 ampoules of 1 c.c. Salyrgan.

Presented by MESSRS. HOFFMAN LA ROCHE.
 6 doz. Redoxon (Synthetic Vit. C).
 1 box Novocain Hcl. gr. $\frac{1}{3}$ and Adrenalin
  gr. $\frac{1}{500}$.
 1 box Strychnine Nit. gr. $\frac{1}{30}$.
 1 box Adrenalin Hcl. gr. $\frac{1}{200}$.
 2 × 100 Digalen "Roche."
 4 × 20 "Sedormid" Sedative Tablets.
 3 × 100 "Allonal."

"Tubunic" ampoule-syringes.

Supplied by MESSRS. A. CHARLES KING LTD.
 1 doz. No. 17 S/S Hypo. Needles.
 3 Evipan Needles No. 1.
 3 Evipan Needles No. 2.
 3 Evipan Needles No. 3.
 2 French's Venesection Needles.
 1 Recordas Syringe 1 c.c.
 6 Mogill's Sprays.
 1 De Vilbis Spray No. 15.
 2 L.P. Needles 20 × $3\frac{1}{2}$ in.
 6 de Caux P.P. Needles.

Presented by MESSRS. H. R. NAPP LIMITED.
 100 tins Ferro-"Hepamult."

Presented by MESSRS. GENATOSAN LTD.
 36 tins Sanatogen.
 6 Mixers.

Supplied by MESSRS. ALLEN & HANBURYS.
 1 hermetically sealed tin containing Rubber Gloves.

Presented by MESSRS. SMITH & NEPHEW.
 6 × 3-in. Elastoplast Elastic Plaster Dressings.
 6 × 2-in. Elastoplast Elastic Plaster Dressings.

1 doz. Elastoplast Extension Bandages 4 in. × 1 yd.
2 tins Assorted Elastoplast First-Aid Bandages.
1½ doz. Elastoplast Wound Dressings 2½ in. ×3½ in.
4 × 3-in. Elastocrepe Super Elastic Cloth Bandage.

Supplied by MESSRS. R. BURNS.
2 " Thomas " stretchers.

Also :
1 Berkefeld Filter.
12 ampoules Sodium Citrate 1 gm. in 4 c.c.
2 Stethoscopes.
1 set Traction Forceps.
1 Catheter.
1 Kidney Bowl.
Vaccine.
Medical and Surgical Books.

Physiology

BY C. B. M. WARREN

INTRODUCTION

THE climbing of Mount Everest calls forth physiological adjustments in the human body which are of great interest for the practical bearing which they have upon the success or failure of the venture. It is coming to be realised that the climbing of the mountain is almost as much a physiological problem as a mountaineering feat. Does deterioration in the physical condition set in when a certain altitude has been reached, despite the fact that acclimatisation may still be going on? Is it possible to climb to 29,002 feet without using oxygen? These are problems which concern particularly the ascent of a high mountain. But perhaps it is worth remembering that the study of high-altitude physiology is beginning to have other practical applications in these days of aeroplanes and ever-increasing travel by air.

Since the main object of the expedition to Mount Everest in 1936 was to climb the mountain, and no provision was made for scientific work to be done as a side-line, only very simple observations could be made. These, nevertheless, may be worth recording, since it is seldom that opportunities for collecting data at altitudes over 20,000 feet present themselves.

MOUNTAIN-SICKNESS

It has long been known that people may be overcome by unpleasant symptoms on going rapidly to a great altitude. The malady is known as mountain-sickness. A person suffering from mountain-sickness complains of a variety of symptoms, some of the commoner of which are difficulty with the breathing, giddiness, headache, and a feeling of nausea which may end in vomiting. And many a mountaineer must at some period of his career have fallen a victim to this bogy of the sport. The condition is due to lack of oxygen as a result of breathing the rarefied atmosphere at high altitudes. It is often acute in onset, and affects only those who ascend rapidly before they have had time to get used to the heights. Thus speed of ascent and lack of acclimatisation appear to be the essential factors for its production, though severe exercise will often precipitate the attack. The acclimatised person rarely suffers from the acute form of mountain-sickness, though on going higher than the altitude to which he is acclimatised he may feel the effects in other ways.

It was during the earlier stages of the march to Mount Everest that acute mountain-sickness was met with. These marches brought us rapidly and steeply from the plains of India on to the high Tibetan tableland, and involved an ascent of 16,000 feet within the first 70 miles. During the reconnaissance in 1935 we all suffered more or less severely with mountain-sickness on reaching Tangu at 12,800 feet, and again two or three days later when crossing the Kongra La. But in 1936 these early stages were taken more slowly, with the result that after a week's stay in the bungalow at Tangu the party went over the pass two days later without serious consequences. Last year, however, the one time in the course of the expedition at which acute mountain-sickness with vomiting did occur was at Tangu on the outward journey. On that occasion the symptoms consisted of severe headache

219

with dislike of the light, nausea and vomiting, and came on a short time after Smythe's return from a climb which he had done near the bungalow. Once the pass is crossed the route to the mountain runs for some 200 miles through comparatively level country, but all the time at altitudes greater than 13,000 feet. Throughout this part of the journey, then, there is plenty of time for acclimatisation to take place. Long before we had reached Base Camp at 16,600 feet we had ceased to be breathless on the slightest exertion; and our headaches had passed away. Indeed, we arrived at Base Camp in high spirits and feeling as well as at sea-level.

ALTERATIONS IN THE BREATHING AND THE RESPIRATORY SYSTEM

One of the most obvious changes associated with life at high altitudes is the difficulty with the breathing. This is most marked when the ascent has been rapid and acclimatisation has not occurred; and still more so, I think, in those who are not accustomed to making mountain ascents. In 1936 most of us noticed breathlessness for the first time on reaching Tangu at 12,800 feet, and this persisted during the crossing of the 16,000-foot Kongra La and for several days thereafter. But in the course of the march to the mountain we became so well acclimatised that no discomfort with the breathing was noticeable at Base Camp at 16,600 feet except when taking fairly strenuous exercise.

The nature of the difficulty with the breathing requires consideration. There was no marked alteration in the *rate* of respiration when at rest, but on the slightest exertion it increased out of all proportion to the amount of exercise taken. Then from time to time one would have to make a forced expiration followed by a long deep inspiration in order to get enough oxygen; but except at such times and during exercise there was no obvious alteration in the *depth* of the

220

respiratory movements, though perhaps experiments with a spirometer might have detected a change. Alteration in the respiratory rhythm known as " Cheyne-Stokes " breathing was frequently observed during sleep. The altitudes at which this change of rhythm appeared were extremely variable even in the same individual. In one person it was present once at 9,000 feet and again later at 21,200 feet. Illness often seems to predispose to it. Wakefulness at night time is sometimes occasioned by the breathing at high altitudes, particularly on going up to a new camp for the first time. Soon after getting off to sleep one wakes up suddenly with a slight feeling of suffocation and has to take one or two long deep breaths in order to get relief. The explanation of this is that during sleep the breathing becomes shallow and the lungs are not properly ventilated. As a result the gas carbon dioxide which is being formed in the body all the time cannot be got rid of in the breath and it therefore accumulates in the blood. If carbon dioxide accumulates in the blood and in the lungs the breathing is powerfully stimulated and there is a feeling of suffocation. By placing a high pillow beneath the shoulders at night the weight of the body is lifted off the chest and the respiratory movements remain unhampered. This is often just enough to get rid of the wakefulness. I discovered the trick when climbing in the Garwal Himalayas and have proved its value since then. The fact that discomfort with the breathing becomes less noticeable as one acclimatises suggests that a mechanism has been brought into play whereby the breathing can be maintained at the new level without conscious effort.

A characteristic which has been described as being peculiar to the native peoples who dwell permanently at high altitudes is the shape of the chest. This is deeper and of greater capacity than that of persons living at sea-level. A greater capacity of the chest, so long as the lungs are healthy and the ribs mobile, would mean that a greater area of the lung was exposed to aeration. In order to see if our own lungs increased their capacity as we went higher we measured the *vital capacity*. To do this the subject is instructed to take in as much air as possible in a single breath. When the chest seems full to bursting-point he is made to blow out the air into a gas meter until he can expel no more. The volume of gas expelled is measured by the meter. In some members their vital capacities had increased at the end of the expedition by as much as 27 per cent., but in others the increase was less marked. This improvement in the vital capacity appears

TABLE I.

Vital Capacity of the Lungs.

	Lachen 8,800 ft.	Base Camp 16,600 ft.	Camp I 17,700 ft.	Camp III 21,200 ft.	Base Camp 16,600 ft.	Tengkye Dz. 13,800 ft.
Individual	23.3.36	29.4.36	5.5.36	26.5.36	16.6.36	27.6.36
C.W.	4.3	4.3	4.0	4.1	4.1	4.3
E.K.	4.0	3.8	4.0	3.9	4.0	4.2
E.W.	4.3	4.6	4.8	5.0	5.0	5.2
E.S.	4.6	4.8	5.0	5.0	5.5	5.6
F.S.	—	3.7	3.7	3.8	4.1	—
P.O.	4.0	4.4	4.1	—	4.4	4.5
C.J.M.	—	4.0	4.2	—	4.8	4.6
H.R.	4.3	5.0	4.9	5.1	5.3	5.4
N.H.	3.5	4.2	4.1	—	—	4.6
P.W.H.	3.5	4.1	4.6	4.6	—	4.3

to be one of the ways in which acclimatisation can be assisted. But it must be remembered that training alone will produce some change, since in athletes the vital capacity is found to be greater than normal. The test is employed by physicians for assessing the soundness of the lungs. It was one of the many tests to which we were subjected by the Royal Air Force Central Medical Board before going out with the expedition. For various reasons no measurements of the chests of the natives living in Tibet were made. The vital capacity test is unsuitable for this purpose since its performance depends for accuracy upon the intelligent co-operation of the subject, and it is difficult to explain in a foreign language how it should be done. We did, however, from time to time, have occasion to examine medically most of our porters, many of whom were Tibetans and hillmen. When making these examinations I noticed that the heart sounds were often difficult to hear, and not only that but the normal area of cardiac dullness was reduced in extent, which would suggest that there was in these people some change in the lungs.

A condition known as clubbing of the fingers is frequently associated with states in which oxygenation of the blood is defective. Barcroft observed clubbing of the fingers in the dwellers at high altitudes in the Peruvian Andes, but we did not find this condition either in the Tibetans we met or in our porters.

From all Everest expeditions there have been reports of altitude sore throats, and both in 1935 and 1936 almost every member of the party suffered. From the point of view of keeping the climbers fit for their task the problem of their prevention is important. Several theories of the cause of the condition have been put forward. Hingston thought that they were due to the rapid breathing of cold dry air. Greene suggested that they were due to an infection picked up from the dust of age-old camps during the journey through Tibet. I think that the following explanation is possible. Normally the throat and nose contain bacteria which are harmless, the normal buccal flora. But by breathing the unusually dry air of the north side of the mountain through the mouth instead of the nose, for when you are panting for breath mouth breathing is the rule, it escapes being moistened by passage through the nose. The result is that the cells lining the upper respiratory passages over which it passes become dried up. In this state they are liable to invasion by the normal buccal flora. In several cases we noticed that the throats were actually ulcerated, and in 1933 Greene observed the same

223

thing. With Shipton the infection spread to his larynx so that he lost his voice and could only issue orders to the porters at Camp III in a hoarse whisper. There was a noticeable improvement in the altitude throats as soon as the moisture-laden monsoon clouds began to pour over the passes from the south on to the East Rongbuk glacier. When climbing in Garwal on the southern slopes of the Himalaya these sore throats were not nearly such a common feature of life at high altitudes. The application of liquid paraffin with a spray, so as to form a protective film over the throat, was tried but found to be inadequate treatment. I can only suggest that an improved mask of the Matthews' respirator type should be used when taking exercise high up. With this mask the moisture in the expired air is condensed on a pad of copper gauze, and then with inspiration the air taken in is moistened and warmed by passage through the gauze. If properly designed the respirator could be worn without there being any obstruction to the breathing.

THE HEART AND CIRCULATION

In 1936, as no one was exposed to the strain of going really high, dilated hearts were not to be expected. Only once was the whole party examined for heart-strain and that was after coming down from Camp III for the first time. On that occasion there were no dilated hearts. Apparently they have been a feature of previous expeditions, and in 1924 Hingston says that all the climbers who had been to high camps showed evidence of them. Their absence in 1936 is due to the fact that no one had a chance of going higher than 23,000 feet.

Irregularities in the cardiac rhythm have been reported, but were not an outstanding feature in 1936. Once when going up to Camp III at a time when I had a sore throat I noticed that my heart was making extra beats at irregular intervals, but this was the only time at which an irregularity in the heart beat was noticed.

The pulse rate was examined particularly with a view to noting alterations in the basal rate. The rates both sitting and standing were also recorded at various altitudes. A large number of determinations were made, but the following table

TABLE II.

Pulse-rate of one individual.

Altitude	Basal	Sitting	Standing
8,800 ft.	63	66	81
15,000 "	63	71	85
16,600 "	63	71	89
20,000 "	67	92	102
21,200 "	73	92	114
21,000 " (three weeks later)	70	90	102

records only a few of these for illustration. The features in the case recorded are : that there is no increase in the basal rate until 20,000 feet is reached ; there is some increase in the sitting rate and a very definite increase in the standing rate as height is gained. These observations are in agreement with the findings of Hingston in 1924.

The basal rate is the number of beats per minute of the pulse when taken the first thing in the morning with the subject lying quietly in bed. Under normal circumstances the frequency remains very constant for each individual. Any effort, such as turning over in bed, will send the rate up. Table III shows the basal pulse rates of eight members of the party at different times during the expedition. In every case except one the rate remained unaltered below 20,000 feet. But in the case of Kempson his rate was constant only below 17,700 feet. In two members of the party the basal pulse frequency remained constant even at 21,200 feet. In six out of eight members of the expedition, then, the heart was

Q

TABLE III.

Basal-pulse Rates of Different Individuals

Place	Altitude	C.W.	P.W.H.	E.W.	P.O.	E.K.	J.L.G.	E.S.	H.R.
Gangtok	6,000'	62	–	–	–	–	–	–	–
Lachen	8,800'	63	63	–	–	58	48	71	61
Tangu	12,800'	62	–	63	–	–	52	70	–
Kampa Dzong	15,000'	63	–	–	–	65	–	70	–
Tengkye Dzong	13,600'	62	–	–	–	62	–	–	–
Base Camp	16,600'	63	–	–	58	64	–	–	–
Camp I	17,700'	63	–	58	–	82	48	–	56
Camp II	20,000'	67	66	83	64	88	–	–	–
Camp III	21,200'	73	66	83	64	102	64	64	56
Camp I	17,700'	61	64	–	–	67	51	–	55
Camp II	20,000'	69	–	–	–	89	68	–	–
Camp III	21,200'	70	–	–	–	90	–	–	–
Camp I	17,700'	62	–	–	–	–	–	–	–
Camp II	20,000'	65	–	–	–	84	–	–	–
Camp III	21,200'	72	–	–	–	–	–	–	–
Tengkye Dzong	13,600'	64	–	–	–	–	–	–	–
Lachung	8,800'	55	–	–	–	–	–	–	–
Tong	4,800'	54	–	–	–	–	–	–	–

working at an increased rate even under conditions of complete
rest whenever they went above Camp I at 17,700 feet. And
this happened not only on their first visits to Camps II and III
but also during subsequent visits when it was known that
they were better acclimatised. Perhaps it is significant that
20,000 feet corresponds roughly to the altitude at which we
noticed other signs of deterioration, such as loss of weight
and lack of appetite.

It is well known that on going to a high altitude there is
an increase in the number of red corpuscles per unit volume
of blood, and a corresponding rise in hæmoglobin content.
Now since the oxygen required by the body for purposes of
life and respiration is carried to the tissues by the hæmoglobin

which is present in the corpuscles, an increase in this pigment will enable more oxygen to be transported. The changes in the blood have always been regarded as one of the most important factors determining acclimatisation. Blood counts have frequently been made at altitudes up to 15,000 feet, and Hingston quotes a few figures from altitudes higher than this on the Pamir plateau. So far as I know counts were not

TABLE IV.

Date	Altitude (feet)	Corpuscles per cu.mm.
April 10	700	4,480,000
May 12	4,390	5,240,000
May 21	8,000	6,040,000
May 28	10,000	6,624,000
May 30	11,960	6,760,000
June 1	12,400	6,800,000
June 21	13,300	7,525,000
June 23	15,600	7,840,000
June 26	16,900	7,640,000
July 27	18,200	8,320,000

made during Everest expeditions until 1936. It should be mentioned, however, that Kellas was able to make a count on his own blood at a camp at 20,000 feet before and immediately after ascending Pawhunri (23,180 feet). Table V shows the number of red corpuscles per cubic millimetre of blood and the percentage of hæmoglobin in one member of the 1936 Everest Expedition. The normal figures at sea-level should be : 5,000,000 red cells per cubic millimetre, and 100 per cent. of hæmoglobin. It will be seen that there is a progressive increase both in the number of corpuscles and in the percentage of hæmoglobin present as height is gained. It will also be noticed that the figures have not returned to normal even three weeks after reaching sea-level again. Seven weeks later they were normal.

Table VI shows the percentage increase in the hæmoglobin of different members of the party as they went above 6,000

TABLE V.

Blood-count and Haemoglobin of one individual.

Date	Place	Altitude	R.B.C.	Hb%
14.3.36	Gangtok	6,000'	4,710,000	93
25.3.36	Lachen	8,800'	4,950,000	96
29.3.36	Tangu	12,800'	4,885,000	96
6.4.36	Kampa Dzong	15,000'	5,110,000	99
11.4.36	Tengkye Dzong	13,800'	5,420,000	105
21.4.36	Shekkar Dzong	14,000'	5,850,000	116
5.5.36	Camp I	17,700'	6,090,000	120
15.5.36	Camp III	21,200'	6,550,000	129
16.6.36	Base Camp	16,600'	6,800,000	134
27.6.36	Tengkye Dzong	13,800'	6,710,000	129
22.7.36	Bombay	S.L.	6,770,000	134
17.8.36	London	S.L.	6,550,000	129

TABLE VI.

Percentage increase in Haemoglobin

Place	Altitude	C.W.	E.W.	E.E.S.	E.K.	J.L.G.	N.H.	F.S.	J.M.
Gangtok	6,000'	0	0	0	0	0	0	0	0
Lachen	8,800'	3	-	9	-	-	0	-	-
Tangu	12,800'	3	3	9	-	-	-	-	2
Kampa Dzong	15,000'	3	25	25	17	-	-	-	-
Tengkye Dzong	13,800'	13	-	-	17	-	9	-	5
Shekkar Dzong	14,000'	25	-	-	-	-	17	-	-
Base Camp	16,600'	-	-	-	21	21	-	33	43
Camp I	17,700'	29	29	39	-	-	-	-	38
Camp III	21,200'	39	44	39	34	40	-	48	-
Base Camp	16,600'	44	-	-	-	-	-	48	-
Tengkye Dzong	13,800'	39	-	28	-	-	21	-	48
S.S.Mooltan	S.L.	44	48	35	-	40	-	-	38

feet. From these figures the individual variations in response to altitude can be seen, and they can be briefly summarised as follows :

1. The maximum increase in the Hb. content of the blood of any individual was 48 per cent. ; three out of the eight members attained this figure : they were E. W., F. S., and J. M. (In the case of J. M. his polycythæmia was twice interrupted by attacks of malarial fever.)

2. The average maximum increase was 36 per cent.

3. In the cases of E. W., E. E. S., and to a less extent E. K., the percentage increase had become marked at the time of reaching Kampa Dzong (15,000 feet). In the remaining five it was delayed until Tengkye Dzong.

4. In the case of E. E. S. his Hb. level appeared to respond more rapidly than the others' to changes in altitude.

The changes in the blood appear to follow closely the stages in our ascent, as can be seen from the chart, where there are two steep rises in the red cell and hæmoglobin curves at a time when there have been two periods of steep ascent. On the same chart another series of figures have been plotted. These represent changes in the reaction of the urine.

The deep breathing which becomes necessary on going high in order to keep up the oxygen tension in the lungs results in carbon dioxide being washed out of the lungs. But carbon dioxide is an acid gas and its loss from the body tends to leave the blood more alkaline. In order to compensate for this tendency towards alkalosis the kidney excretes more alkali, and the reaction of the blood is restored to normal. Since it is difficult to estimate directly these changes in the reaction of the blood an indirect method of doing so was sought. This was by estimating the reaction of the excretion from the kidneys. On the chart an upward deflection in the curve indicates an increase in the pH or alkalinity of the urine. Two peaks of alkalinity are present. Each one appears at a period of rapid ascent and precedes a rise in the blood and

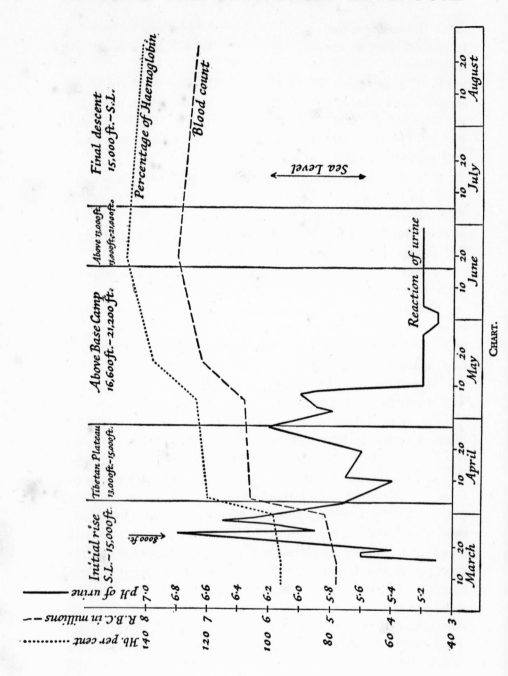

CHART.

hæmoglobin curves. The exact interpretation of these findings is at present difficult and debatable. But this much can be said, that there does appear to be a tendency towards alkalosis at a time when the ascent is rapid and before the blood-count has adapted itself to the new level.

Blueness of the face and lips and lividity of the fingers were noticed at the beginning of the expedition, but curiously enough did not seem to be so pronounced later on. This is remarkable, because people with blood counts which are higher than normal usually become cyanosed or livid more readily. Perhaps we became accustomed to our companions' complexions as one becomes accustomed to new faces.

Muscular Power

Lassitude and a sense of muscular weakness are prominent features of life at great altitudes. They were first noticed at about 12,000 feet on the outward journey, but like the difficulty with the breathing soon passed off as we became acclimatised, only to reappear again when we got to Camp I. Above 20,000 feet there always appeared to be some lassitude. For the first few days at Camp III, for instance, I found that I was always longing to sit down and do nothing. I can only compare the feeling to that sense of weakness which is experienced on first getting up after a long illness. The lassitude, together with a feeling of giddiness, was often particularly noticeable on getting up in the mornings. Although the condition improved after a short time spent at this camp, in my own case at any rate I found that it never disappeared completely. When climbing on the North Col we noticed that the muscles tired more rapidly than at lower altitudes. Indeed, towards the end of our stay on the mountain this lassitude and rapid fatigue on exertion were the only signs of mountain-sickness.

The Mind and Special Senses

At altitudes such as were attained by the 1936 Expedition there appeared to be no diminution in acuity of hearing

231

and vision, though this has been reported on previous expeditions.

There was a very distinct disinclination for serious mental work above about 20,000 feet, which must to some extent be my excuse for not bringing back more information than I have done for this chapter. But apart from this no serious mental changes were noticed. Tempers are said to be irritable at high altitude, but although conditions on the North Col last year were provoking, to say the least of it, we never really quarrelled seriously.

THE DIGESTION

Loss of appetite is a troublesome consequence of life above 20,000 feet. In 1936 appetites were better than usual at Camp III, but even then they were much below normal. During the reconnaissance in 1935 we made a point of writing down the estimated quantities of the various things that were eaten at each meal. On looking at these notes afterwards it was clear that everyone was eating far too little up at the higher camps, although at the time they would stoutly have maintained that they were eating enormously. This failure to take enough nourishment on the part of the climbers was reflected in their weight records. Everyone lost several pounds in weight whenever he went above 20,000 feet for any length of time, and much of this weight was regained on going down to Base Camp for a few days. It is interesting that the porters did not lose weight like the climbers; but this is probably accounted for by the fact that when they are with an expedition they are fed better than normally. This loss of appetite interested me, and I wondered whether it might not be connected with the process of acclimatisation. Is it not possible that the hydrochloric acid which normally should appear in the stomach following a meal is conserved for purposes of neutralisation in the body at high altitudes? For, as we have already mentioned, there is a tendency for the blood to become more alkaline high up, and so any loss of acid from the body, as in the gastric secretion, would still further accentuate this alkalosis; a state of affairs which is the opposite of that required for acclimatisation. If it is true that the hydrochloric acid is retained by the body and not put out during digestion, then the administration of small doses of diluted hydrochloric acid (or even of acid salts such as ammonium chloride) might help to stimulate the appetite.

An attempt was made to detect changes in the acidity of the gastric secretion at two different altitudes by means of a test-meal. The most unpleasant part of the performance of this test is persuading your victim to swallow the stomach tube. It was only fair, therefore, that I should set the example by doing the first test-meal on myself. Wigram, being a student of medicine, volunteered to be the second victim of the experiment. But as he remarked afterwards, the fact that he was given a little icy-cold alcohol down a tube was hardly sufficient compensation for such good nature on his part. In performing a test-meal the subject is made to swallow the stomach tube the first thing in the morning before any food has been taken. The fasting contents of the stomach are then withdrawn and tested for free hydrochloric acid. Immediately afterwards a definite quantity of alcohol (the meal) is run down the tube into the stomach. Then at fifteen-minute intervals samples of the gastric contents are withdrawn and tested for the acid. If no acid appears in the later samples then an injection of histamine is given into the arm, and a few minutes later another sample is withdrawn and tested. This last sample should contain free hydrochloric acid; if it does not the subject is one of those people who cannot secrete the acid at any time. The results of this test performed upon two of the climbers, first of all at Camp I and then at Camp III, are shown in Table VII. It will be noticed that in both cases there was free hydrochloric acid in at least one of the samples following the meal at Camp I,

233

whereas at Camp III there was no acid at any time until histamine had been given.

ACCLIMATISATION

We now come to consider what is the sequence of events in the process of acclimatisation. Breathing becomes deeper

TABLE VII.

Gastric Acidity

	C.B.M.W.		E.W.	
	17,700 ft.	*21,200 ft.*	*17,700 ft.*	*21,200 ft.*
Fasting	o	o	o	o
15 min.	+ +	o	o	o
30 "	+	o	+	o
45 "	+	o	o	o
60 "	+	o		
Histamine	+ +	+ +	+ +	+ +

+ .. *Free Hydrochloric acid present*
o .. *No free acid present*

and more rapid in order to increase the amount of oxygen reaching the alveoli or farthest spaces of the lungs. At first this increased ventilation of the lungs is partly voluntary and for this reason is felt as a difficulty with the breathing. But, as we have already mentioned, the deep breathing causes the acid gas carbon dioxide to be washed out of the lungs, and so tends to make the blood more alkaline. With the loss of carbon dioxide from the circulation, however, the normal stimulus to the breathing mechanism has gone, and so the depth of the breathing dies down again. In order that the deep breathing which is such an advantage to the body at high altitudes may continue, the kidneys after a time learn how to get rid of the excess of alkali from the blood, and thus its reaction is restored to normal. It is in this way that the loss of the acid gas carbon dioxide is compensated for

234

and the breathing allowed to go on at the new level. In addition to this mechanism there is the one whereby the number of red corpuscles is increased in the blood. At first this increase is probably brought about by contraction of the spleen. When this organ contracts red cells are squeezed out from its meshes into the general circulation as water is squeezed from a sponge. A method such as this can obviously be used to increase the number of red cells in the circulation quickly. At a later stage it seems likely that there is actually increased formation of red cells by the red bone marrow, which appears to be stimulated into activity by lack of oxygen. These are the principal means by which the body can adapt itself to the changed state of the atmosphere met with at high altitudes. To what extent these changes are taking place during the climbing of Mount Everest you have in some measure been able to see for yourselves from these pages.

DETERIORATION

Before leaving the subject of acclimatisation in connection with the climbing of Mount Everest something must be said about the deterioration in the physical condition of the climbers which is alleged to set in above a certain altitude. As a result of experiments with animals which were kept at low atmospheric pressures for a long time, Argyll-Campbell and Sir Leonard Hill came to the conclusion that it was useless to attempt to acclimatise to altitudes greater than 21,000 feet by staying for prolonged periods at the higher camps on the mountain. Above 21,000 feet their animals eventually died, and when examined were found to have dilated hearts and fatty degeneration of all their organs. It is possible to argue, of course, that their results with animals need not necessarily have any bearing upon what happens in the human organism under similar circumstances. But it is interesting that after the 1933 expedition it was decided that in future the climbers

235

ought not to stay in the camps above Camp III (21,200 feet) for longer than is absolutely necessary. In 1936, after the first attempt to get above the North Col the whole party retreated to Camp I, having lived at Camp III (21,200 feet) for a period of eleven days on that occasion. Morris and Smijth-Windham were both at Camp I when we came down, and they told me afterwards that we all looked thin and ill when we came into camp. It was also remarkable how we at once began to eat with our accustomed appetites at this camp (17,700 feet). At Camp III most of us had been worried with sore throats, but on going down to lower levels they improved remarkably. The increase in the basal pulse rate which was observed in most of the climbers whenever they went above 17,700 feet has already been mentioned.

To summarise, the evidence which points to deterioration taking place at about 21,000 feet is : loss of appetite, with attendant wasting and loss of weight, which is rapidly regained on going to lower levels ; an increase in the basal pulse frequency which is only present above 17,700 feet ; and in animal experiments the inability to prevent them from ultimately dying with fatty degeneration of their organs.

Have we any evidence that acclimatisation is still going on at 21,000 feet in spite of the fact that deterioration in the physical condition may have started ? To begin with it should be mentioned that we all felt much less distress on our second and third visits to Camp III. The only other evidence is to be derived from the blood counts. Between the time of our first visit to Camp III and our final return to the Base Camp at the end of the expedition there was in most cases a further increase in the red cells and the hæmoglobin-content of the blood. So this much at least can be said, that our later stays at 21,200 feet did not prevent the blood count from continuing to rise. This finding appears to be in agreement with some observations which were made recently by Matthews in the Andes.

Oxygen

BY C. B. M. WARREN

THE OXYGEN PROBLEM

WHEN a man goes to a high altitude he has to breathe an atmosphere which contains less oxygen than there is at sea-level, though the proportion of oxygen to nitrogen remains the same : that is, oxygen still forms 20 per cent. of the atmosphere. What has altered is the barometric pressure, so that the pressure exerted by each of the gases composing the atmosphere has altered also. Oxygen passes from the air in the lungs into the blood which is circulating through those organs as a result of the pressure exerted by the gas, and the amount which is taken up by the blood depends upon this pressure. If the partial pressure of oxygen in the breathed air is reduced, as it is at high altitudes (and in low-pressure chambers at sea-level), then less of it is taken up, the blood leaves the lungs less fully saturated with the gas and so has less to deliver to the tissues. Enough oxygen must be supplied to the tissues if their life and function are to be maintained. It is lack of oxygen to the tissues which gives rise to the symptoms of mountain-sickness and which calls forth the adjustments which are known as acclimatisation.

If a sample of blood is exposed to air containing oxygen at a known partial pressure it becomes partly saturated with the oxygen, i.e. a definite percentage of the hæmoglobin

237

present in this blood becomes converted into oxyhæmoglobin. If the partial pressure is increased the blood will become more fully saturated ; but if it is reduced the saturation will become less complete. A curve can be constructed which will show the relationship between partial pressures of oxygen and the percentage saturation of the blood. This is known as the Dissociation Curve of Oxyhæmoglobin in Blood. On such a curve Dr. Kellas has plotted the calculated alveolar oxygen tensions for altitudes corresponding to a number of well-known mountains (Fig. 1). The curve

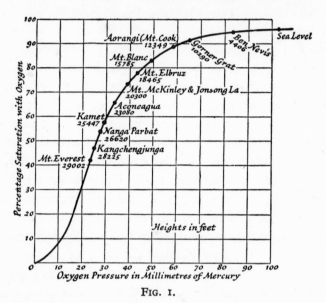

FIG. 1.

shows that up to about 10,000 feet the blood is almost fully saturated with oxygen, but at about 15,000 feet the percentage saturation is beginning to fall. By the time 20,000 feet is reached the curve is steepening rapidly, and with every 1,000 feet rise above this altitude there is a correspondingly rapid fall in the percentage saturation. At a height corresponding to the summit of Mount Everest the degree of saturation is only about 40 per cent. From a consideration of the curve it seems clear that the difficulties in ascending above 20,000 feet will increase considerably ; an observation which is borne out by the accounts of all those who have come back from the higher camps on Mount Everest. So that although the climbers have already struggled to 28,000 feet on the mountain there is no reason to suppose that because they have done so they are bound to be able to climb the last 1,000 feet without using oxygen.

This brings us to a consideration of what happens when the partial pressure of oxygen in the breathed air falls beyond certain limits. Symptoms which are directly attributable to the diminished pressure are met with. For instance, if an airman goes rapidly to a great altitude he loses consciousness without warning. The same thing happens if he is put into a closed chamber at sea-level from which the air is rapidly exhausted. In 1875 Tissandier and his companions made their famous ascent in a balloon from Paris. At 26,500 feet Tissandier lost consciousness. He recovered, to find the balloon descending, but his two companions were dead. It has been suggested that such an accident might happen on Everest, but I do not think it is likely when we consider what happens if the oxygen pressure is reduced more slowly. With a more gradual onset of oxygen-lack the train of symptoms is as follows. The intellect and the senses become dulled without the subject being aware of what is happening. Visual acuity is diminished and sensation impaired. The subject may be in danger and not realise it ; or he may realise his danger and yet be incapable of deciding upon a line of action that would put him in safety. Eventually there is paralysis of the legs and arms, and ultimately loss of consciousness. On the extreme heights of Everest the climber is likely to be brought to a standstill by the fatigue in his muscles (or if you like by actual paralysis) before losing consciousness. He would, however, be exposed to dangers due to mental impairment, such as failure to realise the danger of his position and carelessness in his movements on difficult ground. Apart from the fact that it may not be possible to reach such an altitude as 29,002 feet without using oxygen, I think that the dangers consequent upon mental impairment form the strongest argument in favour of its use on the last lap to the summit.

Oxygen Apparatus and its Use

Whatever type of apparatus is used, its object is to increase the pressure of oxygen in the alveolar spaces of the lungs. This object can be achieved in one of two ways. In the original types of apparatus the outside air was breathed from a bag to which oxygen was added from a cylinder at a fixed rate. The disadvantages of this method are that much of the oxygen is wasted by being expired from the dead spaces of the lungs into the outside air ; that there is an uncomfortable drying of the throat ; and that moisture and heat are lost from the body in the breath. Furthermore, when the ventilation of the lungs increases as it does during exercise the partial pressure of oxygen in the bag will fall. That this apparatus is wasteful of oxygen can be seen from the fact that in order to raise the partial pressure of oxygen in the air at 30,000 feet from 53 mm. of mercury to 110 mm. it is calculated that oxygen must be supplied at the rate of about 9 litres a minute. A partial pressure of 110 mm. of mercury corresponds to an altitude of about 12,000 feet, so that to bring a climber down to this level it would be necessary to supply him with oxygen at that rate. But the body only uses oxygen at the rate of approximately half a litre per minute when at rest and up to 2 litres per minute during exercise, as can be seen from the following table, which was worked out by Zuntz on Monte Rosa. An apparatus of this type was taken by the expedition in 1936. It contained two cylinders of " Vibrax " steel, each holding 750 litres of oxygen, and the reduction valve was set to deliver 6 litres a minute, though it was capable of adjustment to deliver any other quantity. With such an apparatus, then, the supply was 1,500 litres, and this flowing at the rate of 6 litres a minute would last just over four hours. Its weight was approximately 30 lb.

TABLE VIII.

	Oxygen required per minute
Sea level at rest, fasting...............	233 cub. c.
Monte Rosa do.	260 ,,
Ascending glacier on Monte Rosa...	1329 ,,

In another type of apparatus, instead of air being breathed to which oxygen is added, oxygen alone is breathed and the carbon dioxide in the expired breath is absorbed by passing it through a canister containing soda-lime. The breathing circuit is completely enclosed, so that nothing is exhaled into the outside atmosphere. Such an apparatus is similar to that used in rescue work down coal mines and in submarine-escaping apparatus. Its advantages would seem to be that no oxygen is wasted, that heat and moisture are not lost by breathing out into the external atmosphere, and that the pressure of oxygen breathed is the same as that of the external atmosphere (i.e. approximately 250 mm. of mercury at 30,000 feet), a pressure which is well above the partial pressure of oxygen in the atmosphere at sea-level. The apparatus, therefore, should theoretically bring the climber at 30,000 feet down to sea-level conditions. The oxygen-breathing gear was designed and made for us to use on the mountain by Siebe Gorman, the well-known firm of submarine engineers. Two sizes were taken. The smaller of the two weighed 25 lb. and carried a cylinder, made of "Vibrax" steel, of 500 litres' capacity. Supposing the rate of consumption of oxygen when climbing on Everest was 2 litres a minute, then the supply would last just over four hours. The larger apparatus weighed

R

35 lb. and carried a cylinder of 750 litres' capacity, and on the same basis would provide oxygen for a period of six hours. The reduction valve in the respirator was actually set to deliver half a litre a minute, or the amount of oxygen required by the body when at rest ; but by means of an automatic release valve a greater supply could be obtained from the cylinder as required during exercise.

The re-breathing type of apparatus has been criticised on the following grounds : that there is no advantage in bringing the climber down to sea-level conditions, and that such a change may even do harm ; that soda-lime absorbs moisture, so that there is a loss of fluids from the body through the breath ; and that nobody could tolerate having a mask over his face at 28,000 feet. In answer to these criticisms I would first of all point out that if the increase in the blood count is really one of the more important indications of acclimatisation then it seems unlikely that by breathing oxygen for a few hours on end acclimatisation would be seriously affected, for, as we know, it is a matter of weeks and not days before the blood count begins to fall after reaching sea-level. Then, with regard to the moisture which might be absorbed by the soda-lime, I understand that many of the patent absorbing materials, such as "Protosorb," which was used in the apparatus under consideration, are practically non-hygroscopic. And lastly, as far as the intolerance of a mask over the face is concerned, the reply is that with the proper oxygen supply given by this apparatus the climber would not be at 28,000 feet but at sea-level. A mask would indeed even be an advantage, since it would protect the face from the wind and allow it to be muffled up to the eyes with clothing.

The re-breathing respirator was tested both at home in the low-pressure chamber and in Tibet on the mountain. The trials at home were not as thorough as was desirable on account of the limited time at our disposal, and those on the mountain were not made at a sufficiently great altitude to give us any information of great value. But in order to find out what could be done in the apparatus, Shipton took it down to Box Hill and made several ascents of a steep slope in it. At the Box Hill trial he had the apparatus on for an hour and forty minutes in all. During that time he ascended 1,750 feet in the course of $67\frac{1}{2}$ minutes' climbing, so he was climbing at the rate of 1,550 feet an hour, which is very fast. The average angle of the slope on which the trial was made was measured, and worked out at 32 degrees. The surface was wet chalk. The amount of oxygen used during the hour and forty minutes of the trial was just under 250 litres, or half the supply available. A few days later I went to the same slope to test another apparatus, and so had an opportunity of seeing it. I came to the conclusion that a surface of wet chalk set at a steep angle is about the most diabolical place imaginable. I have never wasted so much energy in stepping up only to slide down again as I did in the course of an hour's climbing that afternoon. On the top of it all the apparatus was a trial one and was not working as smoothly as it might have done; in consequence the unfortunate subject of the experiment became half asphyxiated and developed a splitting headache.

The oxygen apparatus was used once or twice in the course of the expedition in order to try it out and to train people in how to use it. This training is most important, and until the climbers can be persuaded to devote a certain amount of time to getting used to the gear and moving about in it, we shall get no further with the oxygen problem. On the slopes of the North Col I climbed in it for a short time and found that I could advance much faster and without the fatigue which normally is experienced at that altitude. It was worn by several members of the party to make ascents of over an hour's duration above Base Camp at 16,600 feet, and no one suffered any ill effects when it was taken off. But the most convincing trial was done at Tangu. Here, before any of us were properly acclimatised, I used the apparatus to climb for at least 1,000 feet up the hillside behind the bungalow. And yet with 35 lb. on my back I was able to climb just about twice as fast as two of my companions who were going without it.

The question which arises is : How should the apparatus be used on the mountain ? Personally I think that to try to make the ascent using oxygen from below Camp V would be impractical and dangerous. I think that it should be used on the last lap only, and then only by a specially trained oxygen party. It would be quite useless and dangerous to let those who feel " anti-oxygen " have a closed type of apparatus up at Camp VI to use in the event of their failure to climb the mountain without it. It has been suggested that oxygen might be used in camp and at night time only, in order to do away with deterioration. But if one really believes, as do some of us who consider the matter from the physiological as well as the mountaineering point of view, that it *may* be impossible for a man to reach 29,002 feet without using oxygen, then such a method of administration achieves nothing towards the attainment of the summit.

A last point which requires consideration is whether a six-hour supply will be sufficient to carry the climber from the last camp to the summit and down again. Shipton has estimated that without oxygen the last 1,000 feet will take about sixteen hours up and down. Now even with 30 lb. on one's back it should be possible to climb at the rate of 500 feet an hour over quite difficult ground when at moderate altitudes without oxygen. We know that this can be done in the Alps, and in the Himalayas people have climbed up difficult rocks with loads of 20 lb. on their backs. If we can produce an oxygen apparatus, then, which will bring the climber down to sea-level when on Everest, even though it does weigh 35 lb. and has only a six-hour supply, he should be able to get to the top and down again within this time.

Since the return of the 1936 Expedition some more trials have been made with oxygen, this time for climbing in the Swiss Alps. These tests have satisfied us that even steep and difficult rocks can be climbed when the apparatus is being worn. Furthermore, the average rate of climbing throughout one of these ascents was as near as possible 800 feet an hour, a speed which suggests that the summit of Mount Everest is within reach with the present oxygen apparatus.

Wireless

BY W. R. SMIJTH-WINDHAM

WHETHER it is proper to invoke the aid of science in an attempt to climb a Himalayan peak is invariably provocative of lively discussion among mountaineers. It will therefore be avoided in this account, where it is merely necessary to recall briefly the occasions upon which wireless has actually been used for such a purpose. From the little information available, it appears that Herr Dyrenfurth, the leader of the International Expedition to Kangchenjunga in 1930, was the first to realise the possibilities of wireless, and took with him a receiver. Even seven years ago, however, wireless components were so fragile that it is hardly surprising to hear that the set reached its destination in small pieces.

It was a big step forward when the 1933 Expedition to Mount Everest took not only two wireless officers, namely Lieut. E. C. Thompson, R. Signals, and myself, but also much costly equipment, with the idea of establishing two-way communication between Darjeeling and Base Camp, Base Camp and Camp III, and Camps III and IV. It was an ambitious programme, for it was not known what would be the effects of altitude and climate, to say nothing of the great barrier of the Himalaya lying across the main link. But good results were obtained.

In 1934 the ill-fated Nanga Parbat Expedition used wire-

246

less, but it is evident that they had learnt no lesson from Everest in 1933, for they had no communication with the outside world, nor with their highest camps. Whether a timely weather forecast would have prevented the disaster that overtook them it is impossible to say, but when in October 1935 I heard that the 1936 Everest Expedition was taking wireless, for which I was to be responsible, I determined that, among the many risks that an assault party must face, lack of the best and most up-to-date weather information should find no place.

On December 3 I landed from India, and soon paid my first visit to the Royal Geographical Society. After being led up three flights of stairs—the lift seldom worked—I was shown into the " Everest " room. An impression of the scene before me, one that was to become very familiar in the next two months, merits a short description. Against the right-hand wall stood a table, at one end of which would be the resourceful Mrs. Wade, busy on her typewriter, and probably chuckling inwardly over the latest item of unpublishable Everest gossip. Beyond her would be Ruttledge, engaged in an interminable telephone conversation about tinned food. The top of the long white table which occupied the centre of the room was always covered with a jumble of letters, photographs, and other oddments amongst which Shipton would be searching. On the small remaining floor space were heaped an assortment of ice-axes, crampons and the rival products of Carter and Lawrie, awaiting selection. Last, but not least, a small window-sill displayed a fine show of sectioned, and already ancient, preserved meats.

Staking my claim at the far end of the central table—not that it made any difference during my absence—I started the work of organising the wireless side of the expedition. *Carte blanche* to buy what was needed was backed by a guarantee of £500 from the Committee. My experience of 1933 and any technical advice that might be obtainable were to be my

247

guides. A chronicle of the next two months would only induce a sense of bewilderment such as I felt at the time. Here I will only sketch the plan of action, for on that depended the selection of equipment, and then describe and comment on the equipment actually chosen.

The Signal Plan

As already stated, my main object was to ensure that weather forecasts, originating at Alipore Observatory, should reach the highest camp in the shortest possible time. For this purpose it would have been best to set up the main station at the expedition's climbing headquarters, Camp III, but even though it might have been possible to transport all the apparatus up the glacier, and to get the charging engine to function efficiently at such an altitude, the risk of Camp III being evacuated during a spell of bad weather made such a scheme unwise. Camp II was to be uninhabited, so Camp I, which, though retaining its old number to avoid confusion, was to be used as the Base Camp, seemed to be the best place for my station. Being thus inevitably separated from the leader, my task would simply consist of relaying messages in both directions between India and Camp III.

Taking India first, the only safe course was to establish a wireless station at Darjeeling, which, besides being nearer than other suggested alternatives such as Meerut and Jubbulpore, had the great advantage of being the only place from which we knew that reliable signals could be received; an enterprise like this was already too full of unavoidable hazards. Through the good offices of the Government of India, and particularly of the Signal Officer-in-Chief, a portion of the Gymnasium at Jalapahar was lent for use as a wireless station, and the services of two N.C.O.'s as operators. Of the latter, Sergeant W. J. Frawley, Indian Army Ordnance Corps, was seconded by the C.O.O., Rawalpindi Arsenal, at my special request, as he had been one of the two Royal Signals N.C.O.'s who had run the Darjeeling Station with such success in 1933 ; the other, L/Cpl. B. Maudsley, Royal Signals, came from my previous unit, " A " Corps Signals, Rawalpindi. Thus the team spirit was well catered for, and if in these pages the Darjeeling station is seldom referred to, it is because it functioned, under this pair, so smoothly and efficiently, that it was soon dismissed from my mind as a possible source of anxiety.

Since the party, apart from myself, included no one with wireless experience, the problem of communication forward to Camp III was less easy. At first glance, a field telephone seemed an ideal solution, but difficulties of laying and maintenance, together with a prohibitive estimated cost of £150, caused the idea to be abandoned. From a wireless point of view, the prospect was hardly pleasing. The direct line between the two camps is badly cut up by offshoots of the North Peak, so that there was little hope of communication by ground wave, while at the short range of six miles it seemed unlikely that good sky wave signals would be possible except in good conditions of the ionosphere. Considerations of portability and simplicity of operation limited the power of the Camp III transmitter so that the chances of being able to use radio-telephony were slender. Clearly there had to be a trained Morse operator at Camp III. To this end Gavin was enrolled and was given as many opportunities as possible of becoming familiar with the apparatus. He, with Ruttledge, Humphreys, and Oliver, was made to attend Morse classes, an occupation remarkably lacking in popularity. The success with which Gavin discharged his unfamiliar duties will appear later.

In 1933 telephonic communication had been arranged between Camps III and IV, which had involved my supervising the laying of a pair of field cables up to the Col. This was uneconomical. The presence of a Signal Officer or other tyro above Base Camp puts an additional burden on the shoulders of the porters, upsets the commissariat, and may even necessitate his being convoyed by climbers who would otherwise be resting. This year I resolved that nothing would lure me above Camp I. Moreover Camp IV was, tactically, only one of the chain of camps above the North Col. During the course of an attempt, the attacking pair would not profit by a weather forecast, no matter how recently issued, that could get no higher than Camp IV. They must take with them, to every camp, light simple equipment that would allow them to keep in radio-telephonic touch with Camp III. Although this principle was only assimilated with difficulty by some, I am convinced of its soundness : it is logical that if wireless is to be used for obtaining information, it must be used right up to the highest camp.

So much for the " Signal Plan." Owing partly to the short time at my disposal, and partly to whichever of the recent political crises was current at the time, I had in some cases to modify my requirements, and take what apparatus was available. Thanks to the enthusiastic co-operation of the makers concerned, I was able to collect the following equipment :

1.   NORMAN LYON 175 C.C. MOTOR GENERATOR

The charging engine was to be operated at a height of 18,000 feet, where the barometer normally is under 15 inches, that is, about half the figure at sea-level. A normally aspirated engine loses power at great heights owing to rarefaction of the air. Mr. L. Mantell, of Solex Ltd., who kindly gave me his advice, put the matter neatly when he said, " What you want to burn is oxygen ; any fool can burn petrol." He strongly discouraged the complication of supercharging, and recommended making up the loss by an increase of compression ratio. In theory a ratio of about 10 to 1 would be required, and this immediately ruled out a side-valve engine. I got into touch with Messrs. Arthur Lyon, whose single-cylinder o.h.v. engine seemed suitable for modification. The com-

250

pression ratio was raised to 8 to 1, retaining a safe working clearance between piston and valves. Coil ignition was substituted for magneto, in deference to vivid recollections of engine swinging in 1933, and the induction pipe was specially lagged to keep it warm. A 12–16 volt, 280-watt shunt-wound dynamo was mounted on the same aluminium bed-plate. Messrs. C. C. Wakefield, having been consulted regarding lubrication, kindly presented 2 gallons of "Patent Castrol Z." The whole, when packed with spares, divided conveniently into $1\frac{1}{2}$ animal loads.

2. ACCUMULATORS

Satisfaction in 1933 led me to go again to the Young Accumulator Company, who kindly presented six 4-volt units of about 90 ampere-hours capacity.

3. CHARGING SWITCHBOARD

This item was built, to my design, by Messrs. Arthur Lyon. The object of the board was to enable two 12-volt accumulator banks to be charged, discharged and metered independently, if need be, or in parallel, by means of switch-gear. It was conveniently mounted, blackboard-wise, on a small easel.

4. BASE CAMP AND DARJEELING TRANSMITTERS

Consideration of the maximum load that could reasonably be handled by the accumulator bank showed that some fifty watts might be put into the aerial by an efficient transmitter on C.W. The use of R/T would have involved a large reduction of the aerial power, and might also have been pre-judicial to secrecy. Two C.W. transmitters were therefore designed and built by Messrs. Stratton of Birmingham. Briefly, they consisted of a crystal-controlled pentode oscillator driving a TZ. 05/20 triode as a neutralised power amplifier, keyed in the grid circuit, and inductively coupled to the aerial. In the case of the transmitter for Darjeeling, where A.C. mains are available, power supply was derived from a " power pack," while the Base Camp transmitter was provided with a rotary converter. Crystal frequencies of 7010, 7020, 7030 and 3720 kc/s were chosen so that in the event of trouble with the Darjeeling transmitter, it might be possible to co-operate with amateurs.

5. BASE CAMP AND DARJEELING RECEIVERS

A special design being unnecessary, two Eddystone " Homelander " receivers were bought. They are 4-valve battery sets, with a built-in loudspeaker. In addition, Sergt. Frawley used a home-made receiver of his own at Darjeeling, with headphones.

6. GLACIER SETS

In working from Camp III to Camp I a very simple and portable installation was essential, and eventually it was found that Marconi S.P.3A equipment suited admirably. The whole outfit is designed to be readily portable without packing, and is very quickly assembled or dismantled. Both transmitter and receiver draw their power from L.T. accumulators and dry H.T. batteries, and communication can be by R/T or C.W. One spare transmitter, for use at Camp I, was ordered in the hope that it might be possible to economise in power input, compared with that of the big transmitter, should conditions be good or should the charging apparatus give trouble. Apart from the main question as to whether sets of such small power could communicate over the route, the difficulties of which have already been mentioned, the only anxiety was lest the accumulators at Camp III should freeze. By relaying charged spares up the glacier, it was hoped that no cell need be discharged to a point at which freezing would be likely. Had we known the sort of season in store for us, we might have spared ourselves the worry.

7. THE HIGH-ALTITUDE 5-METRE SETS

It was clear that the only hope of obtaining sets light enough for the high camps lay in the use of ultra-high frequencies. Fortunately the formation of the upper part of the mountain is convenient in that it provides those direct paths between camps that very short waves demand. Advice from officers of the R.E. and Signals Board sent me to Messrs. Stratton, who had just finished a promising design. Six sets were ordered. As these sets made a notable contribution to Everest technique, a few details may not be out of place. Each complete station comprised :

1 5-metre " transreceiver " in an aluminium case, with the following controls : tuning condenser, Send-Off-Receive switch, filament rheostat and regenerator control. For sending, the two valves functioned as R.F. oscillator and modulator ; for receiving the same two valves acted as super-regenerative detector and L.F. amplifier.

1 Box containing H.T. and L.T. dry batteries.

1 Box containing headphones, microphone and battery connecting cable.

1 Half-wave aerial, made of thin aluminium tubing in three sections, fitting together, with a matched feeder soldered to the centre section.

3 Ex-W.D. haversacks, fitted with clips for attachment to the aerial stays. Filled with boulders, these made excellent anchors for the stays.

The whole outfit weighed 28½ lb., an easy porter load to Camp V. As the sets for Camps VI and VII were likely to have few working hours, their batteries were reduced in size so that their total weight only amounted to 15 lb.—or one porter load at that height.

So much for the main items of equipment. In addition there were the numerous accessories—meters, fuses, tools, spares, wire, to mention only a few—any one of which may make the difference between success and failure when the nearest repair shop is 300 miles away. To weigh future peace of mind against extra weight and expense was often a nice problem. It was, of course, impossible to carry sufficient spares to insure against risk of breakage on the march, but careful packing could minimise this. It seemed wisest to issue detailed instructions regarding the methods of packing required (my 1933 experience was useful here), and to include such spares as might be required in the normal course of wear and tear. The considerations affecting the design of a wireless box are different from those governing the construction of an ordinary expedition store box. The store box, containing perhaps tinned food, should be built so lightly that it is on the point of disintegration on arrival at Base Camp. It must be reasonably thief-proof, but need not be water-proof. A wireless box, on the other hand, must be capable of completing the return journey; its lid must be screwed, not nailed, to permit of investigation of those ominous rattles that develop in the best-packed cases, and, if the screws are to grip after half-a-dozen such openings, a hard wood must be used. This information was given to the manufacturers with the request that they should pack their own apparatus, in the hope that their interest that their products should reach Everest undamaged might ensure a supervision that there was not time to give personally. This plan worked admirably; in particular the Marconi packing department evolved reinforced plywood boxes many of which could have completed the round journey a second time.

As February 7, the date of my departure, drew near, an

ear-splitting roar in the Solex works in Marylebone Road announced that the charging engine was having its carburettor tuned. Although it was found impossible artificially to impose high-altitude conditions upon the engine, more than twice the required power was being developed under sea-level conditions. If this component, my foundation stone, was going to function in similar fashion at Camp I, prospects were rosy.

And so to Delhi, where I was assisted by Captain W. A. Scott, R. Signals, in the conduct of various negotiations, and thence to Calcutta, where members of the Himalayan Club do everything in their power to smooth the path of successive expeditions. In my case there were accumulators to be charged, the despatch of a supply of petrol to be arranged, and divers last-minute purchases to be made. I also paid a visit to Dr. Roy at the Alipore Meteorological Station, to facilitate our wireless liaison later on.

At Darjeeling I found Ruttledge, Morris, and Wyn Harris busy selecting sirdars and porters, and was greeted by the familiar faces of Jemadar Lachiman Singh, Karma Paul and Nursang. The expedition was becoming a reality. Mr. and Mrs. Wrangham-Hardy, to whom Thompson and I owed so much in 1933, were there with their customary welcome, and " What's yours ? " But beyond paving the way for Sergt. Frawley and L/Cpl. Maudsley, there was no excuse for lingering in Darjeeling, and news had come through of the arrival of my boxes at Kalimpong. Those who have read previous accounts will need no introduction to Mr. and Mrs. Odling, in whose visitors' book are the names of every party. I found myself firmly taken in hand on account of a mild attack of dysentery picked up in the plains, dieted on arrowroot, and cured. Open house was kept for all of us ; I say " house " advisedly, for in my experience of India this is the only building I know to which the more usual term " bungalow," with all its implications, does not apply. A pleasant relaxation it was after days spent in the dusty " go-down " in which our stores were collecting.

By the time Kalimpong is reached a certain weight is off the signal officer's mind. During the voyage there has been plenty of time to remember things hitherto forgotten, and, given luck and a long purse, these omissions have been rectified in India. From Kalimpong onwards one is committed, and descends with relief from the theoretical to the practical. A rough knowledge of carpentry and arithmetic is all that is necessary. Here a box, far too large to go on a mule, has to be made into two ; there an already decrepit one demands repair. All must be weighed and numbered, and all painted with a blue and white band to assist identification *en route*.

By this time porters were available for odd jobs. The Darjeeling men, among whom were several old friends, are quite used to an Englishman's Urdu, though a flavouring of Nepali helps. They are so keen that one's efforts are spent, not in encouraging, but in curbing their enthusiasm, and directing it into useful channels. As transport animals are hard to come by in March it had been decided to relay the baggage as far as Kampa Dzong. Most members of the party would motor to Gangtok, and would march with their personal baggage from there. I decided to adhere to a principle adopted in 1933, that the signal officer must never let his own store boxes out of his sight. This policy is seldom popular with the transport officers, but it is perhaps justifiable on the grounds that the signal officer is the only member of the expedition whose reputation is virtually carried on the back of an animal. If the apparatus is to arrive intact it must be carefully loaded at the start of each march, supervised *en route*, and checked at the end. To those who have not seen Tibetan transport conditions the importance of this may be made clear by the following incident of 1933. We had arrived at Chiblung, and had pitched camp in a wind more bitter than usual. On checking our stores Thompson and I missed four cases of Aviation petrol, and presently, after searching the camp, we found a small group of drivers cooking their " tsampa " over a fire nicely shielded from the wind by full petrol tins. They had failed to realise the difference between these and their normal cargoes of wool bales, or perhaps salt. On Sunday, March 14, I took the road to Gangtok by myself, with thirty-six animals carrying wireless gear, and quite a number of others whose loads also required supervision, to say nothing of six ammunition boxes tightly packed with silver rupees. No leg muscles can be too fit for that long pull up from Dikchu to the Tibetan frontier, 16,000 feet in about sixty miles, and the satisfaction of getting into walking trim in good time outweighed the discomforts of the hot, dusty road. I was met on the outskirts of Gangtok by Gavin and Oliver, with suitable refreshment, and escorted via the Dak Bungalow, where half the party was installed, to the Residency, where the remaining six were the guests of Mr. Gould. Little remained to be done, save to arrange for the construction of web carrying straps for the charged accumulators. Six intelligent-looking porters were detailed for their transport, and were given demonstrations of the potency of acid in the hope that the batteries would be treated with respect on the march. As it turned out our total casualties were one hole burnt in a coat, an improvement on 1933, when one day I found to my horror that a metal funnel had been placed across the terminals of a cell, and was firmly welded thereto by the resultant short circuit. Gavin and I unpacked and tested the 5-metre sets, with satisfactory results. Finding that the signals would go " round the corner " even less than we had hoped, we decided to lengthen all the feeders before reaching the mountain, in order to ensure that the aerials could be well sited.

On March 19, having bade a reluctant farewell to the hospitalities of Gangtok, we started the march proper, and on March 24 an entry in my diary reads, " Lachen—found the

S

engine and rotary transformer vilely packed. Re-packed these and other boxes in the hope that they will arrive at Camp I intact, but this seems to be optimistic." In view of my earlier remarks, I should add that it had not been possible to get either of these packed by their makers.

A halt of five days was made at Tangu for purposes of acclimatisation, giving a good opportunity for further experiment with the 5-metre sets, and for instilling my faith in them into the others. Two were unpacked, and on March 27 I ascended the hill behind the bungalow with one set and my servant, Pasang " Picture," so christened when he had carried the camera of the Nanga Parbat Expedition. (If his German friends see this they will be glad to know that, although his hands are badly disfigured as a result of his frost-bite, he appears to suffer no inconvenience in the use of his fingers.) We immediately established first-class communication with the other set, operated by Gavin and Wyn Harris in the bungalow compound. The latter conceived the brilliant idea of giving orders to Pasang Picture to perform various gymnastics on the sky-line above, and even in the head-phones I could hear the roars of applause of the crowd assembled below. After that there was never a lack of volunteers to help to carry the wireless.

The remainder of the march calls for little comment. The daily anxieties of the road look unimpressive on paper, though they were very real at the time. In fact, during the crossing of the twin Bahman Dopte pass beyond Tengkye Dzong, having seen no less than seventeen of my loads unshipped, I grew so despondent that I wrote to Sergt. Frawley, saying that if he never heard me calling he would know why. By the time we made our last major halt at Shekar I was very surprised, on unpacking the Eddystone receiver, to find it none the worse. That evening, a full audience listened to the Empire News from GSH. We had been out of touch with civilisation for over a month, and expected something fresh.

But, amid hoots of derision, the same familiar fare was dished up once more—trouble over demilitarised zones, acrimony over the bombing of Red Cross units, a general election in France, riots in Madrid. I was told to see that better programmes were available in future.

Fortified by the thought that the equipment might work after all, we soon completed the last lap to Base Camp, and April 26 found Gavin and myself busy preparing to make Camp I on the morrow. It had been decided that we should go ahead with all the wireless gear, and sufficient food for two men for six weeks. This done, Camp I would cease to be a drain on transport resources, and all porters would be available for use by the climbing party.

Next day, having finished breakfast, and sat for the customary group, Gavin and I assembled and loaded up the Camp I party. Only five of us were to remain there—ourselves, Gulme and Pasang Picture, our servants, and Pasang Sherpa, who had been promoted head cook on the dismissal of Chung Chung. There were fifty-eight porters carrying wireless (some indivisible loads weighed 80 lb. apiece, but were shouldered without a murmur), twenty more carried equipment for Camp I, and the remainder made up the first " carry " of expedition stores. Excitement was noticeable on all sides ; the porters shared our good spirits. Though the splendid morning may have been in part responsible, it cannot be denied that Everest, perfectly framed by the valley walls, standing as it were alone upon a stage, encouraged us to play our parts. Soon after noon we arrived ; within the next three hours we had laid out the camp, leaving the remaining daylight in which to get ahead of our unpacking programme. Once the sun went down further work was impossible, and my diary records that " at 6 p.m. we had dinner excellently cooked by Pasang Sherpa. Only five of us here to-night, but we are enjoying ourselves immensely." The following morning was spent doing a top overhaul of the engine, which was full

259

of dust. Just before lunch we got it going, to the huge delight of a crowd of Sola Khombu porters who had waited behind to see the fun. Many of them can never have seen an engine before, and the soft " ooh " of the hillman on whose comprehension a new idea has dawned is very well worth hearing. I fear, however, that the crisp note of the unsilenced exhaust may have been wasted on them, though to us it spelt a healthiness for which we gave thanks to those who had taken so much trouble in London. The jet settings were admirable, and as soon as we put the accumulator bank on charge, a short full-throttle run showed that over 300 watts were available, that is, more than 50 per cent. above requirements. The open exhaust had been specified to enable me to hear the engine running wherever I might be in the camp, for sound travels badly in a rarefied atmosphere, but such pessimism was found to be quite unjustified, for the engine scarcely missed a beat in the next six weeks.

That afternoon we started the tedious job of filling the Camp III accumulators prior to their initial charge, and we ended by unpacking the Homelander receiver and listening to the Empire News.

By this time VUF, the Darjeeling station, had started working to a prearranged time-table, and at 8.30 a.m. on April 29 we heard him calling, though our Eddystone transmitter had yet to be unpacked, and its aerial erected. The latter was straightforward enough, for on the dimensions and position of the aerial the layout of the camp had largely depended. It was to be a Hertz half-wave aerial, voltage-fed, and slung between 30-foot masts at right angles to the line to Darjeeling, which, I had reckoned, would coincide with the line of the valley in the vicinity of Camp I. The waves had a clear exit over the Kharta-phu group of peaks, which were too distant to present any serious obstacle. The rotary transformer had been damaged, but a cable home from Lachen had enabled spare brush-holders to be sent to me by

260

air-mail. By the time that these had been fitted, and a broken resistor replaced, the Darjeeling station had finished calling for April 30. I had the rest of the day in which to make things ship-shape, while Gavin occupied himself constructing his famous signpost and Belisha beacon.

On the following morning, May 1, my diary records, " Woke late and missed breakfast, but was compensated by getting through to VUF at 8.20 a.m. on 7020 kc/s (43 metres) and sent two messages announcing our arrival." It was excellent news to be able to report to the others when they moved up from Base Camp later in the day, as well as taking a great weight off my mind. Now that the risks of the march were behind the rest would be plain sailing.

Nevertheless there was still plenty to do. As the transmitter did not like the first aerial, I tried a centre-fed Hertz with matched " flex " feeders. L/Cpl. Maudsley reported " much better—blowing my head off," asked for details, and by the next morning had doubled his signal strength to me. The station was now in regular operation, clearing traffic both ways. In our spare time Gavin and I were busy unpacking and testing the Camp III (Marconi) equipment. Only one transmitting valve had suffered *en route*, and on May 4, in spite of a snowstorm and bad fading, Darjeeling received Morse from the Camp III transmitter at R9 strength.

There remained only the six 5-metre sets to unpack and test. Probably their wiring should have been stronger, more on the lines of a military set, for three were found to have internal disconnections. It should be recorded that Messrs. Exide had sent batteries for the two light-weight sets by air-mail, at considerable expense to themselves, in order to ensure that their already small capacity might not be diminished by prolonged exposure to tropical heat. They had overtaken me at Shekar.

Leaving me at Camp I the party moved up to Camp II on May 6. From there Gavin got through to me using Morse, but not on radio-telephony, giving rise to doubts of the suitability of the rod-type aerials in broken country. These suspicions were confirmed when Gavin moved up to Camp III on May 9, for whereas the Marconi equipment, in reasonable circumstances, is capable of duplex R/T over a range of six miles, even simplex W/T (telegraphy) was difficult to achieve.

The remedy was twofold. Since the Camp III receiver would not tune to 7020 kc/s, I tried using the main transmitter on 3720 kc/s (80 metres), and when Gavin gave me R9 reports, the one spare 5-metre transreceiver was co-opted, and its modulator pentode used as a choke-coupled modulator in the grid circuit of the power amplifier of the big transmitter. It was a " Heath Robinson " arrangement, but it functioned, and henceforth I was able to speak to Camp III except under the worst atmospheric conditions. Secondly, after tests had shown that 5 mc/s (60 metres) was the best frequency for working between Camps III and I, I adapted the spare Marconi transmitter so that instead of working into a Marconi-type aerial and earth-mat system, it used a V-shaped Hertz aerial, current-fed, with the transmitter feeding directly into the centre of the aerial. Safe in the knowledge that the nearest wireless expert was more than 300 miles away, I put the microphone in series with the aerial coupling coil, and again, it worked. The first evacuation of Camp III gave an opportunity of exchanging this modified transmitter with its opposite number, with the result that from now on it took a very bad day to prevent me receiving speech from Camp III.

In view of the success of this experiment, I decided to modify the ex-Camp III transmitter, now installed at Camp I, in the hope that I might be spared the trouble of changing the frequency of the main transmitter several times a day. Gavin had by now become a proficient Morse operator, and so in the interests of efficiency the microphone was omitted, and a simple tapping was taken off to an end-fed Hertz aerial, slung as a high-angle radiator.

This completes the list of major jobs done during my six weeks at Camp I. Nevertheless, the day was always fully occupied. The Nepali having little idea of time, Pasang Picture had orders to wake me as the sun struck the tent. This plan worked well, and gave me time to pull on a sheep-skin coat and a pair of camp boots, and generally to come to life before 7.30 a.m., when I opened up to Darjeeling. They would pass the over-night weather forecast, and possibly an urgent message on expedition affairs, before I had to close down and change over to Camp III at 8 a.m. The weather message went on to Gavin, who would send me a summary of the recent weather there. At about 8.30 a.m. we closed down, leaving half-an-hour to wash, change into flannel trousers, tweed coat and, of course, plenty of Shetlands, and have breakfast. At 9 a.m. the meteorological instruments were read, and a weather report was sent off to Darjeeling. There might also be private messages, with, twice a week, a press telegram of up to four hundred words. Given luck and freedom from interruption, these would be cleared by 11 a.m., and the morning forecast from Alipore would have been received. At 11 a.m. Gavin seldom had much to send, so after he had had the morning forecast he would close down at about noon. The charging engine, which was kept under a canvas cover in the open without coming to any harm, would be warmed up and set to work to restore life to the batteries, a job that normally took about three hours. Meanwhile Pasang Picture and I would clear out the usual accumulation of rubbish from the wireless tents.

While I was alone at Camp I my favourite lunch was tinned ham, boiled potatoes, and slices of raw onion. Such a diet had advantages when exercise was restricted, besides appealing to a palate jaded by altitude. When Morris joined me for convalescence, however, his protests against the onions were so vehement that in future they had to be cooked. In passing, another craving for strong flavours deserves mention. Humphreys, who escorted Morris down, refused most of the lunch prepared for him, but consumed the whole of my only bottle of capers, at the same time telling me how little he thought of the appetites displayed at Camp III.[1]

The afternoon was usually available for maintenance and the carrying out of alterations and experiments. At 5 p.m. I read the weather instruments, and at 5.5 p.m. reopened to Darjeeling to exchange weather messages. Atmospherics, however, making their first appearance at about 10 a.m., would have risen to such a crescendo that D.C. (difficult communication) procedure had to be used; sometimes we failed altogether. At 5.30 p.m. Rugby could be tuned in on 15 metres for the British Official Wireless press bulletin, extracts from which, together with the weather messages, would be forwarded to Camp III at 6 p.m. Gavin and other members would sometimes send down a summary of the day's events. On one such evening Morris and I were able to get the words " Wyn Harris—Shipton—avalanche " above the roar of the interference, but not for another desperate ten minutes were we able to elicit the information that they were *unhurt*.

The sun usually left the camp at about six o'clock, when the temperature fell rapidly. Thick coats and boots were again *de rigueur*; let me commend also the virtues of a portable type of Petromax incandescent lamp, which not only gives a good reading light, but is most effective in keeping a tent warm. Altitude does not seem to worry it, and the mantles have an amazing survival rate.

Pasang Sherpa had built himself a good stone kitchen, roofed by a yak hair blanket. From the darkness of his lair, blinded by smoke and paraffin fumes, he would produce very eatable meals; in fact, he earned such a reputation for the Camp I cuisine that he was presently stolen from us to work at Camp III. The menu of the evening meal, which was eaten at about 6.30 p.m., might be tinned soup, always excellent;

[1] P.S.—Cf. page 209: it *may* have been chutney; if so, the capers suffered the same fate later on.

264

stewed Tibetan mutton, quite palatable after treatment in a pressure cooker, with potatoes and tinned peas ; tinned fruit (or perhaps a jam omelet) ; the whole helped on its way by a tot of Navy rum. At this time our meals were always consumed with gusto ; it was not until the march home, when only the less popular tins remained, that the flesh-pots began to beckon.

Dinner over, there was the choice of gossiping over a pipe in the Mess-tent, or listening to the B.B.C. in the wireless tent. In the latter case, the news was the only attraction, for Camp I had turned out to be badly screened from the direction of England, and local atmospherics robbed music of its programme value. By nine o'clock the camp was usually asleep.

It was a great disappointment that the 5-metre set group could never be put into operation. When, on May 15, Smythe and Shipton occupied Camp IV on the North Col, they were able to open up telephonic communication with Camp III. Shipton afterwards said that he could hear and understand the speech from the far side of the tent when Smythe was operating. This wireless circuit enabled Ruttledge and Smythe to discuss the weather situation, resulting in the decision to evacuate the North Col. There is no reason to suppose that equally useful results could not have been obtained at the higher camps.

After the attempt from the East Rongbuk glacier had been abandoned, and a reconnaissance party had been formed to explore a possible route up the west side of the North Col, permission was given me to accompany the party with skeleton equipment. This consisted of the Homelander receiver, and a modified Marconi transmitter, with the idea of exploring the wireless possibilities of the various camps occupied. As it turned out, observations were only made at what we christened the " North Face Camp," for our stay at the intermediate " Lake Camp " was too brief. On arrival at the former camp, which was situated on the right-hand moraine of the main

265

glacier at a point right in the lee of the North Peak from the Darjeeling direction, it looked as though the chances of communication with Darjeeling were very small. The Marconi transmitter had to send signals over this huge mass with nothing more than a dry H.T. battery to drive it, giving an output of perhaps 5 watts in the aerial. The makers had guaranteed a range of five miles, but this was more than one hundred. Experience led to a choice of 5 mc/s (60 metres), and a half-wave aerial was cut for this frequency. One 18-foot mast was available to support the far end, while the near end was brought in at almost ground level through the tent wall to the set. The lower end pointed towards Darjeeling, and was voltage-fed. The resultant high angle of radiation must have accounted for Darjeeling answering " R 5 " to our first call, and subsequently, on occasion, as much as R 9. The same aerial was used for reception, but it was not efficient in this rôle ; also the screening effect of the North Peak must have been considerable. Nevertheless, the Darjeeling signals were usually of comfortable strength. In these circumstances a regular morning and evening schedule was maintained with Darjeeling during our stay, though naturally the volume of traffic was limited as far as possible.

North Face Camp was entirely unobstructed to the north-west, and this was immediately reflected in a great improvement in the reception of English short-wave broadcasting. My six-by-four Meade tent was often filled to capacity by evening audiences ; in particular we remember almost perfect reception of the first Westchester Cup match.

To sum up, North Face Camp would make an excellent wireless headquarters for an expedition that had decided to use the western route up to Camp IV. It would in any case be necessary to improve the route from Camp I, so that the porterage of moderate-sized boxes should present no difficulty. There should be no important technical or administrative disadvantages to counterbalance the enormous tactical benefit

266

of siting the main wireless station at "operation headquarters." Two miles of light field cable might well be used
to connect with the camp which would be made at the foot
of the Col, whence contact to the high camps could be maintained by ultra-short-wave sets similar to those used this year.

This leads, in conclusion, to a consideration of the problems involved should wireless be thought a necessary part of
a future expedition. First, there is the question of personnel.
For irrelevant reasons, the opinion is held in some quarters
that what flying men call a " ground organisation " is not only
superfluous but encumbers an expedition ; in other words,
the party should consist of none but those who will go high.
Such a policy concentrates solely on attaining the summit, and
excludes all scientific sidelines. Even so, the party might
reasonably hold a knowledge of the trend of the weather to be
an aid to success, and in a civilised country would keep itself
informed by means of a simple receiving set. Not so in Tibet,
where there are no meteorological observatories. The authorities at Alipore have insisted that in the absence of an observatory north of the Himalaya (i.e. one established by the expedition), it is not possible for them to forecast with accuracy the
weather in the Everest region. This means a wireless transmitter which must be somewhere on the glacier, with someone to make and send the observations. To take parapher-
nalia of this sort would be a negation of the policy of the small
party, which, since no two seasons have hitherto been alike,
must rely for its success upon lucky timing of its assault.

If, however, the leader decides that he must base his tactics
on accurate weather information, he must increase his party,
and incur the extra expense of wireless equipment on a scale
similar to that of this year. He cannot economise in personnel,
for although one of his climbers might be technically qualified
to select and install the wireless apparatus, he would not
always be available to ensure that regularity and continuity of
observation which are the foundations of meteorology. At the

267

same time it is strongly recommended that the wireless officer be given an elementary training in meteorological work before leaving England. Not only has unfamiliar language to be learned, but the trained eye is able to give to the reports an accuracy that must have been lamentably deficient in mine.

The technical problems of a future wireless officer will be closely bound up with his expedition's plan of attack. While they cannot therefore be discussed in advance, comfort may be derived from the thought that the alternative approaches to the North Col have now been explored. This year's wireless arrangements could undoubtedly be improved on, but they will furnish a foundation upon which another signal plan can be built. For instance, Darjeeling has twice made an excellent home station, the frequencies and best hours of working being known. Wireless communication between glacier camps has twice been provided, but with a difficulty that should diminish as wireless technique improves. Although ultra-high-frequency transreceivers for use high on the mountain have not been exhaustively tested, their possibilities have been demonstrated ; moreover, the intensive research now being carried out in this field should lead to important developments. Finally, the difficulties of making a charging engine operate efficiently at high altitudes have been overcome. No matter with what care he may choose his apparatus, with what foresight he may make his plan, the wireless officer will still be dependent upon assistance from many sources, from the authorities at home and in India, from the other members of the expedition, and last, but not least, from the porters. If this be given in such generous measure as it was this year, and in particular if he should have the good fortune to enrol such an enthusiastic lieutenant as Gavin, his work will be as enjoyable as it is interesting.

Collecting

BY G. NOEL HUMPHREYS

THE purpose of the 1936 Expedition was solely to get to the summit of Mount Everest, and no botanist or entomologist was taken for the purpose of making collections. The ground that we should pass over had been crossed by previous expeditions, but there is always the chance that even untrained collectors might find something of value, and with this idea we borrowed collecting material from the British Museum so that, should odd moments allow, some collecting might be done.

In Sikkim on our way to Tibet it was early spring. *Primula, Daphne, Magnolia*, willows and *Rhododendron* were in flower. Passing over the Kongra La into Tibet however we dropped back into the depths of winter. The ground was frost-bound. Not a blade of vegetation was to be seen, nor any sign of insect life. The scenery of the plateau of Tibet was magnificent, with its honey-coloured plains, the distant indigo Himalayas, the steely blue sky and the curiously opalescent atmosphere. The mornings were still and bitterly cold. Before noon the wind got up, icy and dust-laden, and the warmth of the sun could not be felt.

The first sign of insect life was on April 17 when, marching from Trangso Chumbab to Kyishong, the first butterfly was seen. On the 25th, on the road between Chō and Rongbuk,

269

they were common. This gave a suggestion of spring, but six days later, when we reached Camp I, there was again neither green vegetation nor insect life, and we were back again in winter. The route along the moraine and glacier to Camp III lay through lifeless country, and the immediate vicinity of Camp III was above the level of phanerogamic vegetation.

On the withdrawal of the Expedition from the eastern slope of the North Col, and our return to Camp I on May 20, there was a change in the landscape ; the tufts of vegetation were tinged with green, though as yet no flower was out. Butterflies and diptera were to be seen, though the number of species was small. The first plant seen in flower was an *Androsace* on May 25, and on that day we started to collect insects. The next day a fall of snow stopped all collecting. On the 27th, under a rock at Camp I, *Primula Caveana* was found in flower, and on the next day a species of *Oxytropis*. Each day now produced a few more flowers and insects, but on May 30 we left Camp I again on the final attempt to re-establish Camp IV. On the failure of this project we, on June 7, evacuated Camp III and travelled via Camp I to Lake Camp. This was at a most beautiful spot with level turf, the only turf we had seen above Chö, a lake and a winding stream bordered with a pink *Sedum* (*S. quadrifidum*). It was at this camp that a lark's nest was found, with two eggs. This nest, perhaps the highest that has ever been seen, was left undisturbed. The lark was identified by Kempson as Elwes's Shore-lark (*Otocorys alpestris* Elwesi). Morris and I stayed at this Camp three days while a reconnaissance was made on the western slopes of the Col. Very few plants were in flower ; *Meconopsis horridula*, for example, was scarcely in bud. There were, of course, no seeds to be collected. We therefore started to pack growing plants in open petrol boxes. These had to be strengthened and the ends drilled to take ropes for attachment to pack-saddles for transport across

270

Tibet. The few plants that could be found in flower were collected and pressed. Also, when it was not snowing, we collected insects ; unfortunately there was not time to dry these specimens properly and the results were not very satisfactory.

On June 12 I joined the party making an attempt on North Peak, travelling via Camp I, where the collections were left, over Camp II to Corner Camp on the east of North Peak. There was no question of collecting during this trip, and by the time of our return to Camp I the Expedition had already started on its return journey.

Much of the country we marched through on our way back across Tibet was desert, but there were oases of level turf dotted with flowers, especially species of yellow *Ranunculus* and a beautiful yellow globe flower (*Trollius pumilus*) with orange anthers. Where the ground was wet but rocky there was a greater variety of flowers, among which a sky-blue *Corydalis* and deeper-blue species of *Microula* stand out in our memory. In more arid country the stony ground, without any carpet of green, was studded with clumps of brightly coloured flowers such as herbaceous *Daphne, Euphorbia, Iris kemaonensis* and that most arresting plant *Incarvillea Younghusbandii*, its flowers lying loosely on the ground like pieces of red rag. On rocky ground in arid regions were typical alpines : *Androsace* and saxifrage, also many crucifers. By far the most beautiful plant we saw in this region was a species of, probably, *Eritrichium* ; enormous grey cushions gemmed with flowers of the intensest ultramarine. Farther still from moisture, in the shifting desert sand, there was, for many square miles, but one plant, the gorse-like *Caragana versicolor*, always nearly smothered by the sand which drifts against it, the tips of its branches protruding from the sand-heap it had accumulated. It reminded me of a plant in Mexico which was described to me by an Indian as " living on the pure juice of sand."

It had been decided that we should return by double marches so as to save the expense of a prolonged expedition. This meant marching up to over twenty miles in a day. We sometimes did not arrive until dusk, and the baggage always arrived much later than ourselves. There was usually a strong wind, and it was impossible to keep candles alight in an open tent, and my tent was so small that it was not possible to kneel in it upright. The difficulty, therefore, of pressing plants was considerable. We collected moths and other insects at night inside the Mess tent, where they had flown, attracted by the light. It was necessary to get up very early in the morning in order to plant in boxes the plants we had dug up the day before. On many days some of the boxes had been knocked off the pack-animals, and these boxes had to be re-planted and sometimes mended. The boxes had also to be watered to prevent them from drying up during the journey. It would, of course, have been far preferable to have collected seeds, but most plants were still only just coming into flower or were still in bud.

In deference to the susceptibilities of the Tibetans we made no collection of animals larger than insects, with the one exception that on high ground, at about 15,000 feet, between Lungme and Kharkhung, we were fascinated by most active lizards scurrying over the sand and diving into their burrows. Some of these we took, and Mr. H. W. Parker, of the British Museum, notes for us that they are *Phryno-cephalus theobaldi* Blyth, a species ranging through Kashmir, Southern Tibet and Eastern Turkestan, and reaching an altitude of 17,000 feet ; usually found in sandy places, living in large colonies, differing from most species of the genus in being cuniculuni and monogamous, living in burrows 8 inches to 10 inches long, and said to be avoviviparous.

On the way out one of the few plants which still had last year's seeds attached had been the *Clematis orientalis*, the only climbing plant in that part of Tibet. On our way back it was in flower. There were three distinct forms : purple-black, yellow and copper-coloured. Unfortunately we never found the last in seed. Several roses were found in seed, and a very few other flowers. It was most tantalising to be dashing through country when a few weeks' delay would have enabled us to make valuable collections. Also, it was sad to leave behind us in bud so many exciting plants which some of us would never see in flower.

The boxes of plants needed constant attention on the way home, and on our arrival were immediately sent to the Royal Botanic Garden at Edinburgh. Some of each kind of the small seed collection were sent to the same garden, and where there was sufficient quantity of seed it was distributed as widely as possible. The collections of insects and pressed plants were sent to the British Museum (Natural History). I am indebted to Mr. J. Ramsbottom, Keeper of Botany, for the list and notes given at the end of this chapter. The Polypetalæ were determined by Mr. E. G. Baker, the first three families of Gamopetalæ by Mr. W. R. Philipson, the remaining Gamopetalæ and Apetalæ by Dr. G. Taylor, and the Monocotyledones and Gymnospermæ by Mr. J. E. Dandy. I am indebted to Mr. N. D. Riley, Keeper of Entomology, for the notes and preliminary lists of insects. The following have supplied the information given : Brigadier W. H. Evans (butterflies), Mr. W. H. T. Tams (moths), Dr. F. W. Edwards, Dr. John Smart, Mr. H. Oldroyd and Major E. E. Austen (Diptera), Mr. G. J. Arrow and Dr. K. G. Blair (beetles), Mr. R. B. Benson and Mr. J. F. Perkins (Hymenoptera), Dr. B. P. Uvarov (Orthoptera), Mr. M. E. Mosely (caddis-flies), Mr. D. E. Kimmins (Neuroptera) and Mr. F. G. M. Westropp (Thysanura).

Among the sixty-seven butterflies obtained by the Expedition were several of especial interest to the Museum on account of their rarity. These were all obtained at altitudes of 15,000 feet or more, and included a single female of

T

Parnassius acco gemmifer Fruhst, which is known only from the region traversed by the Expedition although several other subspecies occur in Tibet. A single male of the very rare and local little Clouded Yellow, *Colias dubia* Elwes, was obtained at the same place and date. This was described by Elwes in 1906 from specimens collected by members of the Tibet Expedition of 1903 at Khamba Jong and Lhanak, and, until a long series of it was obtained by Colonel F. M. Bailey and his brother from alpine Sikkim, remained somewhat of a mystery. A solitary female of the very rare little " White," *Baltia butleri*, which is confined to the Himalayas, was taken on the shelf between Camp I and Base at 17,000 feet on June 15. On June 21, at an altitude of 15,000 feet, at Tashi Gaon two pairs of *Argestina karta* Riley were obtained, and at Doya La, 14,000 feet, on the same day three further males and one female. This species was first met with by the Mount Everest Expedition of 1921, and named on the basis of two males and two females collected on that occasion. Five males and one female were obtained by the 1922 Expedition, but no other specimens are known, and the species appears to be confined to the Mount Everest area. The commonest butterfly at high altitudes appears to have been the Ladak Small Tortoiseshell, *Vanessa ladakensis* Moore, of which twenty-one males and twelve females are included in the collection. Of the closely related Cashmere Small Tortoiseshell there are three males. These species, and also the Small Blue (*Polyommatus eros arene* Fawcett) and a female Swallowtail (*Papilio machaon sikkimensis* Moore), are all strictly members of the palæarctic fauna, the southern boundary of which, in the area traversed by the Expedition, seems to lie somewhere about the 12,000-feet contour line.

The butterflies obtained at lower levels are on the whole less interesting because, being at the northern extremity of their range, they are mostly well known from localities in the Himalayan foothills etc., which have been entomologically species, strongly suggestive of our British species of *Anarta* explored by several generations of collectors. However, amongst them were three males of a big black and yellow species (*Delias sanaca oreas* Talbot) which is very local and by no means common. *Delias* is a genus of " Whites " which reaches its maximum development in the mountains of New Guinea, but the section of the genus to which *D. sanaca* belongs is peculiar to the Indo-Chinese region, where it extends to high altitudes and almost invades the palæarctic region.

A complete list of the butterflies obtained is given at the end of the chapter.

Of the other insects obtained by the Expedition it is far more difficult to give an account, since the groups to which they belong are not nearly so well-known as the butterflies.

The fifty moths brought back contain several new species. There is notably a new Hawk Moth belonging to the genus *Cechenena*, but found by Mr. Tams from an examination of the genitalia to be distinct from the other species of the genus, both of which are very well known. The solitary specimen is a male taken at Chungthang, 3,350 feet, on July 3.

The bulk of the collection consists of Noctuid moths, to none of which is it possible to attach names with certainty. There are, for example, twelve specimens of a species of *Agrotis*, in beautiful condition, taken at Chö, Raphu and Doya La, all at 15,000 feet between June 17 and 20 ; seven of another smaller *Agrotid*, very similar to *A. tritici* in appearance, and three of a third species, which is strongly reminiscent of the English *Agrotis plecta*. These were all obtained also by previous Mount Everest Expeditions, and remain undescribed. Very closely related to these is a single *Lycophotia* near *L. oreas* Püngeler, a central Asian species. To three Hadenine moths it is not possible without considerable labour to assign even their genus ; they represent two species, one of which is also represented in previous collections. The remaining Noctuid is a single specimen of the little black and white that occurs commonly in the Yorkshire and Scottish moors ; it was taken at 17,700 feet at Camp I. The other two Noctuids are unfortunately so damaged as to be unidentifiable. The remaining moths are representative of a number of families. The only Notodontid is a new species of *Ichthyura*, a " Chocolate-tip," which is also represented in previous collections. The Tussock Moths (*Lymantrii dae*) are represented by two males of a species of *Euproctis*, pure white in colour, which is new : these were taken on the same day as the new hawk moth. Geometrid moths are represented by eight specimens. Two of these were the large and common brilliant blue and yellow *Dysphania militaris* Linn., typically Indo-Chinese, and the others are *Discoloxia lilacina* Hampson, three *Stamnodes* representing two species, one of which is near *S. depeculata* Alph. (but too damaged to determine with certainty), a specimen of a species of *Gnophodes* which may be new, and a *Gonodontis* near *G. arida* : all except the *Dysphania* are palæarctic in their affinities. The only other moths are the common Pyralid *Loxostege xuthusalis* Hampson, of which a short series was obtained, and two fine examples of a handsome Goat Moth (*Cossus* sp.) taken at Raphu and apparently new.

The beetles consist almost entirely of species new to science, or which had only recently been described on the basis of the collections made by previous Mount Everest Expeditions. A list is given at the end of the chapter.

Very little can be said of the Bees and Wasps. One sawfly (*Tenthredo* sp.) was obtained at Lingga at 15,000 feet, and another at Tengkye at 14,500 feet ; wasps of the genera *Priocnemis, Sphex,* and Ichneumon flies of the genera *Homocidus* and *Cryptus* were also obtained, the last-mentioned coming from Camp I at 17,700 feet. The bees include a species of *Colletes* from Chungthang, a female *Bombus rufofasciatus* Smith, a *Melecta* from Tengkye, and two *Anthophora pulcherrima* Bingham from Chungthang. The *Anthophora* is especially useful and interesting. Unfortunately the Hymenoptera reached London in poor condition. They serve, however, to emphasise the entirely palæarctic nature of the fauna of the inner Himalayan valleys.

The Diptera obtained compare well with the other orders of insects so far as numbers are concerned, but their preservation, always a difficult matter, has rendered many of them unidentifiable. Two different species of Cranefly, or Daddy-long-legs, were obtained, *Tipula griseipennis* and *T. wardi*, both taken at the Camp at Tang Mochi on July 20 ; both are known only from the Indo-Chinese region. Of the hovering bee-like Bombyliidæ two species again were obtained. It is only possible to refer these to the genus *Bombylius* ; a single specimen of one species was taken at Tashi Gaon, 15,000 feet, on June 21, and a short series of the other at Chungthang, on July 3. At the latter locality also two Robber-flies, *Machimus pubescens*, were obtained, and another specimen of the same genus, but possibly representing a new species or a variety of *M. excelsus*, was collected at Tengkye, 14,500 feet, June 26, 1936. Both these species were included in the collection made at Gyangtse by the Tibet Expedition in 1904. At Camp I, 17,700 feet, two specimens of a Hoverfly, *Scæva* (*Lasiopticus*) *pyrastri*, were taken, as well as another unidentifiable Syrphid and three Tachinid and three Anthomyid flies, which it is not possible to name. Several other flies of these two families, and also some Muscids, including four *Gonia ornata* (Tachinidæ), were taken at Chungthang. These all belong to the families which include the Bluebottles and the House-fly, and would be difficult to identify even if in perfect condition. The zoo-geographical evidence supplied by this small collection of Diptera is entirely in accordance with that provided by the butterflies and moths.

Amongst the few Orthoptera brought back, two species of special interest to the Museum are represented. Two females of the grasshopper *Dysanema irvinei* Uvarov are the only specimens to come to hand since the pair, on which the name was based, collected by a previous Mount Everest Expedition ; it is known only from the Mount Everest region. There is an apparently new species of *Tachycines*, a genus allied to the cave crickets. The other grasshoppers are immature species of *Bryodema* and *Sphingonotus* which it is not possible to name. Had the Expedition been at Lingga and Chungthang, whence these specimens came, a little later in the year, the results would have been much more interesting.

The only dragonfly was a male specimen of *Enallagma cyathigerum*, a small species which occurs throughout the palæarctic region, including Great Britain.

A solitary Ascalaphid captured on July 4 between Chungthang and Singhik appears to belong to the genus *Protidricerus*. It is almost certainly new, and may have to be placed in a new genus.

Trichoptera (caddis-flies) number only six, and belong to two species in two different families. The more important of these consist of two ♂♂ and one ♀ of *Pseudostenophylax himalayanus* Martynov (from Tang Mochi, June 20, 1936, and Gao Gom La, Tanga, July 1, 1936) belonging to the Limnophilidæ, while the other, an unrecognisable *Rhyacophila* species (Rhyacophilidæ), is represented by females from Tang Mochi, June 20, 1936, Lingga, June 28, 1936, and Tashi Gaon, June 21, 1936. *P. himalayanus* was described by Martynov from material in the British Museum, taken by A. E. Hobson at Yatung, Tibet, at an altitude of 4,500 feet, and further material was subsequently taken by Major R. W. G. Hingston at Yatung, at 10,000 feet, during the 1924 Mount Everest Expedition.

There are two Bristle-tails (Thysanura). These were both taken at Camp I, at 17,700 feet. The larger specimen has been identified as *Machilis lefroyi* Silv., taken on June 14 ; the smaller, taken on May 29, is also a *Machilis*, but may be a new species.

278

DICOTYLEDONES

Polypetalæ

Ranunculaceæ

Clematis orientalis L.   Tashi Gaon, June 21.   Kharkhung,
June 24.

Anemone rupicola Camb.   Kharkhung, June 23.

Ranunculus pulchellus C. A. Meyer.   Raphu, June 20.

Ranunculus Cymbalaria Pursh.   Khampa, June 29.

Ranunculus hyperboreus Rottb.   Lake Camp, June 11.

Ranunculus aquatilis L.   Between Tengkye and Lingga,
June 28.

Trollius pumilus D. Don.   Between Chö and Raphu,
June 19.

Violaceæ

Viola biflora L.   Lachen, March 27.

Cruciferæ

Parrya macrocarpa R. Br.   Between Lake Camp and
Camp I, June 11.

Arabis glandulosa Kar. & Kir.   Tang Mochi, June 20.
Khampa, June 29.

Draba glomerata Royle.   Between Lake Camp and
Camp I, June 11.

Draba oreades Schrenk.   Lake Camp, June 10.

Tamaricaceæ

Myricaria germanica Desv.   Between Camp I and Base
Camp, June 15.

Leguminosæ

Thermopsis lanceolata R. Br.   Chö, June 18.   Khampa,
June 29.

Astragalus strictus Grah.   Khampa, June 29.

Astragalus orotrephes W. W. Sm.   Camp I, June 12.

Oxytropis kansuensis Bge.   Khampa, June 29.

Oxytropis microphylla DC.   Camp I, June 7.

    Oxytropis sp. Camp I, May 28.

    Stracheya tibetica Benth. Khampa, June 29.

Rosaceæ

    Spiræa arcuata Hook. f. Between Raphu and Tang Mochi, June 20. Tashi Gaon, June 21.

    Potentilla anserina L. Khampa, June 29.

    Potentilla sericea var. *polyschista* Lehm. Khampa, June 29.

    Fragaria vesca L. *forma.* Lachen, March 27.

    Cotoneaster microphylla Wall. Tang Mochi, June 20.

Crassulaceæ

    Sedum Rhodiola L. Tang Mochi, June 20.

    Sedum quadrifidum Pall. Between Lake Camp and Camp I, June 11.

Gamopetalæ

Caprifoliaceæ

    Lonicera tibetica Bur. and Franch. Tashi Gaon, June 21.

Compositæ

    Erigeron alpinus L. Khampa, June 29.

Ericaceæ

    Gaultheria nummularioides D. Don. Lachen, March 27.

    Rhododendron anthopogon D. Don. Doya La, June 20.

Primulaceæ

    Primula Caveana W. W. Sm. Camp I, May 27.

    Primula consocia W. W. Sm. Camp I, June 12.

    Primula tibetica Wall. Khampa, June 29.

    Androsace sessiliflora Turrill. Camp I, June 12.

    Androsace sp. May 25.

    Lysimachia pumila Franch. Lachen, March 27.

Gentianaceæ

    Gentiana capitata Buch.-Ham. ex D. Don. Lachen, March 27.

    Gentiana leucomelæna Maxim. Khampa, June 29.

Boraginaceæ

   Microula sikkimensis (C. B. Clarke) Hemsl. Kharkhung, June 23.

   Microula pustulata (C. B. Clarke) Duthie. 2,000 feet above Raphu, June 19.

   Microula sp. Khampa, June 29.

   Onosma sp. Kharkhung, June 23.

Solanaceæ

   Scopolia tangutica Maxim. Raphu, June 19.

Scrophulariaceæ

   Hemiphragma heterophyllum Wall. Lachen, March 27. A monotypic genus confined to the Himalayas. This plant is interesting in having dimorphic leaves—one kind orbicular with cordate base, the other needle-like.

   Pedicularis longiflora Rudolph. Khampa, June 29.

   Pedicularis verticillata L. Khampa, June 29.

   Lancea tibetica Hook. f. & Thoms. Chö, June 18. Khampa, June 29. A monotypic genus confined to the Himalayas.

   Oreosolen Wattii Hook f. Between Camp I and Base Camp, June 17.

Bignoniaceæ

   Incarvillea Younghusbandii Sprague. Between Camp I and Base Camp, June 17.

Selaginaceæ

   Lagotis glauca Gaertn. Between Base Camp and Chö, June 18.

Labiatæ

   Phlomis rotata Benth. Chö, June 18. This plant is remarkable for the habit which it has adopted. It is stemless, and the flowers are produced from the centre of the tight rosette of tough leaves.

Apetalæ

Polygonaceæ

   Polygonum sibericum Laxm. Khampa, June 29.

   Rheum globulosum Gage. Camp I, June 16.

Lauraceæ
> *Litsæa Cubeba* (Lour.) Pers. Lachen, March 27.

Euphorbiaceæ
> *Euphorbia himalayensis* Klotzsch. Between Base Camp
> and Chö, June 18.
> *Sarcococca pruniformis* Lindl. Lachen, March 27.

Salicaceæ
> *Salix Daltoniana* Anderss. Kharkhung, June 23.

MONOCOTYLEDONES

Iridaceæ
> *Iris tenuifolia* Pall., a characteristic iris of high Central
> Asia. Between Base Camp and Chö, June 18.

Liliaceæ
> *Fritillaria cirrhosa* D. Don, the common fritillary of the
> Himalaya. Tang Mochi, June 20.
> *Aletris nepalensis* Hook. f. Tang Mochi, June 20.

Juncaceæ
> *Juncus Thomsonii* Buchen., a small slender rush with
> flowers in a dense head. Khampa, June 29.

Araceæ
> *Arisæma Jacquemontii* Bl., a curious plant allied to *Arum*.
> The genus *Arisæma* is rich in species in the Himalaya.
> Tashi Gaon, June 21.

Juncaginaceæ
> *Triglochin maritima* L. Tang Mochi, June 20.
> *Triglochin palustris* L. Khampa, June 29.
> These are the same two species as found in the British
> Isles.

Cyperaceæ
> *Carex orbicularis* Boott, a close ally of the British *C. rigida*
> Good. Khampa, June 29.
> *Kobresia pygmæa* (C. B. Clarke) C. B. Clarke, a minute
> flowering plant allied to *Carex*. Lake Camp, June 11.

Kobresia sp.   Camp I, June 16.
Kobresia sp.   Khampa, June 29.

Gramineæ

Deschampsia cespitosa (L.) Beauv.   Khampa, June 29.
Elymus sibiricus L.   Lingga, June 28.
Poa sp.   Khampa, June 29.

GYMNOSPERMÆ

Ephedraceæ

Ephedra Gerardiana Wall. ex Stapf.   Between Rongbuk and Chö, June 18.   Between Tashi Gaon and Lungme, June 22.   The eastern Himalayan representative of this genus.

BUTTERFLIES TAKEN ON THE EXPEDITION

1. *Papilio machaon sikkimensis* Moore.   1 ♀.
2. *Parnassius acco gemmifer* Fruhstorfer.   1 ♀.   A rarity. July 1.
3. *Pieris napi montana* Verity.   2♂ 1 ♀.
4. *Pieris canidia indica* Evans.   1 ♂ 1 ♀.   Unusually large.
5. *Baltia butleri sikkima*.   1 ♀.
6. *Delias sanaca oreas* Talbot.   3 ♂.   Not common and very local.
7. *Dercas verhueli doubledayi* Moore.   1 ♂.
8. *Colias dubia* Elwes.   1 ♂.   A rarity.   July 1.
9. *Colias fieldii* Menétries.   4 ♂ 3 ♀.
10. *Euplœa mulciber mulciber* Cramer.   1 ♂.
11. *Pararge masoni* Elwes.   2 ♂.
12. *Argestina karta* Riley.   2 ♂ 2 ♀.   B.M. have only 5 ♂ 4 ♀ : peculiar to Everest area.   June 21.
13. *Ypthima sakra sakra* Moore.   1 ♂.
14. *Neptis ananta ochracea* Evans.   3 ♂.
15. *Neptis narayana nana* De Niceville.   1 ♂.
16. *Vanessa ladakensis* Moore.   21 ♂ 12 ♀.
17. *Vanessa cashmirensis æsis* Fruhstorfer.   3 ♂.

18. *Polyommatus eros arene* Fawcett. 2 ♂.
19. *Celastrina albocærulea* Moore. I ♂.
20. *Celastrina cardia dilecta* Moore. I ♂.

COLEOPTERA TAKEN ON THE EXPEDITION

Carabidæ
    Nebria superna Andr.
    Taphoxenus brucei Andr.
    Zabrus malloryi Andr.
    Cymindis longstaffi Andr.
Geotrupidæ
    Geotrupes sp. (probably new).
Melolonthidæ
    Brahmina sp. (probably new).
Elateridæ
    Hypnoidus sp.
Melyridæ
    Genus ?
Tenebrionidæ
    Pachyscelis ænescens Blair.
    Blaps sp. nr. *himalaica* Blair.
    Gnaptorina brucei Blair.
    Læna alticola Blair.
Meloidæ
    Apalus sp.
Curculionidæ
    Ptochus sp.
    Leptomias 3 spp.
    Xylinophorus 3 spp.
Chrysomelidæ
    Swargia nila Maulik.

The Local Name of Mount Everest

BY E. G. H. KEMPSON

THE main evidence for the use of local names for Mount Everest was ably summarised in Col. Sir Sidney Burrard's review of a book by Sven Hedin. This review was published in 1931 by the Survey of India as Professional Paper No. 26. The further evidence advanced here should be read in conjunction with that paper.

During the course of the 1936 Expedition the Head Lama of Rongbuk monastery presented some of the members of the expedition with copies of a booklet that had been drawn up for the use of pilgrims visiting the monastery. It is described as having been printed in the Water-Ape Year, which corresponds to 1932.

This booklet has been translated for me by the kindness of Mr. F. W. Thomas, lately Boden Professor of Sanskrit at Oxford University.

It consists of an Introduction, followed by a general account of the neighbourhood of Rongbuk-dza and references to sites of particular religious interest.

The introduction describes Roṅ-phu-rdza as specially celebrated amongst the eight famous ice-regions of Tibet.

The Earth, originally occupied by evil beings, was after a long time rendered by the holy Vajradhara habitable by heaven-dwellers, chiefly sky-roaming demons. With the growth of Buddhism the countries were brought into order through the instructions of Vajra-yaña teachers. In Tibet came Sroṅ-btsan Sgam-po [c. A.D. 600–650], *an incarnation of Avalokiteśvara; then Khri-sroṅ-rje* [c. A.D. 750–800], *in whose time came many teachers, including Padmasambhava, and blessed many hills, lakes and ice-mountains.*

At that time there was in this province, in the upper part of the valley, a forest called Pha-drug-rgyal-mo [Six-Fathers-Queen, Folk-etymology of Pharuk], *inhabited by wild beasts—hence the name Roṅ-phu-rdza* [roṅ = " defile "]. *In Roṅ-phu-rdza Padmasambhava spent seven months and realised the highest siddhi (spiritual attainment) : he ordained the region to be a place of salvation to all who beheld, heard or thought of or touched it.*

At that time in a place where the auspicious long-lived-five-sisters (Bkra-śis-tshe-riṅ-mched-lṅa), whose esoteric name was Immovable Good Cow (Mi-gyo-glaṅ-bzaṅ-ma) walked the earth, in view, namely of the high, self-create, ice-mountain named Lady Cow (Jo-mo-glaṅ-ma), he exorcised Mi-gyo-glaṅ and the others [i.e. the five sisters] *by his word, and blessed the place to be a chief scene of siddhi. Especially Mkhan-pa-luṅ* [Abbot's Ravine, evidently the valley where is the Rongbuk monastery] *of Sbas-yul he named as taking the lead. It is the auspicious route* [through Sbas-yul] *followed by the Teacher (Padmasambhava) and others.*

By this route arrived [from India] *Mthu-stobs-rnam-rgyal, of the line of pupils of Rnam-rgyal-mgon-po, descendants of the manuscript-discoverer (gter-ston) Rgod-lde. At that time the present Brag-rgya-yan-la* [Precipice-extended-upper pass: this may = Kyetrak, since rgya-brag may well be pronounced kye-drak] *was full of mingled ice and lakes and difficult to traverse; and on one occasion he sat praying that an upper level way, the seat of the Nāga Klu-bsaṅ* [pronounce Lupsang?] *on the*

ridge Rgya-chen-Rdza-dkar-ma [Great-extent-White-Stone =
Dzakar ?] *might serve the needs of attendants, couriers, etc., into
the place of lower Roṅ-phu. Therefore the Śag-thaṅ,* upper
and lower, being of a time later than the way of arriving by
crossing the ice of the left corner of the ridge Jo-mo-glaṅ-ma,
cannot have been known.*

Several points arise from this document. It contains two
references to Chomo-langma. In one Rongbuk is described
as particularly suited to the highest spiritual attainment, being
in view of Chomo-langma. Now those who have been to
Rongbuk can have no doubt that this is a reference to Mount
Everest itself. At Rongbuk the view consists essentially of
one dominating feature, namely Mount Everest. Moreover,
it is the summit that appears so grandly, not merely part of
the range. This answers the objection raised in section 28
of the Professional Paper. In that paper the use of the name
Tchoumou Lancma on d'Anville's map of 1733 was discussed
and the view was held that Chomo-langma referred to some
topographical feature in the country round, but it could not
be asserted that its identity with the summit of Mount Everest
was proved. Whatever may have obtained in the eighteenth
century, we now seem to have evidence that within the last
ten years Chomo-langma is used locally to denote the summit.
This agrees in substance, though not syllabically, with the
terms of the permit originally sent from Lhasa on behalf of
the 1921 Expedition, where reference was made to Chha-mo-
lung-ma. Admittedly the meaning and spelling of these two
words are quite distinct, but as far as pronunciation is concerned, there is enough resemblance for confusion to be
very likely.

---

* *Śag-thaṅ* = *Sake-ding* [of the 1921 Mount Everest book] or *Sakia-thang* [of the
1922 book]: it means "the flat place of Buddha," *Śag* being a known abbreviation
of *Sākya*. It probably denotes a route by the valley of the *Phung Chhu* and the
Doya La.

The only other local written evidence that I have come across I am allowed to publish by the kindness of Mr. J. van Manen, Secretary of the Asiatic Society of Bengal. It consists of quotations from the diary of the Rongbuk Lama.

Leaf 46 : *In the southern part of La-stod* [the upper pass], *there is the interior part of Pha-drug rgya-mo rong* [the intermediate valley of the six fathers] *where there is a mountain called by the general name Jo-mo-glaṅ-ma, which is the place of religious practice of Mi-gyo-glaṅ-bzaṅ-ma, who is one of the five sisters (Bkra-śis tshe-riṅ mched-lṅa).*

Leaf 176 : *Gradually when I was coming via Sa-skya from the summit of the Drong-la (Dong-pass), I saw the snow-mountain called Jo-mo-glaṅ-mahi gaṅs-ri.*

Leaf 287 : *A party of six Europeans arrived here to make an expedition to Gaṅs-ri glaṅ-ma.*

This appears to me to leave practically no doubt that the best-known local name for Mount Everest is Chomo-langma. Whether this should be introduced as the standard name for the mountain I leave to more experienced geographers.

INDEX

U

INDEX

293

EVEREST: THE UNFINISHED ADVENTURE

BY HUGH RUTTLEDGE

PART III

A PORTFOLIO OF THE PICTURES

PLATE I

Mount Everest from the north-east. This photograph was taken by Michael Spender during the 1935 Reconnaissance. On the left is the Rapiu La ; on the right, the North Peak ; below is the East Rongbuk glacier, showing the trough descending from the upper reaches. In this trough was placed Camp II in 1936.

The picture gives a good idea of the condition of the mountain after the monsoon has set in. Local Tibetan evidence is all to the effect that there is very little alteration until the north-west winds of the following spring blow this snow away. The Reconnaissance of 1921, which worked in this region till the end of September, found exactly similar conditions.

PLATE 2

A group of the Expedition taken at Gangtok on March 19, just before they started on the march to Mount Everest.

Back row, left to right :
E. H. L. Wigram, P. R. Oliver, E. G. H. Kempson, P. Wyn Harris.

Middle row, left to right :
C. B. M. Warren, F. S. Smythe, H. Ruttledge, C. J. Morris, G. Noel Humphreys.

Front row, left to right :
J. M. L. Gavin, E. E. Shipton, W. R. Smijth-Windham.

PLATE 3

On the left is B. Karma Paul, the interpreter in Tibetan to the Expedition. He has accompanied every expedition to Mount Everest except the Reconnaissance of 1921. He is a Tibetan by birth but has spent most of his life at Darjeeling, where he runs a motor business. He is an extraordinary linguist, being almost equally at home in Tibetan, English, Urdu, Bengali, Nepali and Lepcha. Being thoroughly conversant with Tibetan etiquette, he has rendered valuable services to all expeditions. In private life he is keenly interested in racing, and when times are good enters a pony for events in the neighbourhood of Darjeeling.

On the right is Jemadar Lachiman Singh Sahi of the 1/3rd Q.A.O. Gurkha Rifles ; an old friend of mine from Almora. He does not usually wear a beard, but this photograph was taken after he had been some time in Tibet. He speaks and writes English exceedingly well, is an excellent organiser and was of the very greatest assistance to Wyn Harris in keeping the expedition accounts. He is related to the old royal family of Askot in the Almora district and his charming manners made him a great favourite with everyone, including the porters.

PLATE 4.—THE SARDARS OF THE EXPEDITION

Back row, left to right :
    Pasang, Tsering Tarkey, Rinzing, Ondi, Tewang.
Front row, left to right :
    Ang Tsering, Nursang, Ang Tarkey, Da Tsering.

Pasang was one of the " tigers " of 1933, and in 1936 only just scraped through the medical examination, his heart being suspect. But he never failed us on the mountain.

Tsering Tarkey was one of the best men we had. He too was a " tiger " in 1933. Most unhappily he fell ill and died at Darjeeling after our return.

Rinzing, " the wild Irishman," was a " tiger " in 1933. He has all the makings of a first-class mountaineer.

Ondi is the " hard case." He recovered from double pneumonia in record time in 1933. More than once he led porters up to the North Col in 1936.

Tewang was my personal servant throughout the expedition. He is the embodiment of quiet efficiency.

Ang Tsering was one of the recruiters sent to Sola Khombu during the winter.

Nursang was Chief Sardar. He has served in the Indian Army, and makes an excellent N.C.O.

Ang Tarkey is probably now the best mountaineer in the Sherpa community. He accompanied Shipton and Tilman in the Reconnaissance of the Nanda Devi Basin in 1934.

Da Tsering was a " tiger " in 1933, since when he has remained mostly at his home in Sola Khombu. He is a fine mountaineer.

PLATE 5

A close-up of Ang Tarkey, who is a most remarkable person. He is very small and knock-kneed, but this does not deter him from being a great mountaineer and load carrier. It has been observed before that, if you put him into a ready-made blue suit, with a purple tie and brown boots, and a Homburg hat, he might pass quite unnoticed in London. Yet his name is already famous in the Himalaya.

PLATE 6.—GURKHA N.C.O.s OF THE EXPEDITION

Lance Naik Lilambar Rana.
Lance Naik Gopal Gurung.

Both are natural-born mountaineers and tremendously keen. Their duties were to help Jemadar Lachiman Singh Sahi in the management of glacier camps, and they did their duty throughout, though eating their hearts out to climb on Mount Everest. They were specially chosen by Major Morris from his old battalion the 2nd Q.A.O. Gurkha Rifles.

PLATE 7

A party of porters being addressed by Major Morris, with the military Nursang in the right foreground. In the middle distance on the left will be observed Ang Tarkey with his mouth wide open and a general appearance of imbecility, entirely belied by his actions. From his appearance I deduce that Major Morris is about to deliver himself of one of those recondite jokes in Nepali which invariably destroyed the solemnity of the proceedings. In the right middle distance Wyn Harris is regarding Ang Tarkey with grave suspicion.

PLATE 8

LEFT. Scenery in Northern Sikkim above Tangu. Here, at an altitude of about 14,000 feet, snowfall is fairly frequent in the evenings of the early spring. I am informed that the tree on the right is a kind of giant juniper.

RIGHT. This is the type of bridge in common use in Sikkim and other parts of the Himalaya. It is constructed chiefly of bamboo, rope and creepers. Very occasionally wire cables are employed but usually ropes, which presumably carry on until an accident occurs. These bridges swing somewhat dizzily above the racing water of the river, and are not appreciated by everybody.

PLATE 9

A view down the valley of the Tista above Lachen. The valley here is steep-sided, and the construction of even a rough track along it must have involved enormous labour. It is constantly broken by land-slips due to heavy rainfall. During the monsoon, from this point southwards leeches give a good deal of trouble to both men and animals.

PLATE 10

LEFT : Wyn Harris trying out oxygen apparatus at Tangu. The Vibrac steel cylinder which holds the compressed oxygen can be seen hanging on the small of the back. The weight of this apparatus was about 35 lb., which, as may be imagined, is a heavy load for a climber to carry anywhere. It is particularly awkward on steep rock, especially in " chimneys " ; and is likely to disturb the balance on slabs. Unfortunately no opportunity occurred to test it at really high altitudes ; there is some uncertainty whether freezing will not occur round the edges of the mask, thereby causing great discomfort to the wearer. On the other hand, when properly adjusted, the apparatus did enable climbers to move without distress at considerable heights.

RIGHT : The acting second Dzongpen of Shekar. This handsome young man rendered valuable service to the expedition, and it was a great pity that on the last evening of our stay there two drunken porters should have damaged his nose with stones. The incident very nearly caused a serious delay in the march, but in the end everything was satisfactorily settled, and this officer accompanied us to the Base Camp, and again on our departure.

PLATE 11

Tangu, the highest rest house in Northern Sikkim at about 13,500 feet. Here the expedition spent several days acclimatising on the surrounding mountains, and testing out oxygen ; and Morris recovered from his attack of malaria.

In front of the porch can be seen the remains of the great masses of snow which accumulate during the winter, rising to the level of the roof.

LEFT TO RIGHT : Panorama made from three photogra
In the centre is Kangchenjau.   On the right is the valley
    In the spring this region is bitterly cold, but sum:
valleys of Sikkim, the grazing being excellent.

n between Gayokang and the Kongra La looking south.
:h the expedition came up through Sikkim.
gs up the shepherds and their flocks from the lower

PLATE 13

Scenery in Northern Sikkim between Tangu and Gayokang. It will be observed that the tree line has now been passed, and there is no vegetation except brushwood. In the background is the great mountain Kangchenjau, climbed by the late Doctor Kellas. The track towards the Kongra La and Sebu La passes round the flank of the hill on the left, leaving Kang-chenjau on the right.

PLATE 14

Gayokang, our last camping place in Sikkim before the passes were crossed into Tibet. It lies at about 15,000 feet, and is occupied by peasant traders and by shepherds during the summer. In the background is Kangchenjau.

Here for the first time we used tents, and began the regular routine of life on the march. A strong, cold wind makes conditions rather hard in the early spring, though nothing like so bad as those on the Phari plain. When we returned in July it was quite warm, and flowers were blowing everywhere. One might have been in Switzerland.

PLATE 15

Our chief means of transport—the yak. This animal stands about thirteen hands, but is very powerful and sure footed. Its normal load is 160 lb. For all its apparent unwieldiness the yak, if it considers that it is over-laden, has no hesitation in bucking off its loads with the utmost agility. Apart from that it is very docile, but nervous of Europeans. The loads are attached to a kind of wood pack-saddle. Yaks are rarely brought below an altitude of 10,000 feet, for their natural habitat is the Tibetan plateau, where they are indifferent to extremes of cold and wind ; they suffer greatly from the heat of the lower valleys.

PLATE 16

Kampa Dzong, at about 14,000 feet, looking north ; on the left is the valley down which travellers come from the Phari plain. Doctor Kellas' grave is on the hill to the right, looking towards the main chain of the Himalaya. In the fore-ground a troupe of dancers is giving a performance which lasted the greater part of a day. On the plain behind them riders in mediæval costume gave a display of horsemanship. The Dzong, or fort at the top of the rock, was designed to withstand sieges, of which doubtless there have been many. Down the rock ridge below it to the left runs a fortified stair-case leading to a spring. It is said that convicted persons used to be thrown from the top of the walls.

PLATE 17

LEFT :   Tibetan dancers at Kampa Dzong.   The chief feature
of their performance is an extremely rapid rotation
which is kept up for minutes at a time and looks very
exhausting at an altitude of over 14,000 feet.

RIGHT :   A Tibetan horseman ready for a tourney at Kampa
Dzong.   These Tibetan ponies stand only about
thirteen hands, many of them are scissor-hocked and
they always have the poorest of food and shelter ; but
they are capable of going tremendous distances at a
fast amble.

PLATE 18

Fording a Tibetan river.   Here can be seen the expedition boxes which were specially packed at home to make up 40-lb. loads for porter transport later on.   Often it is a long business driving the yaks across a river, for they love to stand still and meditate on any convenient sand-bank.

PLATE 19

Typical scenery on the Tibetan plateau, between Kampa Dzong and Lingga. In the background is the Himalayan range.

The predominating colours on this plain during the spring are red and brown, but as soon as the monsoon rains arrive a carpet of green seems to be spread with magical rapidity.

In the foreground is the village of Mendi, which boasts a small but much-prized willow-grove ; also a liquor shop where " chang," or barley beer, encouraged the porters to linger.

The passes by which we crossed into Tibet are away on the left.

PLATE 20

Nearly all small Tibetan villages look like this—the village of Lingga.   This place is surrounded by marshes through which it is very difficult to make any progress during the rainy season. At that time the lake is visited by large numbers of Brahminy ducks and geese.

Here, in 1933, Raymond Greene lost his valuable collection of insects.   Presumably the thief drank the raw alcohol in which they were preserved, but it would require more than that to kill a Lingga villager.

PLATE 21

Tengkye Dzong, about half-way to Everest. When we reached this place black-headed gulls were swimming on the little lake. Here we had a regatta, " the yachts " consisting of Li-Lo mattresses, lashed to a framework of tent struts. The water is very shallow and the yachts were constantly running aground. In the background is the Dzongpen's house, where we were hospitably entertained. On the right are our Mess tents, in which we endeavoured to return the compliment. On the left is the small type of Meade tent of which each member of the expedition had one to himself.

PLATE 22

This picture gives a good general idea of the scenery on the march across the plateau to Mount Everest. It is taken from the top of the Tengkye La, at about 17,000 feet. In the middle distance can be seen patches of barley cultivation, nearly 3,000 feet below.

It is difficult to judge distance by eye, owing to the very clear atmosphere. For instance, the foot of the white hill away on the right is some ten miles away.

The climb on to this pass is dreadfully laborious, owing to the presence of deep sand which has been driven by the west wind on to the lower slopes.

PLATE 23

LEFT : Shekar Dzong, photographed from the little willow grove in which the Dzongpen permitted us to camp on condition that we did not cut any of the wood. Half-way up is one of the two large monasteries, and at the summit are the ruins of an old look-out post. This place withstood a long siege by the Gurkhas about a hundred years ago. From the top Mount Everest can be seen, about fifty miles away. In the foreground is one of the bell tents made for the porters at Cawnpore. It held about twenty men.

RIGHT : A view in the courtyard of one of the Shekar Dzong monasteries.

PLATE 24

A view in a courtyard of a Shekar monastery. The lamas are assembling for a service which will be held in the room on the right. On the left can be seen the supplies of tsampa for the evening meal, and the water buckets from which tea will be made.

The head lamas of monasteries like this are often men of good education who have been trained at or near Lhasa. The ordinary lamas are drawn from villages in the neighbourhood, and have little claim to distinction. Indeed, they are often turbulent, unless kept under a firm discipline such as that which prevails at Rongbuk.

PLATE 25

LEFT : A Shekar Dzong street among the monastery buildings. The whole place is built on rather a steep
hillside, advantage having been taken in a most
ingenious way of every possible ledge.

RIGHT : A view of the Shekar monasteries.

This gives, I think, a good idea of Tibetan architectural
skill. We could see no cracks in the walls, or other evidence
of disintegration, though the general character of the rock on
the Shekar hill is not particularly firm. Presumably it is to
these white buildings that the place owes its name : " the hill
of glass."

PLATE 26

The latest thing in ladies' hats in Tibet. The hats are built up on a framework of wood, into which the ladies' hair is braided. The top portion is of yaks' hair.

Along the edge of the wood are fixed pieces of coral and cornelian.

At the bottom of the photograph can be seen the silver charm-boxes which every Tibetan carries. They contain prayers written on paper by lamas, and are much prized.

PLATE 27

LEFT : A young Tibetan woman dressed for a dance.

RIGHT : An old Tibetan beggar. These men must suffer incredible hardships during the winter, but they seem
very cheerful, and have a considerable repertoire of
songs.

PLATE 28

Tibetan women and children watching a dance. They like being photographed and rarely show any confusion.

The great difficulty is to keep them in a group; they much prefer to surround the photographer and watch him at work. If he has a reflex camera they love poking their noses into the hood so as to see their friends in the ground-glass screen; this provokes shouts of pleasure and much clicking of tongues. Tibetans are usually very kind to children.

PLATE 29

LEFT : A small Tibetan boy who attached himself to the party in the capacity of scullion. He was really quite an artiste with the kind of guitar slung upon his back.

RIGHT : " Neanderthal man," one of the Sherpas who came direct from Sola Khombu to join us at Shekar. He was of a very primitive type and almost inarticulate, but he was a magnificent load carrier. The medical examination which he is here seen undergoing from Humphreys caused him considerable perplexity.

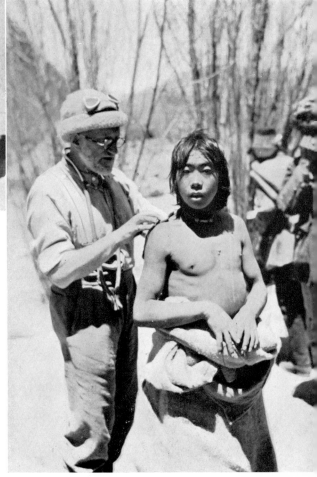

PLATE 30

The old Head Lama of Rongbuk monastery. He is now well over 70 years old, a great age for a Tibetan. He has lived at Rongbuk, at a height of 16,000 feet, almost throughout his life and has a tremendous and well-deserved influence over the neighbourhood, where he is considered to be the reincarnation of a saint. He is a great administrator and a great disciplinarian, as can be seen from the perfect discipline prevailing in his monastery. The Sherpas of Sola Khombu on the other side of the Himalayan range are his parishioners, and they make a point of coming over to Rongbuk at least once a year to secure his blessing. At first he did not welcome the intrusion of Everest expeditions into his valley, where much meditation is the rule, but recently he has come to think there is perhaps a spiritual side to the attempts on the mountain, and last year he volunteered a cordial invitation to return. Behind him can be seen the lovely lacquer-work table at which he sits for the blessing ceremonies. On it are his bell and other instruments of office. In the background are frescoes painted on the monastery wall representing Buddhas and saints.

PLATE 31

Porters being blessed by the Head Lama of Rongbuk monastery. They are dressed in the best clothes they can muster for the occasion, and each man makes some small offering and then prostrates himself. He is then presented with a small scarf and is blessed. All the men regard this ceremony as of the greatest importance.

PLATE 32.—A GROUP TAKEN AT THE BASE CAMP

Left to Right:

Back row :
Smijth-Windham, Oliver, Humphreys, Warren.

Middle row :
Shipton, Smythe, Ruttledge, Morris, Wyn Harris.

Front row :
Gavin, Wigram, Kempson.

Gavin and Smijth-Windham are wearing the high-altitude climbing kit, and Wigram, Kempson and Wyn Harris the warm fleece-lined camp boots. It will be observed that " Tendrup," the Tibetan mastiff, appears to be feeling the heat.

PLATE 33

Mount Everest as we first saw her from near the Base Camp. It will be observed that there was practically no snow on the North Face, and that the north-west wind was blowing a plume of cloud and ice particles away towards Bengal. It is practically certain that Mount Everest must remain in this condition till at least the end of May if a party is to have a reasonable chance of reaching the summit.

PLATE 34

This photograph was actually taken in June, but it shows how Mount Everest looked, almost without intermission, from April 30 onwards. In this condition it cannot be climbed, for snow on the outward-shelving slabs on the North Face is of powder consistency and offers no support to the feet. The slabs cannot be crossed unless they are free from this. In the foreground is the Base Camp at the foot of the terminal moraine of the Main Rongbuk glacier, at 16,800 feet. This camp was not held during the operations except by Karma Paul. Our real base in 1936 was at Camp I, away up a side valley on the left. In the middle distance, almost directly under the summit, is the North Peak.

PLATE 35

Smijth-Windham's wireless transmitting and receiving apparatus in his tent at Camp I at 17,700 feet. On the left can be seen one of the very light transmitting and receiving sets which were intended to be used at the high camps, though in this case it is being used to modulate the main transmitter, seen in the centre. On the right is the " Homelander " receiver, and below the table is the Marconi transmitter which worked Darjeeling from North Face Camp.

Upwards of five hundred wireless messages passed through this tent.

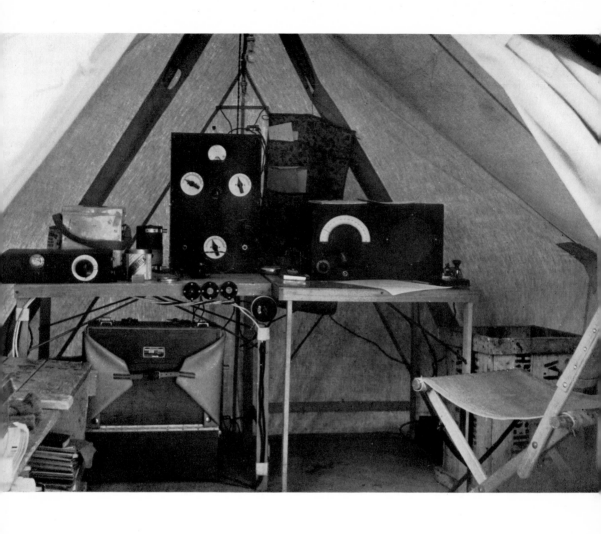

PLATE 36

The wireless battery charging plant, with its switchboard. To assist starting at low temperatures the induction pipe was lagged, and coil ignition was fitted. A compression ratio of 8 to 1 helped to overcome the effects of high altitude.

Mt Everest 1936 Expedition.
Wireless Battery Plant.
Output 400 watts - 18000 ft. up.
Total Weight 110 lbs.
Arthur Lyon & Co.
London.

PLATE 37

The wireless outfit, when packed, made a variety of awkward loads, requiring much supervision on the march.

In the foreground is Ang Tsering, who, as Mess Orderly, never failed to rise to the most unusual occasion.

PLATE 38

LEFT : From Camp I wireless waves have a clear exit
towards Darjeeling over the snout of the East
Rongbuk Glacier.
On the right is the Mess Tent, and the appearance of the cook-house in the centre belies the
excellence of the meals that came from its smoke-
filled interior.

RIGHT : Gavin, a master of improvisation, wasted no time
in making himself a dressing-table at Camp I.

PLATE 39

A sunset view at Camp II, at nearly 20,000 feet. Oliver is cutting steps up one of the great ice séracs, the base of which is away down out of sight in a trough in the glacier. It took him about four hours to complete this difficult climb.

Within half an hour of the taking of this photograph everyone had retreated to his tent, for sunset at this altitude brings a great fall of temperature. Fifty degrees of frost have more than once been recorded here.

PLATE 40

"Kellas' Rock Peak," from Camp II. This peak has often appeared in newspaper illustrations over the title "Mount Everest." It is over 23,000 feet high, and was climbed by the Reconnaissance party in 1935. It will be seen that some of the glacier ice séracs are beginning to melt under the influence of the hot midday sun.

PLATE 41

Ice-pinnacles on the East Rongbuk glacier showing the effect of the hot midday sun. It is not altogether easy to account for the existence of these pinnacles, for the slope of the glacier is not severe at this point and the ice is not therefore much crevassed. The most likely explanation seems to be the combined action of sun, wind and snow.

PLATE 42

More ice-pinnacles on the East Rongbuk glacier and the easy way up the " trough."   In June the latter is sometimes full of water from melting ice, and a way has then to be sought to left or right.

PLATE 43

At this point in the "trough" a little lake has begun to form and the party is therefore obliged to cut steps along the base of a pinnacle.   A slip into the water would make things very uncomfortable for the victim as his clothes might freeze hard when he got out on the open glacier beyond.

PLATE 44

A view from the point where the open upper glacier is reached; looking down the trough in the direction of Camp II. In the background is " Kellas' Rock Peak," which was climbed during the Reconnaissance of 1935. At the point where the photograph was taken difficulties may occur on a windy day as parties are constantly exposed to severe conditions after enjoying the shelter of the trough.

PLATE 45

Wigram's party ascending the upper part of the East Rongbuk glacier towards Camp III during a blizzard.

They were going up from Camp II, where stores were needed while we were storm-bound between May 31 and June 3 ; these stores they brought back with them after a very hard day. There is not much detail in this photograph : that is the measure of the prevailing conditions. Most of our pictures are likely to give the impression that there is perpetual sunshine on Everest ; the reason is that very few men are able to take photographs while a storm is blowing, as the wind and cold and driving snow make that a painful and even dangerous undertaking.

PLATE 46

The North Col from Camp III, 21,500 feet ; the height of the face of the Col is about 1,200 feet. The way up from the camp lay along the moraine to the right, then on to the comparatively flat ice at the foot of the slopes in the middle of the picture, then again to the right behind the ice-slope in the middle distance behind the rock cliffs, up on to the plateau about half-way up, and then left along the big shelf, finishing with a steep climb up on to the Col to the left of the cloud. This "cloud" is really snow which is being blown by a violent wind from the western side, to drop down on the eastern slopes. The way up to Camp V is on the left.

PLATE 47

Mount Everest seen from Camp III, 21,500 feet. The summit is directly above the tent. This photograph gives some idea of the heavy snowfall on the mountain in 1936, which rendered the climb impossible. Owing to the camera having been tilted upwards, the slope of the North Ridge in the middle distance looks very much less steep than it actually is. In a good season the rocks of the north-east shoulder on the left would have been almost completely black.

PLATE 48

Porters carrying up to Camp IV on the top of the North Col. Most of them are still on the long traverse, but those in the foreground are commencing the steeper ascent to the crest. It was the dangerous condition of the slopes on this traverse which eventually cut us off from Camp IV. The avalanche which nearly killed Wyn Harris and Shipton occurred near the point at which the most distant figures are visible.

PLATE 49

LEFT :   Smythe and Oliver climbing the last steep section to the crest of the North Col.   In the background can be seen the great north-east shoulder of Mount Everest, about 27,000 feet.   This is seen to be under deep snow.

RIGHT :   Camp IV, at 23,000 feet on the North Col.   This camp was fully established and occupied on May 15, but had to be evacuated, as it turned out for good, on May 18.   The crest of the Col here is completely exposed to the north-west wind, but in 1936 there was not enough of this wind, and snow accumulated very fast, rendering further progress impossible   All these tents, and equipment and stores, are still on the North Col, where they are doubtless slowly sinking into the ice.   The two tents in the foreground were allotted to this camp ; the tent in the background was intended for the higher camps.

PLATE 50

Mount Everest and the North Peak from the Main Rongbuk glacier. On the right is the north-west ridge of Mount Everest, which is clearly both long and difficult. At the time this photograph was taken the wind had cleared a good deal of snow off the mountain, but it was all back again next day.

On the left is the North Peak.

PLATE 51

The view looking up the Main and West Rongbuk glacier from the corner where a side valley leads to Camp I. The way to the west side of the North Col lay up the valley on the left. In the background is the magnificent peak Pumori, " the daughter peak," named after Mallory's daughter. It has not yet been climbed.

PLATE 52

A view up the West Rongbuk glacier from Lake Camp. The monsoon is evidently in full force.

In the foreground are the séracs or ice-pinnacles of the Main Rongbuk glacier, flanked by the moraine up which we went to explore the west side of the North Col.   The Lingtren group of peaks is to the left.

PLATE 53

The magnificent Lingtren Peaks from near Lake Camp. Shipton and Bryant made some very good ascents in this group during the Reconnaissance of 1935, obtaining some splendid photographs of Mount Everest. They narrowly escaped disaster on an ice-ridge, where a corniche broke away and carried Bryant with it. Fortunately Shipton was able to hold him on the rope.

PLATE 54

The North Face of Mount Everest from near Lake Camp. The great couloir or gully can be seen descending below the left-hand edge of the summit. The highest point so far reached, in 1924 and 1933, is just to the left of the black band of rock below the summit. The band at this point is about 200 feet in height. On the left of Mount Everest is the North Peak, round the flank of which we went to see the west side of the North Col.

PLATE 55

The North Peak and the east ridge of Mount Everest from Peak 21,120 above the Rongbuk glacier. This and the next three photographs were taken by L. V. Bryant, the New Zealand mountaineer, during the Reconnaissance of 1935, when he and Shipton were climbing in the Lingtren group. The west side of the North Col lies in the gap between the North Peak and Mount Everest.

PLATE 56

Nuptse, the high peak on the south side of the Khumbu glacier in Nepal, taken from the same view-point as the last. On the left is the lower portion of the great north-west ridge of Everest. Between it and Nuptse lies the Khumbu glacier, the head of which is directly under the West Face of Everest.

PLATE 57

Mount Everest from the same view-point as the last two.
This photograph shows practically the whole length of the
north-west ridge of the mountain. Clearly this would be a
very long and difficult line of attack. The North Peak is on
the left, and part of the western slopes of the North Col can be
seen in the gap between it and Everest.

PLATE 58

Mount Everest and Lhotse (the South Peak) from Lingtren Nup, 21,610 feet. The summit of the North Peak is emerging from the clouds on the left.

This photograph indicates how very steep is the North-west Face of Everest (seen to the right of the summit).

PLATE 59

The West Face of the North Col as first seen by the Expedition of 1936. We have just arrived out on the upper part of the main Rongbuk glacier, expecting to go on to the Lho La away to the right. But the approach to the West Face of the North Col is so evidently worth close examination that we have halted and are now preparing to ascend as far as possible towards the Col.

Unfortunately within an hour of the time when this photograph was taken the clouds began to come up from Nepal on the right, and the climbers were not able to get farther than the bergschrund which can be seen at the foot of the final slopes. North Face Camp is out of sight on the left. Above, also on the left, is the North Peak. The slope ascending to the right from the Col itself is the North ridge of Everest.

This photograph was taken by the Houston Mount Ever
Flight of 1933. It shows the final pyramid and summit
Mount Everest from the north. On the left is the north-e
arête descending towards the shoulder. At the bottom
the left-centre of the picture are the slabs on which an assa
party would arrive after crossing the head of the great coul

seems likely that a way can be found up the centre of the
amid almost directly below the summit, where there are
siderable patches of snow. Just right of the centre the great
·th-west ridge descends from the summit.   On the right is
 very steep north-west face, which is actually in Nepalese
·ritory.

   [*By kind permission of the Houston Mount Everest Flight.*

PLATE 61

The North Face of Mount Everest from North Face Camp at about 19,000 feet. The north-west ridge of Mount Everest descends to the right. To the left of the summit, just underneath the cloud, can be seen the Second Step, on which Odell thinks he saw Mallory and Irvine in 1924.

PLATE 62

A last view of the North Face of Mount Everest taken shortly before we left for the march home. By that time the monsoon was so heavy that any further climbing was out of the question. The mornings were often sunny and bright, but these clouds invariably came up before noon and dissolved in heavy snow in the evening and night.

PLATE 63

The final group, taken on the day after the party crossed over from Tibet into Northern Sikkim, on the return march.

LEFT TO RIGHT:

Back row

Warren, Oliver, Humphreys, Kempson, Wigram, Gavin, Smijth-Windham.

Front row :

Shipton, Smythe, Ruttledge, Wyn Harris, Morris.